American Commonwealths.

VOLUME 17

RHODE ISLAND

AMS PRESS
NEW YORK

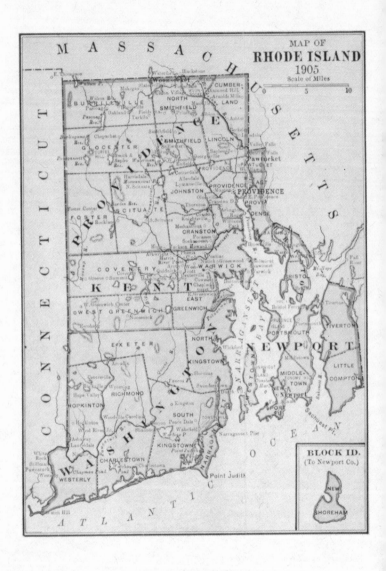

MAP OF
RHODE ISLAND
1905
Scale of Miles

BLOCK ID.
(To Newport Co.)

NEW
SHOREHAM

American Commonwealths

RHODE ISLAND

A STUDY IN SEPARATISM

BY

IRVING BERDINE RICHMAN

AUTHOR OF "RHODE ISLAND:
ITS MAKING AND ITS MEANING"

BOSTON AND NEW YORK
HOUGHTON, MIFFLIN AND COMPANY
The Riverside Press, Cambridge
1905

Library of Congress Cataloging in Publication Data

Richman, Irving Berdine, 1861-1938.
  Rhode Island: a study in separatism.

  Original ed. issued as v. 17 of American
commonwealths.
  Bibliography: p.
  1. Rhode Island--History. I. Title.
II. Series: American commonwealths, v. 17.
[F79.R53 1973]   917.45'03'4   72-3749
ISBN 0-404-57217-0

Reprinted from the edition of 1905, Boston and New York
First AMS edition published, 1973
Manufactured in the United States of America

International Standard Book Number:
Complete Series: 0-404-57200-6
Volume 17: 0-404-57217-0

AMS PRESS, INC.
New York, N.Y.   10003

PREFACE

UPON the formative period of Rhode Island history, the author of the present study has dwelt at length in " Rhode Island : Its Making and its Meaning," published in 1902. The period in question was characterized by a separatism that was intense, but subsequent periods have by no means been wanting in this feature, and it is largely the object of the present book to point out the influence of separatism in determining the course of events in Rhode Island during the eighteenth and nineteenth centuries.

Within the current year there has been published by Dr. Edward Channing, of Harvard, volume one of a history of the United States. This volume, at page 412, contains the statement, that all existing histories of Rhode Island are " full of prejudice against Massachusetts." The statement would seem to commit Dr. Channing to the dictum that no historical writer may speak with severity — discriminating severity even — concern-

ing the general attitude of early Massachusetts
toward early Rhode Island, without incurring the
charge of prejudice. Outside of the Bay State
severity against early Massachusetts intolerance
(*vide* Osgood and Andrews) is evidently not considered by American historians an indication, *per
se*, of prejudice, nor is it evidently so considered
by such European scholars, English, Swiss, and
German, as Doyle, Bryce, Borgeaud, and Jellinek.
The possibility remains that in his dictum, that
all histories of Rhode Island (because of severity
toward early Massachusetts) are filled with prejudice, Dr. Channing is right and others, American
and European, are wrong; but, as affecting the
weight of the dictum, the circumstance can hardly
be overlooked that Dr. Channing, by birth, education, and persistent environment, is a Massachusetts man.

Animated with the hope that as one possessed
of no relationship, ancestral or contemporary, to
New England, his work may be found reasonably
impartial, the author desires to make acknowledgment for valuable aid to his friends, Mr. Clarence
S. Brigham, librarian of the Rhode Island Historical Society; Mr. George Parker Winship,
librarian of the John Carter Brown Library; Mr.

William E. Foster, librarian of the Providence
Public Library; Professor William MacDonald,
of Brown University; Mr. William P. Sheffield,
Jr., of Newport; Dr. Frank G. Bates, of Alfred
University, New York; and Mr. Reuben G.
Thwaites, of the Historical Society of Wisconsin.

I. B. R.

MUSCATINE, IOWA, September 23, 1905.

CONTENTS

THE smallest [of the New England colonies], Rhode Island, had features all its own; . . . the rest were substantially one in nature and origin.

FRANCIS PARKMAN, *Montcalm and Wolfe*, vol. i, p. 25.

PART I

AGRICULTURE AND SEPARATISM
1636–1689

RHODE ISLAND

CHAPTER I

NARRAGANSETT BAY

Geography — Discovery — Present-day Environment

BEFORE the age of Roger Williams Rhode Island was separatist. It was so in its geography. It consisted of a strip or section of territory — a continental or mainland section embracing Narragansett Bay — and of a series of formations within the bay constituting a section of islands.

Within present boundaries the greatest length of the Narragansett Bay commonwealth is forty-eight miles, and its greatest width thirty-seven. Its area, including the bay, is nearly thirteen hundred square miles. The bay itself comprises about two hundred square miles, and is broken into lesser bays, and into straits and channels, by its groups of islands. Of these islands Prudence, Conanicut, and the island of Aquidneck, or Rhode Island, are the largest. The entire coast line (bay and sea) extends four hundred miles, and adjacent to it in South Kingstown, Charlestown, and Westerly the lands are low and marshy. To the northward and westward there is a gradual increase in elevation, the highest point — 805 feet — being attained at Durfee's Hill in Glocester.

Narragansett Bay forms the outlet for three considerable Rhode Island streams, — the Blackstone (Seekonk), the Woonasquatucket, and the Pawtuxet, — and the Atlantic Ocean for a fourth stream, the Pawcatuck. These streams are interrupted by falls and rapids, and in the days of the first settlers were bordered by strips of luxuriant grass land. Aside from the river meadows and coast marshes, the surface of aboriginal Rhode Island was stony or sandy and covered by a thick growth of forest.

Passage from the mainland to the islands, and from the islands to the mainland, was in the early days often difficult and sometimes dangerous, a fact to which official records and private diaries bear concurrent testimony. That Providence and Newport, therefore, should develop on divergent lines is not surprising; although in calm weather the physical bond between them must have been of a closer nature than would have been supplied by as many miles of Indian forest trail.

In a letter to Francis I of France, dated July 8, 1524, Jean Verrazano describes the shores and islands of Narragansett Bay, a spot upon which he had come, in the spring of the year named, in searching for a channel through the American continent to the regions of Cathay.

" Weighing anchor," he says, " we sailed eighty
leagues toward the East, as the coast stretched in
that direction, and always in sight of it; at length
we discovered an island of a triangular form,
about ten leagues from the mainland, in size about
equal to the island of Rhodes, having many hills
covered with trees, and well peopled, judging from
the great number of fires which we saw all around
its shores; we gave it the name of Your Majesty's
illustrious mother [Luisa].

" We did not land there as the weather was
unfavorable, but proceeded to another place, fifteen
leagues distant from the island, where we found a
very excellent harbor. . . .

" This region is situated in the parallel of Rome,
being 41 degrees 40 minutes of north latitude, but
much colder from accidental circumstances and
not by nature, as I shall hereafter explain to Your
Majesty, and confine myself at present to the
description of its local situation. It looks toward
the south, on which side the harbor is half a
league broad; afterwards upon entering it, the
extent between the coast and north is twelve
leagues, and then enlarging itself it becomes a
very large bay, twenty leagues in circumference,
in which are five small islands, of great fertility
and beauty, covered with large and lofty trees.
Among these islands any fleet, however large,
might ride safely, without fear of tempest or
other dangers. Turning towards the south, at the

entrance of the harbor, on both sides, there are
very pleasant hills, and many streams of clear
water, which flow down to the sea. In the midst
of the entrance, there is a rock of free stone [Goat
Island], formed by nature, and suitable for the
construction of any kind of machine or bulwark
for the defense of the harbor."

But Verrazano possibly was not the first European to visit the bay in question. As early as the
tenth century, according to Norse tradition, Leif,
son of Eric, sailed from Greenland to the west
and south and wintered upon the New England
coast at a point which he called Vinland, on a bay
identified by the Danish scholar Rafn as that of
Mount Hope. In the opinion of the enthusiastic
Rafn, the Old Stone Mill at Newport, the mill
which Governor Benedict Arnold had built about
1675, and of which he makes repeated mention in
his last will and testament, was of Norse construction.

After Verrazano, map-makers were wont to des-
ignate Narragansett Bay as the Bay of St. Juan
Baptist, although Verrazano himself had chris-
tened it the Bay of Refuge. It remained the
Bay of St. Juan until 1614, when a Dutchman,
Adriaen Block, emulating the brave Henry Hudson, who fourteen years before had sailed up the
lordly North River, appeared off Point Judith in
a little ship of sixteen tons. Block touched at the
three-cornered island which Verrazano had named

Luisa, and gave to it his own name, Block —
Block Eylandt. He then carefully explored the
Bay of St. Juan, calling it Nassau. The west
passage he called Sloop Bay, and the east passage
Anchor Bay. A small island, believed from his
account of its location to have been Hope (it lay
to the west of Aquidneck), he described as " een
rodtlich Eylandken."

For sketches of the Indians of the Narragansett
region we are indebted to both Verrazano and
Block. At the time of Block's visit the Wampanoags, or Pokanokets, would seem to have been in
occupation of the principal islands of the bay, and
the Mohegans and Nyantics of the mainland to
the west. Later on the Narragansetts, who abode
between the Mohegans and Wampanoags, extended
their dominion to the eastward. By 1636, the
date of the coming of Roger Williams, the Narragansetts had established a suzerainty over the
Wampanoags, but on the west they were held in
check by the warlike Mohegans and Pequods,
the latter an invading tribe from the north. Of
all the tribes of southern New England, the Narragansetts were the most numerous — eight or ten
thousand souls ; and their chief sachems, the aged
Canonicus and youthful Miantonomi, were men
of exceptional astuteness. Of unusual qualities
also were the chief sachems, respectively, of the
Wampanoags, Mohegans, and Pequods, — Massasoit, Uncas, and Sassacus.

Occupation of Rhode Island on the part of the English was first by an agricultural class, and next by a class that was commercial. In recent years it has been by an industrial class. The agricultural-ists, who never formed a very numerous group, dis-persed themselves over Aquidneck and through the valleys of the Seekonk, the Woonasquatucket, the Pawtuxet, and the Pawcatuck, and became (in the more remote sections) ignorant, superstitious, and prejudiced. With the decline of agriculture, the best representatives of the group entered commerce, or, after the Revolutionary War, migrated northwest-ward into Vermont and New York; and those left behind — the less energetic — tended yet more to degenerate into a class of poor whites.

Availing themselves (as they freely did) of the fresh water meadows and salt marshes for their cattle and horses, and of the woods and barrens for their swine and sheep, the Rhode Island agri-culturists made no great impression on the Narra-gansett wilderness outside of Aquidneck; and with the development of commerce the impression made was still less, for commerce tended to draw popu-lation (the best of it) to the commercial centres — Newport and Providence. With the rise of manu-factures the river valleys became scenes of greater activity than ever before; but in the interior, away from the valleys, there reigned a solitude that was profound. Agriculture now became markedly de-pressed, and the depression has not as yet been dispelled. Mr. Josiah B. Bowditch, after a review of the census figures for 1900, concludes that the farming population of Rhode Island to-day is no greater than it was in 1790. Some towns, as, for example, West Greenwich, have declined from as early a date as 1748.

To take one's station on a Rhode Island hill and permit one's glance to traverse the Narragansett Bay region, is to behold a commonwealth occupied in its main valleys (those of the Blackstone and Pawtuxet) and along its coast line by an active population of nearly four hundred thousand souls and its back country by an inactive population of not much to exceed thirty thousand souls. This back country, moreover, one would perceive to be a country of hills and forest. "The huge rollers," observes Mr. Clarence Deming, "stretch to the horizon in endless rise and slope . . . and over all is laid the thick mantle of the woods, unbroken save by one or two brown houses on a distant hill, or by a clearing so infrequent and small that it accents the ocean of forest. . . . Swift and clear streams pour through the valleys, fed by springs and sustained in drought by the swamps; the underbrush is dense, and through vast areas all but impenetrable, with such cover for quail, partridge, and woodcock as seems to challenge the most destroying energy of the pot-hunter; the wildest of wild flowers, such as the cypripedium, grow by the very roadside in their season; lakes and ponds, reputed

to have good black bass fishing, show hardly a
dwelling on their shores or a boat on their waters.
. . . Old taverns, lodging no guest and with no
welcoming host, front the highways, the dim ghosts
of old revelry seeming to peer through shattered
pane and shutter. Half the farmhouses are deserted and in every degree of infirmity. The
houses where families yet abide are in the decrepit
stage of unpainted clapboard, sagging rafter, and
wry fence. . . . But saddest of all are the decay-
ing monuments of what was once a region of lively
and expansive industry — a whole mill village
deserted. . . . In wildest Rhode Island the abandoned mill jostles closely the abandoned farm, and
both have gone down together before the industrial
wave which has swept the smaller factories to the
railroad and shore and hived the workers in the
greater shops under higher productive organization."

Of course amid a scene of desolation such as
this there are to be encountered types of character
all the quainter from their surroundings. Impressed with the fact, Miss Esther B. Carpenter,
in 1887, published a delightful series of character
sketches — "South County Neighbors." The men
and women she depicts are survivals from the
pristine Narragansett stock with its "Old Jobs"
and "Young Jobs" and its "Uncle Simons;" its
"Alzadys," "Celindys," and "Lovisy Anns;" its
"Oseys" [Osiannas], "Pashes" [Patiences], and

"Phylutys." "Now, neighbor," Uncle Simon was wont to remark, "what d' ye think makes Squire Potter and Squire Hazard always talk to me wheresumever they see me?" "Why, I don't know, Uncle Simon." "Well, neighbor, I'll tell ye. 'T is to draar knalidge — yes, to draar knalidge." It was (we are assured by Miss Carpenter) a favorite hypothesis of Simon's that if he could only have talked with King George the Revolution need never have occurred.

But, to pursue a query propounded by Mr. Deming, "What does the future hold for Rhode Island's west, where nature is so fast overgrowing man, where meadows and sown field year by year shrink, where the woodlands expand, and the farm problem of Yankeeland repeats itself in its superlative degree? Will the rich sporting patroons, who have begun to buy up the forests by the square mile at a dollar or two an acre, realize their hopes of a paradise of rod and gun? Will the strange expanse of the very penumbra of busy cities be given over at last to the well-watched preserves of the sportsmen's clubs and syndicates? Will it in the maturing of the science of forestry, now in bud, become the source of lucrative timber supply? Or as populations outside wax and a refluent stream of wealth pours on the picturesque sites of New England, will remote posterity see the semi-wilderness cut by electric roads, the truck farmer or tenant driving back the forest, the lands grown

fat and costly, and every scenic hilltop crowned
by the homes of the rich? To such surmise," says
Mr. Deming, " whether of economist, nature lover,
or sportsman, the deepening solitudes of wildest
Rhode Island give no reply."

Possibly not, but Professor N. S. Shaler of Harvard confidently predicts a time when, by reason
of the exhaustion of more available lands, the
lands of New England, especially those of a marshy
character, will be widely reclaimed. Be that as it
may, " Rhode Island's west " — its sparsely peopled, its intensely individualistic and separatist,
west — is even now exerting a preponderant influence in Rhode Island affairs. The nature and
tendency of that influence are reserved for consideration in our last chapter.

CHAPTER II

1. *Founding of Providence and Warwick*

THE age of Roger Williams in Rhode Island centres about six historic names and four geographical points. The names are Roger Williams and William Harris; William Coddington and John Clarke; Samuel Gorton and Anne Hutchinson. The points are Providence and Warwick on the Rhode Island mainland, and Newport and Portsmouth on the island of Aquidneck.

Roger Williams was born in London about 1603. His parents were James and Alice (Pemberton) Williams, and the occupation of his father was that of merchant tailor. Of his boyhood years we know nothing. Our first glimpse of him is obtained in 1620, when he was a lad of seventeen. Williams (probably with a view to a livelihood) had learned shorthand, and for the purpose of practicing his art had obtained permission to attend sessions of the Court of Star Chamber. Here, by his alertness of mind and openness of heart, he won the regard of Sir Edward Coke — the grim Sir Edward who, as chief justice of the Court of King's Bench, had in 1616 withstood to his face on a question of prerogative the pedantic James the First. Of Williams Coke straightway became the patron, and as such he in 1621 secured for him admission to the Charterhouse School, an institution then newly founded and of which the jurist himself was one of the overseers. In 1652 (long after the death of Coke) Roger Williams sought to enter into correspondence with a surviving daughter, Mrs. Anne Sadleir of Standon, Puckridge, but the dame — grim by disposition like her illustrious parent and incensed at Williams for his iconoclastic religious views — bound his letters into a package and indorsed upon it : " This Roger Williams when he was a youth would in a shorthand take sermons and speeches in the Star Chamber and present them to my dear father. . . . Full little did he think that he would have proved such a rebel to God, the King and his country. I leave his letters that, if ever he has the face to return into his native country, Tyburn may give him welcome."

From the Charterhouse Williams went to Pembroke College, Cambridge, where he graduated in 1626. His inclination at first was for the law, but the times were times of theology, and in 1629 he was filling the position of chaplain to Sir William Masham of Otes, in Essex. While thus employed he fell deeply in love with a niece of Lady Barrington, the Lady Barrington being an aunt to Oliver Cromwell. Williams's love affair was not prosperous. He had, it is true, won the heart of the maiden to whom he aspired; but in the eyes of Lady Barrington he was a match altogether unsuitable for one of her family, and his passion was frowned upon. In complete despair he wrote to the obdurate lady on May 2, 1629: "We [his sweetheart and himself] hope to live together in the heavens though ye Lord have denied that union on earth." But this was not all that he did. Cambridge, where he had attended college, was in Cambridgeshire, one of those eastern counties of England into which there had long been migrating from Holland Anabaptists and Mennonites imbued with the idea of severance of Church from State. With this idea Williams himself had become impressed; so much so, indeed, that he had thought it not unimportant to acquire a knowledge of the Dutch tongue. In his present situation, therefore, — crossed in love and a rebel against episcopacy, — he began to bend his gaze across the sea to a new land: that land whither already had departed the Separatist congregation of Nottinghamshire Pilgrims, and whither the Winthrop company of Puritans from Lincolnshire were soon to set out: a land, moreover, tenanted by a race wild, fantastic, and in need of Christianization — the land of the Massachusetts Bay.

On February 5, 1631, Roger Williams disembarked at Boston from the ship Lyon; and as though to emphasize the entirety of his renunciation of bygone days and dreams, he disembarked

accompanied by a wife, Mary (*née* Barnard), and
without having visited Stoke House to say farewell
to Sir Edward, his patron, whom indeed at this
time it would scarcely have been prudent for him
to face. In New England — first at Salem, then
at Plymouth, then at Salem again — Williams
found himself constantly and from the first in
opposition to prevailing ideas. Where he had
thought to find, if not his own conceptions, at
least room for the assertion of those conceptions,
he found a hierarchy of ministers and elders and
a stiff ecclesiastical discipline; a hierarchy and
discipline to which the distinctively secular agency,
government, was in practice subordinated. Yet
the conceptions held by Williams were not such —
all of them — that any government of the day
could wholly have passed them by. They involved
opposition to the charter of the colony because it
recognized the king rather than the Indians as the
source of title to lands; a delicate point at the
moment, for the king was then seeking a pretext
for recalling the charter. They involved opposition
to the autonomy of the colony under the charter,
for they were antagonistic to judicial oaths by
which that autonomy was sought to be confirmed.
Some things, however, they involved that the
government (had it been secular) could well have
tolerated: for instance, that the civil magistrate
ought not to be empowered to punish sins as such,
offenses purely against God — the acts forbidden

in the first table of the Decalogue ; that, in other words, magisterial power should extend only to the punishment of misdemeanors and crimes, offenses against man — the acts forbidden in the second table of the Decalogue. Upon this principle there was to be founded the commonwealth of Rhode Island.

The final result of the clash between Roger Williams and Massachusetts was that on October 9, 1635, Williams was ordered to depart within six weeks out of the jurisdiction of the Bay, as one having " broached & dyvulged dyvers newe & dangerous opinions, against the aucthoritie of magistrates," and having " writ lres of defamacōn both of the magistrates & churches." Afterwards the sentence of expulsion was so far modified that Williams was permitted to remain in Salem until spring. But inasmuch as by private discourses and exercises he continued " to draw others unto his opinions," it was decided in January, 1636, to send him to England. The plan was revealed to the culprit in season for him to thwart it by evading Captain John Underhill, who had been charged with its execution, and soon, amid cold and deep snow, he, with his servant Thomas Angell, was on his way to the lodge of his friend Massasoit, the sachem of the Wampanoags.

In the spring of 1636 Williams broke ground for a habitation at Seekonk (East Providence), on the east bank of the Seekonk River. Here he was

joined by three companions, among them William
Harris. The party would have remained where
they were, but were warned away as trespassers by
Plymouth, and in the summer removed to Mooshassuc and began to lay the foundations of Providence.

The arrival at Seekonk of William Harris was
an occurrence most significant for the Providence
settlement. Williams and Harris had come to
Massachusetts in the same ship, but by temperament and training were antipathetic to a degree.
Williams was an idealist; Harris was a realist.
The former was generous, full of compassion, and
not altogether practical. The latter was keen,
hard, and regardful of personal advantage. The
Providence which together they succeeded in creating partook of the characteristics of both; and
throughout the lives of both, lives lasting almost
to the end of the seventeenth century, was racked
by the dissensions of themselves and of their respective adherents.

Among the motives which had inspired the coming of Roger Williams to America was a desire to
convert the Indians, " to do the natives good." At
Plymouth the newly arrived clergyman had early
made friends with Massasoit; and as a result of
excursions into the Narragansett country, during
which he had carefully studied the Algonquin
tongue, he had entered into relations with Canonicus and Miantonomi. When, therefore, he and his

companions — a party of five — found themselves
at Mooshassuc, Williams was master of the situation. The Indians knew him and respected him,
and in the fullness of their knowledge and respect
executed to him on March 24, 1638, a conveyance
of a township of land on the Mooshassuc and Pawtuxet rivers. It was the intention of the grantee
to devote the gift to charitable uses. He meant to
make of it in part a mission station, and in part a
basis for a communal society composed of persons
" distressed for conscience." To the latter design
he probably was led by the circumstance that persons distressed for conscience — persons harassed
at Plymouth or at the Bay — were already congre-
gating about him.

But just here William Harris began to assert
himself. He was willing that idealism, in the form
of affection, philanthropy, and religion, should win
from the Indians a tract of land ; but he was not
willing that the land so won should remain " a
common stock " for the benefit of all " distressed "
comers. Individual ownership was what he sought,
and by October 8, 1638, he had so far " wearied "
Williams by importunities that the latter executed
to twelve men — Stukeley Westcott, William Arnold, Thomas James, Robert Cole, John Greene,
John Throckmorton, William Harris, William Carpenter, Thomas Olney, Francis Weston, Richard
Waterman, and Ezekiel Holliman — a deed constituting the twelve (along with the grantor) a

"fellowship" in the Indian grant. The deed did
not create a partnership; it created a corporation.
But to convert the corporate holding largely into
holdings in severalty was the work of but a little
time. In fact, during the same autumn so much of
the Indian grant as lay upon the Pawtuxet River
(a portion called the "Pawtuxet Purchase") was,
by agreement between the proprietaries, parti-
tioned into several tracts.

The government which under Williams was first
instituted at Providence was by "masters of families." The masters met once a fortnight and dispatched business "by mutual consent." By August
or September, 1636, there had been admitted into
the community a body of "young men, single persons." The government now was rendered more
definite by a stipulation, concluded between the
early comers and "young men," that the latter
were to be subject "in active and passive obedience" to the orders of the major part of the
"present inhabitants, masters of families, incorporated into a town, and such others as they should
admit, only in civil things." In 1640 a board of
five disposers, or selectmen, was established, to
"be betrusted" with general matters, and a system of arbitration was set up. In the above mentioned cautious and tentative contrivances the individualism implied in the doctrine of Soul Liberty
or Freedom of Conscience was sought as fully as
possible to be carried into the domain of politics.

There were no magistrates ; there was no constable. As Williams had written to Governor John Winthrop of Massachusetts in 1636, "the face of magistracy did not suit with [the] condition [of the settlement]."

In March or April, 1641, Samuel Gorton appeared in Providence. He was a man of some pretensions to family, and, like the father of Roger Williams, a London clothier. He also was a theologian — one of those extreme products of the Reformation in whom the age abounded ; men and women actuated toward the large mysteries of life, redemption, and immortality by a spirit of daring challenge, and just enough schooled to obscure their lucubrations by garbing them in Hebrew imagery. As an extremist, Gorton believed in Freedom of Conscience. Hence in politics he was an individualist ; but to his political individualism there was imparted stability by the circumstance that he was a profound admirer of the English common law. Wherever that law was enthroned and observed, there for him was civil liberty ; and wherever it was not enthroned, or was not observed, there for him was civil tyranny.

Up to the time of his advent upon the Mooshassuc, the life of Gorton in New England had been a succession of small tempests. At Plymouth, where, in 1637, he had removed from rigid Boston, he had had an altercation with the magistrates over their treatment of his serving maid for " smiling in church ; " with the issue that in December, 1638, he had been banished for " contempt." From Plymouth he (Roger Williams like) had made his way, through " snow to the knee," to Portsmouth, on the island of Aquidneck. Here, within a brief time, he had become involved in behalf of another serving maid — one charged with assault — and in due course (for his own defiance of authority) had been banished to the mainland. But Gorton's career, though thus a series of contentions, was not altogether a madness. At Plymouth the proceedings in restraint of the levity of his servant were to him ecclesiastically tyrannous as against conscience, and civilly tyrannous in that (as conducted) prosecutor and judge, contrary to English law, were one. At Portsmouth none of the proceedings were to him justifiable, because on Aquidneck the government was neither of royal nor popular origin, but " set up of itself."

The reception accorded to Gorton by Roger Williams was far from cordial. He demanded that the fugitive, as a condition precedent to admission to the town fellowship, exculpate himself from the charges brought against him at Portsmouth ; and in this demand he was sustained vigorously by William Arnold. Gorton, on his part, found the situation at Providence no more worthy of respect than on the island. A few men, without authority from the king of England, or from any source other than themselves, were (with their families) occupying houses distributed along a narrow highway skirting the Mooshassuc and called " the towne street." Besides a house-lot, these men owned each a six-acre pasture or arable field; and as a body (as a fellowship or corporation) they owned all the rest of Providence. And not only so, but thirteen of them were owners, each, of a great estate on the Pawtuxet. Surely this was all wrong, all an illegal monopoly, and should be overthrown.

Gorton had been accompanied from Portsmouth by various disciples, and he made further converts at Providence. In his train now were Randall Holden and John Greene; and the entire party — after bringing the settlement so near to revolution that Roger Williams, who at first " in Christ's name had withstood [the intruder]," at length gave up the contest and seriously bethought himself of flight to the island of Patience — settled down at Pawtuxet. At Pawtuxet, however, there were the Arnolds — William and his son Benedict; and the Arnolds were of no mean order of ability. Their best energies were at once directed to the task of ridding the region of the burden of Gorton.

Already in 1641 Massachusetts had let fall the pregnant hint that it might operate for quiet and good order on the Mooshassuc and Pawtuxet if the more substantial inhabitants were to subject themselves to the jurisdiction of the Bay. So in the autumn of 1642, the Arnolds and their family

connections made subjection in the name of Pawtuxet, and notice of the fact was promptly conveyed to Gorton by Governor Winthrop. The
Gortonists had been neatly circumvented, and in
January, 1643, they, after dispatching to Boston
a letter stigmatizing the Puritans as a merciless
Jewish brotherhood, removed to Shawomet. Shawomet was a district embracing what to-day are
the towns of Warwick and Coventry. It was obtained by the Gortonists from Miantonomi and
two local sachems, Pumham and Sacononoco.
Gorton possessed something of Williams's faculty
for ingratiating himself with the Indians, and his
purchase of Shawomet marked the beginning of a
friendship between himself and Miantonomi that
was to be provocative of much.

Having forced Gorton from Pawtuxet, the Arnolds next resolved to force him from Shawomet.
Massachusetts had served their purpose once, it
should be baited to do so again. In May, 1643,
Pumham and Sacononoco were taken by Benedict
Arnold to Boston, and, offering to submit themselves and Shawomet to the jurisdiction of the
Bay, were graciously received. Pumham acknow-
ledged that he had signed a deed for Shawomet to
the Gortonists, but professed to have been driven
to the act through the sinister influence of Samuel Gorton over Miantonomi, his overlord. Accordingly both Gorton and Miantonomi were
summoned to appear and show cause why the Gor-

tonists should not be evicted from their holdings as trespassers. Furthermore, commissioners were sent to Shawomet and Pawtuxet to inquire into conditions on the spot, and to take in writing the answers of the local sachems to a series of interrogatories on the ten commandments. If Massachusetts became sponsor for Pumham and Sacononoco, it must be on a satisfactory profession of their faith. The profession proved to be satisfactory, and on June 22 a formal deed of submission from the Indians was accepted.

Miantonomi obeyed the summons to Boston, but Samuel Gorton did not. The latter in September (pursuing a favorite method) reduced his views to writing. These views were that the head of the State in Massachusetts was an " Idol General — a Satan transforming himself into an angel of light;" and that his subjects " lived by blood " through persecutions. " If," continued the epistle, "your sword be drawn, ours is girt upon our thigh."

In this plain challenge to arms, Gorton perhaps was indiscreet. At all events Massachusetts, the next month, put in the field a company of soldiers and advanced on Shawomet. The Gortonists took refuge in a log house where they fortified themselves, and to the fortress the invaders laid siege. A lively fire was directed upon the structure without harm to the inmates, but, after a few days, the latter — upon (as they always insisted) a promise of " safe conduct " — consented to accompany the besiegers to Boston; in a word, capitulated. At Boston the Gortonists were put on trial, not as would be supposed for trespass, or for anything connected with title to the Shawomet lands, but for heresy. If they could be convicted of that, all else would naturally follow. They were convicted, and death well-nigh became their portion. In lieu of death they were thrust in chains and set at hard labor. At length, in the spring of 1644, their presence becoming an embarrassment, they were liberated; but with the understanding that they were to betake themselves forever from the soil of Massachusetts, Providence, and Shawomet.

When, in January, 1643, Miantonomi affixed his hand to the deed of Shawomet to Gorton, he little foresaw that virtually he was affixing his hand to a warrant for his own undoing; but so it proved. On May 19, 1643, the New England Confederation was formed. It embraced Massachusetts, Plymouth, Connecticut, and New Haven. Of these colonies Connecticut was on the border and had suffered severely from the Indians. It responded in alarm to every rumor of an Indian uprising and kept urging upon Massachusetts action concerning the Narragansetts, against whom the jealousy of its own Indian allies — the Mohegans — constantly bred charges of treachery.

Massachusetts, in 1640 and again in 1642, had investigated like charges, and, finding them without foundation, had become convinced of the good-

will of the subjects of Canonicus and Miantonomi ;
but after the sale of Shawomet to Gorton its attitude changed. The presumption now in the mind
of the Bay — now that Miantonomi had cemented
a friendship with Gorton, with Gorton the heretic,
Gorton " the beast," Gorton " the blasphemer " —
was converted from one of innocence to one of
guilt. Accordingly, when in July, 1643, Miantonomi, as the result of an attack upon the Mohegans, was made captive by them and held pending
a decision as to his fate by the United Colonies,
Massachusetts, acting the part of a Pontius Pilate,
surrendered the unfortunate sachem — its own oft-
tried friend — unto the vengeance of Connecticut
and its allies. Miantonomi was condemned to death,
and on a day in September, at a spot near the present Connecticut town of Norwich, was slain by
Uncas the Mohegan, with a war-hatchet.

2. *The Pequod War ; Portsmouth and Newport.*

On the part of the Pequods — the most warlike
of the New England Indian tribes — a hostile attitude toward the English had early begun to be
manifested. By the summer of 1636 this attitude
had become so marked that Massachusetts, fearing
the consequences, set to work to secure the friendship of the Narragansetts. With the latter (through
the earnest and hazardous labors of Roger Williams) an alliance was formed. The Pequods thus
placed in isolation were, on the morning of May 26,

1637, surprised in their stronghold on the Mystic
River by the combined forces of Massachusetts and
Connecticut, and almost to a man delivered to the
sword.

The destruction of the Pequods removed from
the Narragansett region all immediate peril from
the Indians; and winning in the aspect of its woods
and waters as by nature the region was, it held
forth in its unsettled parts a seductive and insist-
ent invitation to the pioneer. Those to accept the
invitation were a band of refugees from Boston —
the Antinomians. Not long after the banishment
of Williams there had arisen at Boston a spirit of
strong reaction against the formalism, the rigid
ecclesiasticism, of Massachusetts. Here and there
protests began to be heard regarding the Puritan
doctrine of salvation by works as inculcated on
Sabbaths and Lecture Days by the pastor of the
Boston Church, the Rev. John Wilson. Anne
Hutchinson and her brother-in-law, John Wheelwright (both from near Boston in Lincolnshire)
were the most pronounced of the innovators; but
John Cotton, the associate of Wilson, was himself
an innovator; and even Sir Henry Vane, who in
1636 had been chosen governor, was an anti-legalist.

With a view to settling doctrine and restoring
discipline, there was held at Cambridge in September, 1637, a synod of the Massachusetts churches.
The movement was so far effective that it bridled
Cotton; but neither Mistress Hutchinson nor John

Wheelwright was cowed by it, and in November both were brought to trial as fomenters of sedition — disturbers of the civil peace. Wheelwright was found guilty and at once banished. Mistress Hutchinson, too, was found guilty, but banishment was deferred until she should have been tried by the Boston Church for heresy.

As a result of the proceedings above described, and of an order by the Massachusetts government for disarming such persons as sympathized with the victims, a considerable party of Boston people, headed by William Coddington and John Clarke, set forth in March, 1638, to seek to the southward a more congenial place of abiding. The party had Delaware in view, but owing to detention at Cape Cod were enabled to hold (through their leaders) a conference with Roger Williams at Providence. At Williams's suggestion, and by his aid, there was obtained on March 24 a deed from Canonicus and Miantonomi " to William Coddington and his friends united under him " for Aquidneck (the island of Rhode Island) in Narragansett Bay ; and hither the Antinomian company straightway repaired to lay the foundations of Portsmouth.

William Coddington was born in Boston, England, in 1601, and in his native town was a man of substance and position. When the corporation of Massachusetts Bay was formed, he was made one of the assistants or council, and later became treasurer. On the trial of Anne Hutchinson for sedition, he boldly withstood Winthrop, John Endicott, and the clergy. John Clarke was born on October 8, 1609, in Bedfordshire. He was by calling a physician, and his general education was unusual for the time. On arriving at Boston in 1637, he, like Williams before him, was astounded at the bigotry which he found enthroned, and immediately began casting about him for a more liberal retreat. Now that a retreat had been found, the next step was to erect a government; and it seems to have been a step somewhat summarily taken. Indeed, at first, the Antinomians did little else than re-erect the Jewish system whence they so lately had fled. Already at Providence they had chosen Coddington chief magistrate under the title of Judge, and upon their occupation of the island no change was made until January, 1639, when three elders (John Coggeshall, Nicholas Easton, and William Brenton) were chosen " to assist in the execution of justice and judgment."

In the nature of things a theocracy on the island of Aquidneck could not long endure. Antinomianism in the very term implied oppugnancy to forms. It was of the spirit, and the spirit must be free. Then, too, on Aquidneck, Antinomianism was succored by the influence of two extraordinary personalities — Anne Hutchinson and Samuel Gorton. The former had come to Portsmouth (where her husband William Hutchinson had preceded her) at the conclusion of her trial for heresy, — a trial

in the issue of which she had been pronounced
excommunicate and delivered up to Satan,— and
Gorton had come fresh from his legal tussle with
the magistrates of Plymouth. So pronounced now
was the latitudinarian tendency that it alarmed
both Coddington and Clarke. On April 29, 1639,
they, together with their more immediate friends,
— William Dyer, Thomas Hazard, and Henry Bull,
— abandoned Portsmouth, and, proceeding to the
southerly end of the island, established a new settlement — Newport.

At Newport the system of government by judge
and elders was reinaugurated, and to the judge
there was accorded "a double voice." At Portsmouth, meanwhile, ideas essentially Antinomian
were given scope. The community made formal
acknowledgment of King Charles I and (perhaps
as a concession to Gorton) adopted the common
law. They elected, for one year, a chief magistrate (William Hutchinson) and eight assistants
or councilmen, and established quarterly courts
and trial by jury. The separation of the two island
towns lasted until March 12, 1640, when, discovering that separated they were weak, they
resumed the original union. Separation, however,
had taught to each a lesson — the lesson taught
of old by Menænius Agrippa. At Portsmouth it
had taught that radicalism may be too radical
and end in anarchy. At Newport it had taught
that conservatism may be too conservative and end

in tyranny. The government which the reunion brought into effect was characterized by wise features of both radicalism and conservatism. There were to be a governor and deputy-governor and four assistants — all annually chosen. The governor and two of the assistants were always to be chosen by one of the towns, and the deputy-governor and two of the assistants were always to be chosen by the other of the towns. There also were to be chosen, annually, two treasurers, a secretary, two constables, and a general sergeant. Nor did the work of statesmanship stop here. In 1641 the State was formally declared a democracy under the control of the "Body of Freemen orderly assembled, or the major part of them," and no one was to be "accounted a delinquent for Doctrine" who kept the civil peace. Already there had been adopted the common law with its scheme of magisterial courts, courts of quarter sessions, and jury of the vicinage.

Now that the island of Aquidneck had become a political entity, the contrast between it and the entity (or *non*-entity) Providence was marked in the extreme. By Providence there was symbolized individualism both religious and political — a force centrifugal, disjunctive, and even disruptive. By Aquidneck (and especially by the Newport part of it) there was symbolized collectivism — a collectivism thoroughly individualized as to religion, but in politics conjunctive and centripetal. On Aquidneck, as at Providence, the employment of the people was agriculture — swine and sheep breeding, the breeding of horses, and dairy farming. Agriculture everywhere tends to separatism; and in early Rhode Island it emphasized the individualistic bent imparted by the idea of Freedom of Conscience. During the age of Roger Williams that which we are bidden to contemplate on the shores of Narragansett Bay is a struggle for supremacy between separatism and collectivism.

3. *Providence Plantations — the Patent of 1644.*

When pondering the question of reunion with Portsmouth, the Newport government had instructed Mr. John Clarke and Elder Nicholas Easton " to inform Mr. Vane by writing of the state of things here, and desire him to treate about the obtaining a Patent of the Island from his Majesty." Nothing had resulted, and in 1642 it was decided to send to England a representative — Roger Williams.

Williams, because of the decree forbidding his presence in Massachusetts, set sail in 1643 from New York in a Dutch ship, and late in the summer or early in the autumn reached London. Here he met Sir Henry Vane, — the young Sir Henry whom he had known in Boston in 1635, now prominent in the councils of the Long Parliament, — and through Vane he came to know Oliver Cromwell. The affairs of the colonies were in charge of a Parliamentary board at the head of which was Robert,

Earl of Warwick. To this board application was made by Williams for a patent of incorporation for the Narragansett settlements — Providence, Portsmouth, and Newport; and on March 14, 1644, there was issued a patent under the appropriate seals. The instrument empowered the inhabitants of the settlements in question to " govern and rule themselves by such a form of civil government as by voluntary consent of all, or the greater part of them, they should find most serviceable ; . . . the laws . . . of the said plantation to be conformable to the laws of England, so far as the nature and constitution of the place would admit."

Seemingly all was well. But since 1641 there had been sojourning in London two ardent representatives of Massachusetts — the Rev. Thomas Welde and the Rev. Hugh Peters. Hearing of the mission of Williams in quest of a patent, they early had taken measures to thwart it. By dint of contriving, they, on December 10, 1643, had obtained (under the signatures of nine members of the colonial board — one member less than a majority) a patent whereby there was added to the bounds and limits of Massachusetts the "tract of land . . . called the Narragansett Bay in America." The Narragansett Patent, as it was designated, was sent to Boston in 1645, and there made the basis of a claim to the whole of the unoccupied part of the Narragansett region ; but the insufficiency of the instrument was too obvious to admit of much parleying, and the claim under it was unsuccessful. One fact it made manifest; namely, that Roger Williams had come to England none too soon.

With his own patent in possession, Williams returned to Providence in September, 1644, and his coming was made the occasion of a demonstration at Seekonk. He was met by a small flotilla of canoes, and triumphantly escorted home. But those who escorted him were all from Providence. None from the island participated in the act of welcome. Williams had been sent abroad to procure a patent for Aquidneck. It is not recorded that the people of Providence had even expressed a wish for a patent. When, therefore, the agent for the island returned bearing a patent which not only coupled Aquidneck with Providence, but bestowed upon the infelicitous combination the name " Providence Plantations," Coddington and his friends were little pleased. They exhibited their chagrin by postponing to the latest practicable moment recognition of validity in the instrument which had been secured. So far did they carry resentment that upon learning, just before Williams's arrival, of the step which he had taken, they hastened to apply to the New England Confederation to be received into alliance. " I desire," wrote Coddington to Winthrop on August 5, 1644, "to have either such alliance with yourselves or Plymouth, one or both as might be safe for us all." To this intimation the confederation replied declining an alliance, but counseling subjection ; and here for a season the matter dropped.

Although Coddington and his friends were loath to accept the Roger Williams patent, there were others upon the island who deemed acceptance the wiser course, and on May 19, 1647, a general convention was held at Portsmouth to organize for Providence Plantations a government. In this convention Providence was represented by ten delegates, but in the main the convention was probably a Landsgemeinde or popular gathering of freeholders. A year later the freeholders met again, this time at Providence ; and in 1649 and 1650 further meetings were held. In October, 1650, the Landsgemeinde was superseded by a court of representatives.

The work of the several conventions consisted in creating a government, legislative, executive, and judicial, and in adopting a code of laws. Legislative power was vested in the freeholders through a committee of six from each town, called the General Court. A measure might originate with a single town or with the General Court, but was only to become a law upon adoption by " the Major parte of the Colonie." In 1650 this device was so far modified that the General Court was given " the full power of the General Assemblie " or freemen, but must submit its acts to the freemen for possible rejection. In its modified form the device was that of the Swiss Referendum. Executive

functions were made to devolve chiefly on the presiding officer of the General Court, called " the
President." The president was to be aided by four
assistants, one from each town; and besides these
officers there were to be a treasurer, a sergeant, a
general recorder, an attorney-general, and a solicit-
or-general. A " Generall Courte of Tryalls," composed of the president and assistants, was instituted.
It was to exercise original jurisdiction in graver
criminal cases and in cases arising between town
and town, between residents of different towns,
or between a town and a resident of a neighbor-
ing colony. Likewise there was instituted trial by
jury. The code of laws which was adopted (the
Code of 1647) is noteworthy in a high degree. By
it the death penalty was limited to a few heinous
offenses; banishment and imprisonment for debt
were repudiated; divorce might be granted only
for adultery; and the maritime code, " the Lawes
of Oleron," was declared in force.

The Code of 1647 was the work of the people
of Aquidneck. It embodied their organizing and
systematizing spirit and thus wrought for collectivism. But in its framing there were not overlooked
the claims of particularism. Providence, in commissioning its ten delegates to the Portsmouth
convention, had been at pains to instruct them to
make known its wish " to have full power and authoritie to transacte all [its] home affaires," and
the wish was both made known and regarded. A

bill of rights, containing the familiar provisions of Magna Charta in defense of personal liberty, was passed. In the sessions of the Court of Trials the magistrates of the town where the court was held were empowered to sit with the general magistrates for " councile and helpe." The court, furthermore, was to sit permanently in no one town, but, as also (after 1652) the General Assembly, was to make the circuit of the towns, beginning with Newport. Warwick, which had not been named in the patent, was accorded the privileges of the other towns; and in order that the one underlying principle in which Providence, Portsmouth, Newport, and Warwick were agreed — the supreme *raison d'être* for their several and collective existence — might be duly emphasized, the Code of 1647 was drawn to a conclusion thus: " Otherwise than what is . . . herein forbidden, all men may walk as their consciences persuade them, everyone in the name of his God."

The first president of Providence Plantations was a Newport man, John Coggeshall; but upon the island William Coddington had been almost continuously chief magistrate, and in May, 1648, he was chosen president. He however did not come forward to accept the office. He was too busily engaged in intriguing for the admission of Aquidneck into the New England Confederation. Indeed, in September, 1648, he and a few others formally petitioned the confederation to be received in "a

firme and perpetuall League of friendship." The
petition was rejected, and in October Coddington,
accompanied by his daughter, set sail for England
to make trial what he himself might be able to do
toward obtaining for the island that autonomy
which it had failed to receive at the hands of
Roger Williams. In London Coddington met Sir
Henry Vane and Hugh Peters. The latter had
become a preacher to the Council of State, and
through his aid, perchance, the Aquidneck magnate
gained an introduction to the council itself. At all
events, he laid before that body a petition in which
he described himself as the " discoverer and owner "
of the islands of Aquidneck and Conanicut in
Narragansett Bay, and asked to be confirmed in
his title to these islands and to be made governor
over them. The petition was referred in March,
1651, and, despite protests from Edward Winslow
in behalf of Plymouth, was so speedily acted upon
that by April 3 Coddington found himself appointed governor of the two islands for life — a
veritable king in miniature, with power to select a
council of six, to administer law, and to raise forces
for defence.

Short lived was his glory. In August, 1651, he
reached home. Meetings forthwith were held at
Newport, Providence, and Portsmouth. On every
hand there was shown a determination to secure a
revocation of the new and revolutionary patent.
Accordingly, in November, Roger Williams for

the mainland and John Clarke for the island were on their way to the mother country. There they met Vane and Cromwell, and on October 2, 1652, an order was obtained directing that Providence Plantations continue under the government authorized in the Roger Williams patent until further commanded.

Roger Williams returned from England in 1654; but although news of the revocation of the Coddington patent had been received in the Plantations in February, 1653, the mainland and the island were found still to be maintaining a divided existence. Samuel Gorton had filled for one year the office of president of the mainland towns, and in 1652 a law had been enacted by these towns, providing that "whereas there is a common course practiced amongst Englishmen to buy negers that they may have them for service or slaves forever," it be ordered that "no black mankind, or white," may be forced to serve any man or his assigns longer than ten years. On the island Coddington had been met by armed resistance, and, forced to seek safety in flight, had in April, 1652, at Boston, signed a disavowal of exclusive personal proprietorship of the island lands. In 1653, the island, anticipating a future source of wealth and power, had commissioned privateers in the war then in progress between England and Holland.

It remained for Williams, by virtue of a severe arraignment of the colony under the hand of Sir

Henry Vane, and by virtue of an eloquent and
moving appeal under his own hand, to effect a
reunion of the island with the mainland. Formal
articles of agreement were ratified on August 31,
1654, and on September 12 Roger Williams was
elected president of the rehabilitated commonwealth. As for William Coddington, his last hope
was extinguished when, in March, 1655, Oliver
Cromwell, now Lord Protector, wrote that the colony were to proceed in their government " according to ye tenor of their charter formerly granted."
A year later the Newport magnate put his hand
to the declaration: " I William Coddington, doe
freely submit to ye authoritie of his Highness in
this Colonie, as it is now united, and that with all
my heart."

The struggle against collectivism, by which the
first period of Rhode Island history is characterized, was a struggle not confined to bodies politic
such as the mainland and island. It extended to
religious sects. Providence from the first had been
Anabaptist. At Newport the original Antinomianism had gradually been tending to Anabaptism
and Quietism. Upon removing to Aquidneck, Anne
Hutchinson had become Anabaptist; so much so
that, impelled by distrust of the collectivistic spirit
of Coddington with its longing after the United
Colonies, she, in 1642 or 1643, had removed to
East Chester, New York, where she and all her
family, save one, had fallen a prey to the Indians.

In Roger Williams Anabaptism had, in 1639 or 1640, become Seekerism, the *ne plus ultra* of religious individualism ; and in William Harris secularism (by reason of the poverty of the man — land was an inconvertible asset) had become a kind of anarchism. In 1657, during the presidency of Williams, Harris, because of his advocacy of the doctrine that " he that can say it is his conscience ought not to yield subjection to any human order amongst men," was arrested and tried for high treason. By 1651 Anabaptism on the island was grown distinctively aggressive. In July three Anabaptists — John Clarke, Obadiah Holmes, and John Crandall — boldly ventured into Massachusetts with their practices. They were seized, and one of them (Holmes) was scourged for his temerity with a three-thonged lash.

To Anabaptist aggressiveness there succeeded the more intense aggressiveness of the Quakers. The sect began coming to Boston from England in 1656. Driven from that town by stripes, they were received at Newport. In September, 1657, the New England Confederation upbraided Providence Plantations for its course. At this time Benedict Arnold was president, and his reply was : " We have no law whereby to punish any for only declaring by words their minds and understandings concerning the things and ways of God as to Salvation and an eternal condition." Between 1656 and 1660 many were the Quakers that from the

convenient harborage of Aquidneck essayed the
wrath of the Bay and of its high priest of persecution, John Endicott. Among them were Mary
Clarke, Christopher Holder, John Copeland, William Brend, William Robinson, and Marmaduke
Stevenson; but the most noteworthy of them all
was Mary Dyer. She was wife to the secretary
of the colony, William Dyer, and though sweet of
disposition, had, under Anne Hutchinson, her pre-
ceptress, become so infatuated an individualist, so
relentless a challenger of theocratic pretensions,
that she can hardly be regarded as possessed of
perfect mental balance. By reiterated baitings of
Endicott she provoked her own death, and on June
1, 1660, was hanged on Boston Common.

Rhode Island and Providence Plantations — The Charter of 1663

On March 13, 1644, the General Court of
Aquidneck changed the name of that island to
the "Isle of Rhodes or Rhode Island." No little
discussion has from time to time been occasioned
by surmises as to the origin of the name; but
Roger Williams, writing in 1666, remarked that
"Rhode Island, like the Isle of Rhodes, in the
Greek language is an island of Roses;" and deri-
vation more authoritative we perhaps shall not be
able to discover.[1] At all events, in 1663, when

[1] In the *English Historical Review* for October, 1903, Mr. Louis
Dyer, of Oxford, England, advances the theory that the name

John Clarke was negotiating with the restored
monarch Charles II for a royal charter for the
Narragansett Bay colony, he was careful to repay
Williams for his assumption (in the Patent of
1644) of the name " Providence Plantations" by
placing before the latter, in the new instrument,
the name " Rhode Island."

The restoration of Charles, which took place in
1660, was for the Narragansett Bay settlements
an event of the first importance. Now that the
king was on his throne, the question arose, What
validity has the Patent of 1644? It was felt that
measures to secure a royal charter should be taken
without delay. John Clarke was in England, where
he had lingered on private business after the return of Roger Williams in 1654, and to him in
1661 there was sent a commission as agent for the
colony in its new undertaking. Clarke set earnestly
to work, and on July 8, 1663, the charter was issued.
It was conveyed to the Plantations by Captain
George Baxter, and on November 24 the freemen
assembled at Newport to inspect the instrument
and to hear it read. It was taken by Baxter from

" Rhode Island " is merely a translation of the Indian name for
the island of Rhode Island — Aquidneck. "Aquidneck," observes
Mr. Dyer, " the island in the bay, was englished into Road or
Roads Island. The prevalence in the early texts of the spelling
Road goes to confirm this account of the matter. . . 'Roade
Island is' (we read in a document dated in 1661 [Richman's
Rhode Island, vol. ii, p. 239]) 'a road, refuge, asylum, to evil
livers.' " From the above Mr. S. S. Rider strongly dissents in
Book Notes, vol. xx.

its box, and by him " with much becoming gravity held up on hygh to the perfect view of the people." It then was read aloud and returned for safe keeping to its receptacle. The alterations which it effected in the existing constitution were not fundamental. Boundaries were made more certain ; Freedom of Conscience was elaborately confirmed ; the president was superseded by a governor and deputy-governor ; the assistants were increased from four to ten ; the General Assembly was made to consist in the governor (or deputy-governor), the assistants, and a body of deputies to be chosen, six from Newport, four each from Providence, Portsmouth, and Warwick, and two each from all other towns ; the courts were left much as before, but the Court of Trials was made a fixture at Newport.

In obtaining for their government and jurisdiction the sanction of a charter from the king, it was hoped by Rhode Islanders to insure for themselves the toleration and, perchance, respect of their neighbors on the east and on the west. But so it did not turn out. By both Massachusetts and Connecticut the charter was deemed a sword rather than an olive branch. Since the acts of subjection on the part of the Arnolds, and of Pumham and Sacononoco, the Bay and Plymouth (one or both) had asserted a claim to eastern Rhode Island, including the island of Aquidneck. These claims were practically disallowed in 1665, when commissioners of the king fixed the eastern littoral of Nar-

ragansett Bay as the western limit of any possible
claim by Plymouth; and the whole question was
settled in 1746–47, when, by a final decision of the
crown, Massachusetts (the heir in 1691 to Plymouth
territory) was obliged under the charter to surrender to Rhode Island the border towns of Cumberland, Warren, Bristol, Tiverton, and Little
Compton.

But it was with Connecticut that the principal
difficulty was encountered. On the return of the
Gortonists from Boston in 1644, they found a temporary asylum at Portsmouth. Thence Samuel
Gorton was summoned by Canonicus to an impòr-
tant conference. The Narragansett Indians, observing that the Gortonists had been liberated by the
Puritans, came to the conclusion that the former
must be identified with the stronger party in England (where war was known to be in progress), and
the Puritans with the weaker. They therefore, as
against the weak Puritans (by whom Miantonomi
had been put to death), decided to espouse the cause
of the strong Gortonists, and desired of Gorton that
he would make record of a formal act of subjection
by them to the English sachem. The record was
duly made on April 19, and in December Samuel
Gorton, together with Randall Holden, was on his
way with the document to the shores of a distracted
realm.

During the period of the English Commonwealth
the act of subjection by the Narragansetts to the

king was of course entirely void of effect. Oppression on the Indians by the Puritans increased rather than diminished.

The territory chiefly occupied by the Narragansett nation was that part of the present State of Rhode Island south of the south line of Warwick and Coventry. It was a region of stony soil, but its lagoons and streams were well supplied with fish. As early as 1640 or 1641 Richard Smith, a Gloucestershire man, had built a trading house at Cawcamsqussick (Wickford); and in 1645 or 1647 Roger Williams also had come hither to trade. In January, 1657, the easterly part of so much of the present town of South Kingstown as lies west of Boston and Point Judith Necks was purchased from the Indians by a company of Newporters called the Pettiquamscutt Company; and in June, 1660, a further company of Newport men purchased Misquamicutt (Westerly). The purchase by the Pettiquamscutt Company — an association comprising among its members one stanch Bostonian, John Hull[1] — gave Providence Plantations occasion to reflect, and in 1658 there was passed a law forbidding purchases from the Indians without consent of the colony. In 1661 confirmation of the Misquamicutt purchase was secured; but for a purchase made in 1659 by a company of Massachusetts

[1] The other members of the company were Samuel Wilbor, Thomas Mumford, John Porter, and Samuel Wilson. Afterwards Benedict Arnold and William Brenton became members.

men, called the Atherton Company, confirmation was not even asked.

The objects of the Atherton association were two-fold: to obtain a vast tract of land, and to place this tract under the jurisdiction of Massachusetts or Connecticut. In the attainment of their first object they secured, in 1659, Indian deeds for Quidnesset (northeasterly North Kingstown) and Namcook (Boston Neck); and in 1660 they secured from Ninigret, the Nyantic, and other sachems, an Indian mortgage upon all the unoccupied lands of Narragansett. The mortgage was given to insure to the association repayment of an indemnity which had been exacted from Ninigret by the United Colonies, but which the association had artfully assumed. Under the mortgage (in 1662) the association undertook to perfect a title by foreclosure. The same year the second object of the Atherton Company was seemingly effected through a charter issued by the crown to Connecticut for territory extending on the eastward to the "Narragansett River."

The agent principally concerned in negotiating the charter for Connecticut was John Winthrop, Jr., son of the early governor of Massachusetts, and Winthrop had been made a member of the Atherton Company. The issuing of the Connecticut charter narrowed controversy, for thereby Massachusetts, which had been claiming a part of Narragansett as land conquered from the Pequods, was completely ousted. As between Connecticut and Rhode Island, the jurisdiction of the latter over Narragansett was at the last moment sought to be saved by John Clarke by a stipulation, concluded between himself and Winthrop, that wherever in the Connecticut charter the eastern boundary of that colony was described as fixed by the Narragansett River, the words " Narragansett River " should be taken as signifying Pawcatuck River — the western limit of Rhode Island under the Patent of 1644.

Out of the Clarke-Winthrop stipulation there grew a controversy as prolonged as it was bitter. In 1665 Sir Robert Carr, Colonel George Cartwright, and Mr. Samuel Maverick, as commissioners of the king for settling the royal authority in New England, visited Rhode Island, and while there they met in council the sachems of the Narragansetts. They found them enraged at Massachusetts and the United Colonies because of the indemnity mortgage and pretensions of the Atherton Company. They also found them possessed of a lively recollection of the submission which, in 1644, they as a nation had made to King Charles I. Under these conditions, and privately instructed as the commissioners were by Lord Clarendon, they annulled the Atherton mortgage, and placed the Narragansett country (entitled the King's Province) under the administrative authority of Rhode Island. This act, however, by no means put an

end to the claims of Connecticut. These claims
were asserted and reasserted. Sustained in 1683
by a royal commission headed by Edward Cran-
field, they were rejected in 1687 by Sir Edmund
Andros. Sustained again, in 1696, by the attorney-
general of King William, they were yielded vol-
untarily in 1703 (out of policy) by Connecticut
itself. Revived in 1723, they were abandoned forever in 1728. Meanwhile, in 1674, Rhode Island
had erected the Kings Province into the town of
Kingstown, and in 1677 had detached from Kingstown the town of East Greenwich.

The men to whom the preservation of Narragansett to Rhode Island is mainly to be ascribed
were Samuel Gorton, Randall Holden, and the
John Greenes, father and son. Gorton and Holden, as a result of their journey to England in
1644 with the sachems' deed, obtained an order
permitting the reoccupation of Shawomet (Warwick). Afterwards (1660) William Harris, whose
appetite for land was insatiable, had, under certain deeds from the Indians (called "confirmation
deeds"), obtained color of title to a wide area for
the Providence town fellowship and the Pawtuxet
proprietors. Some of the Pawtuxet land (under
the " confirmation deeds ") extended south of the
north line of Warwick, and this circumstance led
to a union on the part of the Gortonists with Roger
Williams to resist Harris.

In 1677 Holden and John Greene, Jr., visited

England, but gained no permanent advantage. In 1679 Harris set forth for the same destination. He did so not merely in his own interest, but as the authorized agent of Connecticut and the Atherton associates to further their pretensions to Narragansett. While on the way (January, 1680) the ship in which he was embarked, the Unity, was captured by Algerians, and he himself was made a slave and held for ransom. Piteous were the letters which Harris sent home to his family and friends. "I pray you therefore," he wrote on April 4, "to stir up both parties to send bills of the said sum 1191 pieces of eight and 5 royals. If the sum fail, or the time, it is most likely to be my death ;— for then I fall permanently into the cruel man's hands that hath like to kill me already." The money was secured and sent, and in the winter of 1680–81 Harris was given his freedom, but the boon came too late. On reaching London, the victim of Algerine barbarity died from exhaustion. Had he lived, the cause of Connecticut would have been powerfully advocated. That he did not live, that through the labors and pains exacted of him he perished, is significant of the vigor and pertinacity with which he was withstood.

In the midst of the struggle for Narragansett (indeed, much as though in mockery of it), there broke forth King Philip's War. The conflict was one which long had been impending. Little by

little the Pokanokets — the people of the region
once ruled by Massasoit — had been crowded to
the westward and had grown sullen and suspicious.
Causes, too, in the case of the Narragansetts had
been making for alienation. First there was the
execution (never to be forgotten) of Miantonomi.
Next there was the fruitless and disappointing
submission and resubmission of the nation to the
Stuart kings. It was the English of the United
Colonies that chiefly were responsible for the unhappy situation ; but the time had at length come
in New England when it was realized by the Indian that he and his white brother were not com-
patible, could not dwell together, but must contend
for supremacy.

The immediate occasion of hostilities was the
death of Wamsutta or Alexander, the elder son of
Massasoit. In 1662 Alexander had been arrested,
by order of the governor of Plymouth, on suspicion
of conspiracy, and during his detention had died
of a fever. It was thought by the Indians that he
had been poisoned. His successor was his brother
Meatacom or Philip. It was resolved by Philip to
avenge Alexander's death, and in June, 1675, he
withdrew into the country of the Nipmucs (central
Massachusetts), leaving behind him a trail of fire
and blood. At this time the war sachem of the
Narragansetts was Canonchet, a son of Miantonomi. The war begun by Philip was regarded by
Canonchet as an opportunity to avenge the death

of his parent, and he lent what aid he could against Plymouth and Massachusetts. In December the three colonies — Plymouth, Massachusetts, and Connecticut — invaded the Narragansett country. Assailing the Indians in their stronghold or fortified village, they inflicted upon them a crushing defeat. Early in 1676 the dispersed Narragansetts burned Warwick and a portion of Providence. In their advance on Providence they destroyed "Study Hill" in Cumberland, the abode of William Blackstone, an eccentric recluse of the Church of England and friend of Roger Williams. As for Williams himself, it is the tradition that on the approach of the savages he fearlessly met them, staff in hand, and sought to dissuade them from further acts of devastation, but in vain.

In April Canonchet was captured and put to death. His executioner, strangely enough, was Oneko, son of Uncas, the destroyer of Miantonomi. The final event in King Philip's War was the killing of Philip himself by a force under Captain Benjamin Church of Plymouth. Driven from point to point, Philip, in June, concealed himself in a swamp at the foot of his ancient fastness of Mount Hope. Church was told of his whereabouts, and, secretly investing the spot at night, startled his prey. The entrapped sachem made a bold dash for liberty, but was shot through the heart by one of Church's men, and fell headlong in the mud and water.[1]

[1] King Philip's War left the Narragansett Indians much reduced

Rhode Island as a colony took little part in King Philip's War. The cause was the dominance of the Quakers. Antinomianism on Aquidneck had now been merged in Quakerism. The early families — the Coddingtons, the Eastons, the Clarkes, the Bulls — nearly all had become Quakers. In 1672 George Fox himself had visited Newport, and his presence had been made by Roger Williams (who still was enough of a Puritan to

and dispersed. By 1707 Ninigret (the head of the tributary Nyantics) was the only sachem of Narragansett affiliations with whom the Rhode Island government could treat. With him, accordingly, on March 28, 1709, an agreement was made by which all of the vacant Narragansett territory (the region which had been sought to be appropriated by the Atherton Company) was conveyed to the colony, except a tract eight miles square in Charlestown, which was kept as an Indian reservation. In 1713 an act was passed by the General Assembly inhibiting sales within the reservation save by consent of the colony. In 1759 the inhibition was removed. In 1763 various members of the Narragansett nation made complaint that, through the removal of the inhibition, their sachem (Thomas Ninigret) was rapidly dispossessing the nation of all its lands. The colony therefore interposed, but the alienation of lands (especially upon long leases) was not much checked, and in 1792 a committee was appointed to establish regulations. By 1791 the whole number of Narragansetts in Charlestown had dwindled to two hundred and fifty, and by 1833 to one hundred and ninety-nine, of whom only seven were of the genuine blood. In 1880 the tribal relations of the Narragansett nation were abolished and rights of citizenship were conferred upon the members. — *Opinion of the Justices of the R. I. Supreme Court relative to the Narragansetts*, January, 1898. *A Statement of the Case of the Narragansett Tribe of Indians as shown by the Manuscript Collection of Sir William Johnson*, compiled by James N. Arnold, 1896.

detest the heresy of the " inner light ") occasion
for a challenge to public debate. Fox had departed
before the challenge could be delivered to him, but
it had been accepted by his associates, John Burn-
yeat, John Stubbs, and William Edmundson. On
August 9 a tumultuous controversy — one which
Williams had come all the way from Providence
in an open boat to conduct — had been held in the
Newport Quaker meeting-house.

By the Charter of 1663 there was imparted to
Rhode Island, despite the machinations of Massachusetts and Connecticut, stability both territorial
and administrative. Under the instrument, collectivism gained over separatism. The several towns
were reduced in their privileges, and the colony
became for the first time an entity. So far did
the process of integration extend that Block Island
(which down to 1662 had been an appanage of
Massachusetts) was in 1664 incorporated with
Rhode Island, and in 1672 erected into the political division New Shoreham.

4. *Sir Edmund Andros and the Quo Warranto.*

At the end of the seventeen years during which
England had been ruled by Parliament or by
Cromwell, the American colonies — particularly
Massachusetts — had grown well-nigh independent
and had developed a considerable commerce. They
had traded without hindrance with the friends and
enemies of the mother country; with the Dutch

more especially; and their freedom (in words attributable to Roger Williams) had perhaps been for them " a sweete cup," rendering them " wanton and too active." Now that the monarchy was restored, it became the royal policy — a policy inaugurated by Clarendon — to curb colonial pretensions.

The curbing was to be in two directions : in that of Puritan religious intolerance and in that of disregard of the acts of Revenue and Navigation. So far as Massachusetts was concerned, the king's commissioners had in 1664 endeavored to change the basis of the suffrage from church membership to property, and to secure recognition for the book of common prayer, and of a right in the crown to try revenue cases ; but with little result other than to provoke hostile demonstrations. In Rhode Island there of course was no religious intolerance, and the colony possessed little commerce; so the crown was content with the situation. Nor perhaps would a different feeling have arisen had it not been for the renewal of difficulties with the Netherlands. But difficulties were renewed; and when, in 1674, peace at length was declared, the exasperation of the English crown and merchants at the disloyal trading spirit of the colonies, which had dwelt on gain while Monk struggled in the Channel with De Ruyter, was intense.

The revenue acts, breach of which had been complained of by the commissioners, were acts passed respectively in 1660 and 1663 (12th and 15th of Charles II) ; and they so far restricted colonial trade as to prohibit, with slight exception, the direct importation of European commodities into the colonies. Such commodities must be carried thither by way of England. The acts in reality imposed no particular hardship on the colonies, for England was for most things the best purchasing market in any event. Indeed, in one important respect the acts were positively beneficial. Under them trade with the colonies might be conducted only in English built or British colonial built ships, and for the building of such ships the colonies themselves (especially in New England) were well adapted. More than aught else, therefore, breach of the acts was an expression of resentment on the part of colonial importers and shippers at being required to abandon the easy, convenient, and long - established practice of employing the ubiquitous Dutch bottoms.

In 1675 and 1676 the English merchants — London silk mercers and others — petitioned the crown for redress against New England as the " mart and staple whereby the navigation of the kingdom is injured ; " and the same year Edward Randolph was sent over, as agent for the Lords of Trade and Plantations, to make an investigation. He visited several of the colonies, and in 1678 his position was strengthened by an appointment as collector and surveyor of customs. Thenceforth his every

effort was put forth toward securing what he knew
the crown desired, namely, proof of violations of
law and privileges on the part of the chartered colonies sufficient to justify an annulment of the charters themselves. As a result of his toils, the charter
of Massachusetts was annulled in 1684. In 1685
he was instructed to "prepare papers . . . upon
which writs of *quo warranto* might be granted
against Connecticut and Rhode Island."

Randolph promptly complied in a document
which alleged, in the case of Rhode Island, that
the colony disregarded the laws of England and,
like Massachusetts, "violated the Acts of Trade."
A writ accordingly was issued, and in May, 1686,
the collector (who for a season had been in England) reached America with it in his possession.
It was served in June, and the General Assembly,
loyal to the last, voted " not to stand suit with his
Majesty but to proceed by . . . humble address
. . . to continue our humble privileges and liberties according to our charter." It had been the
plan of the crown to unite Massachusetts, New
Hampshire, Maine, Plymouth, and Narragansett
into a royal province; but in February, 1685,
Charles II had died, and under James II, his
successor, there was provisionally adopted a
plan whereby Massachusetts, New Hampshire, and
Narragansett were placed under the government
of a " President and Council." The president
was Joseph Dudley of Boston, and for a short

period Narragansett, which had been organized as Kingstown, was fated to bear the name of Rochester.

On June 3, 1686, the whole of New England was created a royal province under Sir Edmund Andros as governor in chief, and the chartered liberties of Connecticut and Rhode Island seemed by the act forever to be forfeited and concluded. Late in the year Andros made official announcement of his authority to receive the surrender of the Rhode Island charter, and in 1687, while on a visit to Newport, he demanded the instrument. It, however, had been put out of the hands of Walter Clarke, the governor, and could not be found. In Rhode Island the rule of Andros was little noteworthy. The General Assembly, taking advantage of the separatist spirit still strong in the commonwealth, had in 1686 sought to devolve political authority on the several towns ; had sought, in other words, to meet danger (after the manner of some forms of crustacean life) by resolving the threatened organism into its integral and elemental parts. How far the plan might have succeeded cannot be told, for in April, 1689, on news of the abdication of James II, New England rose against Andros and imprisoned him. In Rhode Island government was reëstablished under the charter in February, 1690, with Henry Bull as governor ; and in 1693 (December 7) the attorney-general of the crown rendered a formal opinion that in point of law nothing stood in the way of a confirmation of the charter by William and Mary.

With the flight of James from Whitehall the age of Roger Williams comes fully and finally to a close. Since 1643, the year of the founding of Warwick, the four geographical points — Providence, Portsmouth, Newport, and Warwick — had grown slowly. At Providence and Warwick the people still pastured their cattle and horses, and turned loose their depredating swine. Rarely did they get news of the outside world, and none of them, save William Harris, achieved anything like the position of a magnate. At Newport sheep and horses were bred, and men such as William Coddington, William Brenton, Nicholas Easton, and Henry Bull, identified themselves with picturesque estates which, in "Coddington Cove," "Brenton's Neck," "Easton's Beach," and "Bull's Point," have perpetuated their names. By 1686 the population of the island was perhaps twenty-five hundred. That of Providence was perhaps six hundred, and that of Portsmouth and Warwick together, perhaps eight or nine hundred.

As contrasted with each other, the island was refined, flourishing, aristocratic, while the mainland was primitive, poor, and plebeian. Yet despite the limitations of an agricultural existence — an existence ameliorated at Newport after 1660 by intimations of commerce — the age of Roger Williams in Rhode Island was a great age. For the first time in human history State had wholly been dissociated from Church in a commonwealth not utopian but real. For the first time the fundamental idea of modern civilization — that of rights of man as a being responsible primarily to God and not to the community — had been given an impulse powerful and direct.

As for the six historical personalities about whom the age centred, all now were dead. Anne Hutchinson, the vindicator of faith against works, had died in 1643. John Clarke, the procurer of the Charter of 1663, had died in 1676. Samuel Gorton, the founder of Warwick and defender of Narragansett, had died in 1677. William Coddington, the first Newport magnate, had died in 1678. William Harris — more even than Coddington the Mammon of the group — had died in 1681. The last to pass away was Roger Williams himself. He died between January 16 and May 10, 1683, aged about eighty years.

PART II

COMMERCE AND COÖPERATION

1690–1763

CHAPTER III

PAPER MONEY

Canadian Expeditions — The Ten " Banks " — *Trevett vs. Weeden.*

KING WILLIAM, who with Mary his spouse came to
the English throne in 1689, was a ruler who knew
thoroughly his own mind, and that mind was to
diminish in the world the disproportionate power
of France under Louis XIV. He purposed to
make war upon Louis ; and as war would involve a
clash between the French and English in America,
it became part of his policy to dispose the American colonies into groups, and to place the control
of each group (for military ends) in a single hand.
Thus Massachusetts, Connecticut, and Rhode Island were constituted a New England group under
the military control of Sir William Phips.

Of the policy of King William, however, the
part spoken of was conspicuous for ill success.
Neither Connecticut nor Rhode Island (because of
its charter) would recognize in Phips the least
authority. Then there was France. Already Count
Frontenac had hurled bands of savages against
New York, New Hampshire, and the dwellers on
the Penobscot. Schenectady had fallen in massa-

cre, and Boston itself had not been without alarm.
In 1692, therefore, the English government gave
urgent direction that a conference be held at Albany. Most of the colonies — distant Maryland
included — sent delegates, but Rhode Island did
not; nor did it respond to a direct appeal for help
addressed to it in 1693 by the governor of New
York, Benjamin Fletcher.

In fact, throughout the whole of King William's
War (1690–1697) the Narragansett Bay colony
furnished aid neither to Phips nor Fletcher, and
one at least of its pleas in apology must excite a
smile. Owing, it said, to the undeterminated state
of its eastern boundary, Massachusetts was enabled
to " detain from it several of its towns," whereby
it was " incapacitated." But another plea Rhode
Island offered which was honest and in large measure a justification. " May it please your most
excellent Majesty," the General Assembly wrote to
the king in 1693, " *this your Collony is a frontier
to your collonies in New England, by sea.*" Rhode
Island and the Sea is a topic that awaits us with
the next chapter, but we may here pause to reflect
how truly this early official letter struck the key-
note of Rhode Island history in the eighteenth
century. Privateering gave rise to hardihood and
skill upon the wave ; hardihood and skill brought
to Narragansett Bay wealth from the West Indies ;
and by wealth there was built up that Newport
which, throughout the three decades just preced-

ing the Revolution, surpassed New York for trade
and quite eclipsed Boston for culture.

The death of William in 1702 left Louis XIV
to be dealt with by Queen Anne, and the queen
(by Marlborough's help) waged war against him
from 1702 to 1713. In the earlier stages of the
war Rhode Island failed to meet demands for men
made by New York and Massachusetts; but in
1707 it changed its attitude, furnishing, at the
request of Massachusetts, militia and a ship in the
abortive expedition against Port Royal. This action it emphasized in 1709 by cheerfully responding with its quota and with two ships of war for the
contemplated Vetch-Nicholson expedition against
Canada; and again in 1710 it was at hand with
more than its quota and with three warships for
the second and, this time (as it proved), successful
Port Royal expedition. From 1707 to 1763 — a
period marked by the disastrous invasion of Canada
in 1711, the disastrous attack upon Cartagena in
1741, the brilliant capture of Louisburg in 1745,
and by the whole series of struggles ending with
the conquest of Canada in 1763 — Rhode Island
was pervaded by a martial spirit, a spirit involving
of necessity much also of the spirit of coöperation.

In 1710 (during the governorship of Samuel
Cranston) the cloud like a man's hand appeared.
In that year the colony, staggered by the cost of
its military undertakings, voted an issue of bills of

credit for £5000. These were to mature in five years and were to be redeemed in specie. To insure redemption, an annual tax of £1000 was laid for the period during which the bills were to be outstanding. In making the issue in question, Rhode Island followed the example of Massachusetts, a colony which in 1690 had had recourse to bills to meet the demands of its soldiers disappointed of booty in Canada. Cotton Mather quaintly condones these demands, observing: " *Arma tenenti, omnia dat, qui justa negat;* " and in truth it is difficult to see what course other than to pledge its good faith was open either to Massachusetts or Rhode Island in the circumstances in which both were placed.

Harm for Rhode Island lay not in a small issue of redeemable bills of credit; it lay in the taste of the joys of credit *per se* — unlimited credit — which these bills were the means of affording a hungry demos. In 1710 the colony was not beyond the agricultural stage; it had few merchants; its predominant class were landowners; and what is more these landowners were land poor. Add the fact that in the eighteenth century the nature of money and of the relation of money to credit was in general ill understood, and it is not surprising that in Rhode Island the demos (the landowners), balked of a circulating medium, should at the first opportunity have gone credit mad.

A second issue of colony bills came in the year 1715, and this issue differed from the first. The bills (£40,000) now no longer were secured by tax levy, but by mortgages upon land. Any person wishing to supply himself with money might mortgage his land to the government and receive bills to the amount of his mortgage. Upon the bills he was to pay five per cent interest, and the principal represented was to be met in ten years. Here evidently was a contrivance that exactly fitted the Rhode Island landowner's case. Such owner had plenty of land; this land he could convert into money by help of the government; and when the day should arrive for converting the money back, he might get an extension of time. What the landowner did not perceive was that the land in which he abounded had, by reason of lack of demand, little immediate or convertible value. When put in pledge to the colony, it was not an available treasury asset. Had it had convertible value, the owner could have sold it, or borrowed upon it upon easy terms in the open market, and the government need not have been involved.

Between 1710 and 1751 there were nine several "banks" (as the loans upon land security were called) floated in Rhode Island; and what these "banks" typified for the colony was distinctly a rake's progress. At first (1715) the "bank," like the bill of credit, was honestly resorted to as a means of meeting the cost incurred in Queen Anne's War. Next (1721, 1728, 1731, 1733, and 1738) it was resorted to as a means of postponing liquidation and so of keeping the people satisfied; although, to put a better face upon the operation, stress was laid on bounties, on the opportunely ruinous condition of Fort Anne (afterwards Fort George) at the entrance to Newport Harbor, and on the likewise opportunely ruinous condition of the Newport jail.

By 1731, when the total amount of bills outstanding exceeded £120,000, uneasiness began to be shown. Depreciation had set in to such an extent that silver, which had been worth eight shillings an ounce, now rose to twenty. Besides, counterfeiting was becoming a vexatious grievance.[1] But there was another cause for the gathering alarm. Rhode Island was no longer wholly agricultural. At Newport mercantile interests were waxing strong. Accordingly, on the 25th of June, just after the General Assembly had decreed a "bank" of £60,000, Governor Joseph Jenckes, relying upon an order-in-council issued in 1720, requiring the

[1] Under date of February 17, 1729, John Comer makes note in his diary of "a number of persons found in ye act of counterfeiting ye bills of credit of this colony." These persons had, as they expressed it, "unanimously joined in a League and Contract, to use our best endeavors in our respective places to make and put off without discovery a quantity of paper money." The "League" was concluded thus: "God save ye King, prosper our progress herein, and keep us from all traitors. . . . Then each and every one of us taking ye Bible in our hands swore by ye contents thereof, to observe these Articles of Agreement." It further appears from Comer's diary that on April 28, 1729, Nicholas Oatis, one of the "League," "stood in ye pillory and had his ears clipt for making money." — *R. I. Hist. Coll.* vol. viii.

royal assent to acts for the emission of bills of credit, interposed a veto. A storm at once arose, and the governor, backed by such representative Newporters as Abraham Redwood, William Ellery, John Freebody, Nathaniel Kay, Daniel Ayrault, and others, appealed for justification to the king.

The situation was one of interest. Never before had a Rhode Island governor presumed to try to checkmate the General Assembly. So to presume, indeed, was revolutionary of Rhode Island ideas — an attack upon the colony's individualistic democracy. As it proved, the old principles were entirely safe. The king decided, first, that by the Rhode Island charter the governor himself was " a part of the Assembly," hence void of power against it; and, second, that by the charter the crown even had no discretionary power of repealing laws in Rhode Island. All laws enacted there were valid, save such as contravened the laws of England.

The foregoing decision but served of course to encourage the supporters of the credit system, and under the régime of the Wantons and of Governor William Greene the launching of "banks" went merrily on in the years 1740 and 1744. These years were years of war, and as such afforded to the scheme of " banks " a better pretext, for now perhaps Fort George did require repairing, and of a certainty there were required both ships and men. Still depreciation was only accelerated; nor could it be brought to pause by the device of inscribing upon the bills their declared value in gold and silver. So serious had the depreciation become by 1746 that the Assembly was forced to raise the qualification of voters from two hundred to four hundred pounds, in order to keep the franchise within anything like its original limits.

All this was bad enough, but it was not the worst. In 1747 Parliament appropriated £800,000 to reimburse the colonies for their outlay in the expedition against Louisburg, and Massachusetts with its proportion of the sum proceeded to redeem in part its outstanding paper. It at the same time passed an act prohibiting the circulation of the bills of the other colonies within its borders. Here was a further blow to Rhode Island money, a blow fraught with bankruptcy for not a few.

The strength of the landholding class around Narragansett Bay and the fatuous blindness there of nearly everybody else, excepting a few merchants at Newport, is illustrated by an elaborate defense of paper money addressed by Governor Richard Ward to the Lords of Trade on January 9, 1740. The governor confessed to bills outstanding in the aggregate of £340,000 ; but calling attention to the trade of the colony, which was represented by one hundred and twenty sail, drew the hardy inference that " if this colony be in any respect happy and flourishing, it is paper money and a right application of it that hath rendered us so."

With 1750 Rhode Island in its financial "progress" came to a turning point. In the month of August a " bank " of £50,000 was ordered by the lower house of the Assembly. Counterfeiting was made punishable with death, and the Assembly adjourned to reconvene in September. On September 4 a petition bearing seventy-two signatures, signatures of substantial, intelligent men — of the Freebodys, the Ayraults, the Harrisons, the Redwoods, the Tillinghasts — was forwarded in desperation to the king.

" The currency or instrument of commerce of a country [declared the petitioners] being the standard and measure by which the worth of all things bought and sold are established and determined, it ought to be fixed invariably, otherwise property can neither be ascertained nor secured by any plan or method whatsoever." Five allegations were then categorically put forth: That the currency of Rhode Island had sunk in value " above one half in seven years;" that the colony had now outstanding in bills £525,335; that these bills " ought to be drawn in by a tax;" that so far from levying such a tax the house of deputies had just passed a vote for £50,000 of further bills; that of the bills outstanding £390,000 had been secured by mortgages upon land, and that a strong reason for the authorization by the deputies of the £50,000 more of similar bills was that, in the general plethora, landowners might be en-

abled to discharge their mortgages for a song.
The petitioners humbly prayed that his Majesty
would prevent the government of its colony of
Rhode Island "from emitting any more bills of
credit upon loan" without his Majesty's permission.

The prayer was effective. In 1751 Parliament
passed an act forbidding all further "banks," •
and permitting the issue of bills of credit for but
two objects, — current expenses of the colony and
expenses arising from the exigencies of war. Bills
for the first object might run two years, and for
the second, five. Provision for redemption must
be made at the time of issue; there was to be no
legal tender feature, and the royal approval was
to be a *sine qua non*.

By means of bills of the character indicated,
Rhode Island was enabled, without serious strain,
to meet its proportion of the cost of the expedition projected in 1755 against Crown Point; and
when, in 1756, there were received from England
six chests of silver and one of gold as a partial
reimbursement of outlay, the money was promptly
used for redemption purposes. In 1763, at the
end of the struggle for Canada, gold and silver
coin were made by act of the Assembly the only
lawful money in the colony. The recovery by
Rhode Island of sanity upon the money question
was remarkably swift; as swift almost as had
been the recovery by Massachusetts of sanity upon
the question of witchcraft. Moreover, throughout

the war of the Revolution Rhode Island maintained its good reputation. In 1776 it with great docility accepted the recommendation of a committee of the New England States to emit no unnecessary bills of credit, but rather to levy taxes or borrow; and, in 1780, acting upon a resolution of the Continental Congress, it passed a measure so equitably adjusting between debtor and creditor the complexities growing out of Continental currency that its course was widely imitated.

For the reformed commonwealth, as for the reformed individual, lo, the pitfalls and temptations! For Rhode Island the temptation now to be recorded was sore indeed.

In launching its first "bank" the colony had been moved by a cry for money, a convenience, rather than by a cry for bread, a necessity. In 1786, when the tenth and last "bank" was launched, bread to an alarming extent was the object sought.

In this situation what the enlightened part of the people desired to do was to grin and bear misfortune; what the unenlightened part desired to do was to secure immediate relief. In 1785 the General Assembly (still in the hands of the commercial class) rejected a petition for an emission of paper. In 1786 the General Assembly, now divided between the commercial class and their

opponents the agriculturalists, gave strong signs
of regarding paper as not the worst of evils. Newport and Providence thereupon presented strong
protests, and again the movement for paper
received a check. But in 1786, at the spring
election, the agriculturalists carried all before
them, and an Assembly was elected pledged to
paper as the only means of relief.

The triumph of the agriculturalists on the
money question was in reality the triumph (tem-
porarily) of the old individualism over coöperation.
It was a reactionary step, and, like most steps of
the kind, culminated in extremes. The new Assembly, on convening, passed an act for the
launching of a " bank " — the familiar old bank
of the years 1710 to 1750 — for £100,000. But
the old bank was made· fresh by a clever device.
Should any creditor refuse to accept its bills in
payment, the debtor might secure a discharge by
depositing bills in the amount of his debt with
one of the judges of the Superior Court or of the
Court of Common Pleas. It nevertheless was part
of the device that, upon the completion of the
deposit, the judge must cite the creditor personally
to appear within ten days to receive his money ;
and under this provision many and diverting were
the incidents. The natural order of things (as in
" Alice Through the Looking Glass ") was entirely
reversed. Instead of debtors seeking to escape
their creditors, creditors now were seeking franti-

cally to escape their debtors. Haggard and harassed, the pursued creditor found (we are told)
asylum in his attic; or perchance leaped headlong
from a convenient window.

But two months were required to demonstrate
that existing measures would not prevent a depreciation of the new bills. An act, therefore, was
passed imposing a penalty of one hundred pounds
upon any one who should refuse to accept them at
their face value in exchange for commodities. This
act made clear the wisdom of those who had counseled a policy of endurance rather than one of
credit. Merchants closed their stores. People left
the State. Food became scarcer than ever. Uncon-
vinced still, and wrathful at opposition, the agriculturalists got together in town meetings and farmers'
conventions and arranged for a convention which
should be representative of farmers throughout the
State. By this body, to which sixteen towns sent
delegates, it was advised that the paper money
laws be " supported." And supported they were
to the bitter end.

At a special session of the General Assembly
held in August, 1786, at Newport, there was created
a court for the trial of complaints against creditors.
The court consisted of not less than three judges
drawn from the Superior Court or Court of Common Pleas, and was to convene at any time upon
three days' summons. There was to be no jury,
decision was to be by majority vote, and from such

decision there was to be no appeal. The one-hundred pound penalty for refusing to give commodities for paper was reduced, but the reduction was largely offset by a provision that upon the conviction of a creditor sentence was to be put immediately into execution. Neither delay nor suspension was to be permitted. Against the above described sweeping attack by the legislature upon personal liberty, the commercial element, through the deputies from Newport, Providence, Bristol, Warren, and New Shoreham, made vigorous protest, but absolutely to no effect. It remained for a poor Newport butcher — a man so poor that within a month he had received town aid — to vindicate Magna Charta by precipitating one of the most memorable trials in American history.

The butcher referred to was John Weeden. In September, 1786, he refused a piece of paper currency tendered him by John Trevett in payment for a piece of meat. Trevett at once filed a complaint, and the case was heard before the judges of the Superior Court on September 25. The defendant was charged with a violation of the statute, and this charge he met by a threefold plea : first, that the statute had expired (a technical contention based on the ambiguous wording of the act); second, that the matter complained of had been made triable before a special court uncontrolled by the supreme judiciary ; and third, that the statute was unconstitutional and void, because

by it there was denied to the defendant a trial by
jury.

Weeden's counsel were James M. Varnum of
East Greenwich and Henry Marchant of Newport,
men of the highest standing and best talent. Varnum addressed the court first, and in opening said:
"Well may a profound silence mark the attention
of this numerous and respectable assembly! Well
may anxiety be displayed in every countenance!
Well may the dignity of the bench condescend to
our solicitude for a most candid and serious attention, seeing that from the first settlement of this
country until the present moment a question of
such magnitude as that upon which the judgment
of the court is now prayed hath not been judicially
agitated!"

The first two points of the plea for the accused
were dwelt upon briefly. The third — that of denial
of trial by jury — was elaborated exhaustively and
with deep feeling. It was Varnum's contention that
trial by one's peers (the mode of trial secured to
every Englishman by Magna Charta) had been
established in Rhode Island by the charter of the
colony, which provided that the inhabitants "should
have and enjoy all liberties . . . of free and natural subjects . . . as if they . . . were born
within the realm of England." American independence, it was averred, did not affect the matter, for
the colony charter had been retained and was in
force as the constitution of the State. With this

point settled there remained but one other. Who
in a given case was to decide whether an in-
habitant — a citizen — had been deprived of a
chartered right? "Have the judges a power to
repeal, to amend, to alter laws, or to make new
laws?" asked the advocate. "God forbid! In that
case they would become legislators." "But," he
continued, "the judiciary have the sole power of
judging of laws . . . and cannot admit any act of
the legislature as law which is against the constitution." Here was the whole case for the accused,
and it was a strong one.

But strong on the constitutional point as Weeden's case was, the point itself was hardly (as Varnum had claimed in his exordium) one never before
" judicially agitated " in America. A single court
prior to this time (the Supreme Court of New Jersey in 1779) had weighed the question of the competence of the judiciary to declare an act of the
legislature void on constitutional grounds, and had
found unanimously in favor of such competence.[1]

[1] The New Jersey case was *Holmes vs. Walton*, 4 Halstead,
N. J., 444. (See *Am. Hist. Rev.* vol. iv, p. 469.) *Trevett vs. Weeden*,
although not decided upon constitutional grounds, is often quoted
as if so decided. (See Cooley, *Constitutional Limitations*, 4th ed.
p. 196; Bryce, *The American Commonwealth* (earlier editions), vol.
i, p. 244; Arnold, *History of Rhode Island*, vol. ii, p. 525; McMas-
ter, *History of the People of the United States*, vol. i, pp. 337–339
(but see vol. v, p. 398); Fiske, *The Critical Period of American
History*, p. 175; Channing, *The United States of America*, p. 119.
The true ground of the decision (lack of jurisdiction) was stated
in 1883 by Judge Thomas Durfee of Rhode Island in his " Glean-

In *Trevett vs. Weeden* the Rhode Island judiciary waived the constitutional point, and, tacitly indorsing the plea of the accused that the body charged with the trial of the offense was not the Superior Court, but one specially constituted, dismissed the complaint before it for lack of jurisdiction.

ings from the Judicial History of Rhode Island" (Rider's *Hist. Tract No. 18*, p. 52). It was also stated by Mr. S. S. Rider in 1889, in a review of Bryce's *American Commonwealth* (*Book Notes*, vol. vi, p. 41), and in 1902 by Mr. E. C. Stiness in his " Struggle for Judicial Supremacy in Rhode Island," contributed to Edward Field's *Rhode Island at the End of the Century*, vol. iii).

What makes the New Jersey and Rhode Island cases of surpassing interest is a consideration of an historical nature. Until these decisions were made, it was an open question in America whether the courts (state and national) would, in gauging legislative power, follow English Parliamentary precedent, or the *dicta* of certain English judges. According to Parliamentary precedent, the legislature (Parliament) was an omnipotent body bound by no set of fundamental principles. According to the *dicta* of a few English judges, " the Common Law doth control Acts of Parliament." Thus Lord Coke (the patron of Roger Williams) in Bonham's case (8 Rep. 114) and Chief Justice Hobart (Hobart's Reports) held that the common law was supreme over Parliament. In *Trevett vs. Weeden*, Varnum cited both Coke and Hobart, as also Plowden and Bacon's Abridgment (iv, 635), in support of his contention that the legislature was bound to regard constitutional limitations. Presumably similar citations were made in *Holmes vs. Walton*. The American courts, therefore, chose at the very outset (1779 and 1786) to indorse the *dicta* of judges like Coke, Hobart, Plowden, and Bacon, in support of the common law (constitutional law) rather than to follow the strict precedent of English Parliamentary practice. On the whole subject the reader is referred to an admirable paper by Judge Charles B. Elliott of Minneapolis, printed in the *Political Science Quarterly* for June, 1890.

At first the dismissal — construed as it was as a
vindication of both Weeden and honest money —
promised ill consequences. Rhode Island's individualistic democracy was shocked profoundly; more
so than it had been at the attempted exercise by
Governor Jenckes of the veto power. Was it then
true, it was indignantly asked, that in Rhode Island
the ruling element was no longer the people? Were
governors and judges to set themselves up against
the General Assembly? Not if the General Assembly rightly gauged its power. Paul Mumford,
Joseph Hazard, Thomas Tillinghast, Gilbert Devol,
and David Howell — the five judges who had heard
the now famous case — were summoned promptly
to appear before the Assembly and to assign the
reasons of their judgment. The court (so the summons recited) had declared an act of the supreme
legislature unconstitutional and void, and such
adjudication " tended to abolish the legislative authority." Howell, the youngest of the judges, but a
Princeton graduate and the only trained lawyer
of the court, explained that the act had not been
declared unconstitutional. He at the same time
proclaimed it the right of the bench to pass upon
the constitutionality of any legislative act. At
length the Assembly, counseled by the attorney-
general (William Channing, father of William
Ellery Channing), brought itself to declare: " As
the judges are not charged with any criminality
in rendering the judgment upon the information

Trevett vs. Weeden, they are discharged from any further attendance upon this Assembly, on that account."

At the spring election of 1788 Hazard, Tillinghast, and Howell all failed of reëlection; but such evidences of spleen proved to be only the dying convulsions of the paper money party. By 1789 (when the legal tender statute of 1786 was repealed) death had quite supervened; not, however, before Rhode Island's reputation had been smirched; nor before a Connecticut poet had sung in jeering distich, —

> " Hail realm of rogues, renowned for fraud and guile,
> All hail ye knaveries of yon little isle.
>
> .   .   .   .
>
> The wiser race, the snares of law to shun,
> Like Lot from Sodom, from Rhode Island run."

CHAPTER IV

RHODE ISLAND AND THE SEA

Piracy and Bellomont — The Wantons and Privateering — Colony
Sloop Tartar — The Spanish Main.

IF, down to 1759, the wars with France and Spain
led in Rhode Island to the manifold woes of paper
money, these same wars, together with the great
French war of 1756, led to other things as well.
They led through privateering to the golden age
of Newport. They led also, through the same
means, to an American navy.

It was in May, 1690, that Rhode Island waged
its first fight upon the sea. A French privateering fleet of seven small sail had captured Block
Island. For a week the captors had rioted there,
plundering and maltreating the inhabitants and
threatening a descent upon Newport itself. In the
emergency Captain Thomas Paine, a Newport
seaman, manned two sloops with ninety men and
sought the enemy. He soon fell in with five sail,
and, running into shallow water to avoid being
surrounded, gave battle against odds. The French
captain bore down in melodramatic style, wishing
himself "damned if he did not board immediately," but was repulsed and after two hours of

musketry combat withdrew. The day following, when Paine would have renewed the attack, his enemy put hastily to sea, scuttling a prize laden with wines to expedite his progress.

The year 1690 was that of the beginning of King William's War, but it was by no means that of the beginning of Rhode Island's familiarity with privateering. As long ago as 1653 the island of Rhode Island had sent out vessels against the Dutch; and since 1680 captains bearing questionable West India commissions had found the shores of Narragansett Bay not inhospitable. In fact, the redoubtable Paine was of this class, for in 1683, on arriving at Newport in command of a ship commissioned from Jamaica, he had escaped arrest only by the timely interposition of Governor William Coddington.

The report as to Paine which the deputy collector at Boston sent to England may well have elicited the letter which in 1684 was dispatched by the king to Rhode Island, commanding the enactment of a law for the " suppressing of privateers and pirates." At all events such a law was passed. But law or no law, the business of privateering (now piracy) at Rhode Island was not lessened, and by the close of King William's War, in 1697, it was to attain proportions truly formidable.

From 1690 to 1695 John Easton was governor at Newport. From 1696 to 1698 the governor was Walter Clarke. Both Easton and Clarke were

Quakers, and as such purposely inactive with regard to the war then in progress. But during the
entire decade, 1690 to 1700, John Greene was deputy-governor. Upon him as emphatically a fighting man there devolved the task of prosecuting the
conflict — a task which, as Rhode Island did virtually nothing on land, consisted mainly in commissioning privateers. Greene in some respects was a
unique character. He was a strong Gortonist, and
in that capacity had rendered important public
service by withstanding Harris and the Atherton
Company. But his Gortonism was avowedly Antinomian in the extreme. There was involved in it
the doctrine that, provided a man were at one with
God inwardly, it mattered not what his mere outward conduct might be; " he might [if he chose]
do what a beast might do." So, in commissioning
privateers, Greene with tranquil "inwardness"
took no bonds and kept few troublesome copies of
papers. The fact that these privateers in many
instances turned out piratical craft is something
which may or may not have been anticipated.

Nathaniel Coddington, register of the local Court
of Admiralty, charges Deputy-Governor Greene
with having commissioned thirty privateers during
the year 1694. Among them was a barque commanded by John Bankes and a brigantine commanded by William Mayes. Apropos of Mayes, the
Lords of Trade advised the Governor and Company
of Rhode Island in 1697 that it was reported that

their colony was "a place where pirates were ordinarily too kindly entertained;" and it is true that in 1699 the return of Mayes from the Red Sea "with vast wealth" was eagerly awaited. But Bankes is of more interest to us than Mayes, for he had as a partner or companion the famous Rhode Islander, Thomas Tew.

The vessels of Bankes and Tew — the latter vessel a large sloop with accommodations for eighty men — lay side by side at Newport, and the strife to fill a berth in either was intense. Says Coddington : " Men come from all the country round ; servants left their masters and sons their parents ; many hid themselves on board ; it may be with a griefe spoken the endeavors some men made to send away the youth of the land." " Of these men," Coddington continues, "our good governor [Easton] laboured to hinder the wicked designs." And again : " All the vessels had great guns mounted ; no cost was spared for small arms and powder. . . . The discourse was generally that they were bound to Madagascar, but some [thought] they were to go to the Red Sea [1] where the money was as plenty as

[1] " We [a band of English pirates] came early in 1696 to Liparan Island at the mouth of the Red Sea, where three more sail of English came to us, one commanded by Thomas Wake, another, the Pearl, William Mues [Mayes] commander, fitted out at Rhode Island, the Amity, Thomas Tew commander. . . . They all joined partnership, putting Captain Every [Avery] in command. . . . After five or six days the Moors' ships, twenty-five in number, passed them in the night; but hearing of this from a

stones and sand, saying the people there were infidels, and it was no sin to kill them." Bankes got away in due form by Greene's connivance; but Tew made the mistake of applying for a commission to Easton, and the further mistake of offering the governor a *douceur* of £500. He did not get his commission, so put to sea without a clearance. He joined forces with the noted pirate Mission; established a colony in Madagascar; resisted the Portuguese; amassed an immense fortune; and returning to Newport paid the owners of the vessel in which he had sailed fourteen times the cost of their adventure.

One day a pirate more desperate even than Tew appeared — Joseph Bradish. In 1698 Bradish was boatswain's mate on board the ship Adventure,

captured ketch they resolved to follow them. . . . Steering for Surat we caught up one of the ships which we took after she had fired three shots, she had £50,000 or £60,000 on board in silver and gold. We shortly afterwards spied another ship, mounting forty guns and carrying (as was said) 800 men. She stood a fight of three hours and yielded."

" We kept possession of both ships, and all the crew, except one man, boarded her by turns, taking only provisions, necessaries, and treasure, which was very great, but little in comparison with what was on board; for though they put several to the torture they would not confess where the rest of their treasure lay. They took great quantities of jewels, and a saddle and bridle set with rubies designed as a present for the Great Mogul. Several of the Indian women on board were, by their habits and jewels, of better quality than the rest." [Report by the secretary of the East India Company to the Lords of Trade concerning acts of piracy committed in the Indian seas in the spring of 1696. — *British State Papers — America and West Indies — 1696, 1697.*]

bound from London to Borneo. Winning twenty
men to his design, he awaited his chance, seized
the vessel, put ashore part of the crew on a desert
spot to starve, and made all sail for Block Island
— that same Block Island which in 1690 had been
so gallantly rescued from piratical hands by Captain Paine. But in the estimation of the Block
Islanders there evidently were pirates and pirates.
One kind came (as had come the French) to plun-
der and lay waste; another kind — the Bradish
kind — came to find shelter and to divide spoil.
The latter were welcome. Capture, however, over-
took Bradish, and he was lodged in jail in Boston.
He soon contrived to escape, and with fine discrimination as to places fled back to Rhode Island.

Throughout the period covered by King William's War and the deputy-governorship of Greene
it was well-nigh impossible in Rhode Island to
secure the apprehension, the detention, or the conviction of any person for piracy. Pirates resorted
there, spent their money there, even married there.
Arrests, it is true, were sometimes made, as in the
case of Robert Munday and George Cutler of the
Henry Avery crew, who were unable to account for
money and East India goods in their possession;
but escape by connivance of jailers was more certain than arrest, and when it was sought to indict
the jailers grand juries were wont to indorse " ig-
noramus " upon the bills. Indeed, by 1699 so perfect a haven for freebooters had Narragansett Bay

become that certain of the associates of the never-to-be-forgotten William Kidd were making it their asylum. Among them was the murderous James Gillam. Also among them was our own worthy Captain Thomas Paine, soon to be enrolled a founder of Trinity Church, Newport. To him, in his unobtrusive abode on the island of Conanicut, Kidd from his jail in Boston sent a messenger for gold ; and by him the aforesaid messenger was intrusted with " seven bars."

But the day of reckoning was at hand. Seriously aroused by complaints and threats from the Great Mogul of India, the English government had resolved to suppress piracy. In March, 1697, the Earl of Bellomont was appointed governor of New York, Massachusetts, and New Hampshire, with powers of captain-general over Rhode Island and Connecticut. Shortly afterwards Peleg Sanford was appointed judge of admiralty for Rhode Island. In 1653, during the war with Holland, the island of Rhode Island had established an Admiralty Court ; and in 1694 the colony, as a convenience for condemning prizes, had (until the king's pleasure should be further known) revived the institution. When Peleg Sanford presented his commission as admiralty judge by royal appointment, judicial offices conflicted. The governor, Walter Clarke, solved the point for the present by taking the Sanford commission and keeping it.

In May, 1698, Clarke was succeeded as governor by his nephew, Samuel Cranston, and soon Edward Randolph, surveyor-general of his Majesty's customs in America, visited Rhode Island. There followed a series of stinging dispatches to Cranston from the Lords of Trade demanding sight of the commissions and bonds (mostly non-existent) under which privateers had been sent out by Deputy-Governor John Greene, and notifying the governor of the deputing of Lord Bellomont as a special agent of the crown to inquire into the local "disorders and irregularities."

Bellomont's inquiry was conducted by himself at Newport in September, 1699, and when concluded an elaborate report of it was sent to the Lords of Trade. The report was scathing. It declared that the colony usurped and exercised admiralty power contrary to the charter; that the prosecuting attorney was "a poor, illiterate mechanic;" that John Greene, the deputy-governor, was "a brutish man of very corrupt or no principles in religion;" that his commissions to privateers were made out "to the captain or his assignees," hence to anybody and everybody; and finally, that "the government was notoriously faulty in countenancing and harboring of pirates who had openly brought in and disposed of their effects, whereby the place had been greatly enriched." Cranston, meanwhile (awakened to the peril in which the colony stood), was eating exceedingly

humble pie before both the Lords of Trade and
Bellomont, — " begging a favorable construction
in what of weakness may appear in us, we being
a plain and mean sort of people; " or, as he further expresses it, " an ignorant and contemptible
people."

Before Bellomont's report could be acted upon,
its author died at New York and Joseph Dudley
was appointed governor of Massachusetts. This
appointment was made in 1701. It carried with
it, as in the case of Phips and Bellomont, power
over the Rhode Island militia, and there was soon
annexed a power of vice-admiralty.

Dudley, in 1705, revived against Rhode Island
Bellomont's charges. But now, with war begun,
the disposition of the home government to be critical of the maritime ethics of its privateering colony
was perceptibly lessened. Nor should it be overlooked that at this juncture the London agent of
Rhode Island was the accomplished William Penn,
nor that Penn's relations with Queen Anne were
those of a trusted courtier.

Clear as the culpability of Rhode Island is with
respect to piracy, one fact should be emphasized:
no governor of the colony was ever actually caught
trafficking in official favors. Even Deputy-Governor John Greene — whose explanation to Bellomont of the negotiable and unbonded commissions
issued by him to Mayes, Bankes, and the others,
was that the recipients were good home folk, hence

presumably *sans reproche* as they certainly were
sans peur — probably gained little by his malle-
ability. In the early eighteenth century piracy was
rife all along the Atlantic coast, and Rhode Island
sustained to it relations less odious than did New
York or the Carolinas.[1]

[1] Extracts from the official correspondence of Lord Bellomont and of Governor Benjamin Fletcher: —

" I find that those Pyrates that have given the greatest disturb-
ance in the East Indies and Red Sea, have been either fitted from
New York or Rhode Island, and mann'd from New York. . . .
And Capt[n] Tew that had been before a most notorious Pirate
(complained of by the East India Company) on his returne from
the Indies with great riches made a visit to New York, where
(although a man of most mean and infamous character) he was
received and caressed by Coll: Fletcher, and they exchanged presents, as gold watches ette, with one another," etc. [New York,
May 8, 1698, Bellomont to the Lords of Trade. *N. Y. Col. Docs.*
vol. iv, p. 306.]

" I am informed by Mr Randolph, Surveyor General of the
Customs, that R. I. pretends to a Jurisdiction of a Court of Admiralty, and that they have seized a pirate there with his money
and designe to try him and perhaps acquitt him. I know not yet
what priviledge they have by their Charter, but I am well informed what constant encouragement they give to Pirates to come
in there, and bring in their spoils, and likewise what connivance
is made to the breach of all the Acts of Trade, and from thence
it may be concluded that there will be but very faint prosecu-
tions in a Court of Admty of their owne enacting," etc. [New
York, July 1, 1698, Bellomont to the Lords of Trade. *N. Y. Col.
Docs.* vol. iv, p. 334.]

" We are very sensible of what your Lordship writes about
the partiality and favour to pirates in R. I." [Oct. 25, 1698,
Lords of Trade to Bellomont. *N. Y. Col. Docs.* vol. iv, p.
414.]

" Capt Tew had formaly rec'd a commsn from the Govr of

With the passing of the peril from Bellomont
and Dudley, Rhode Island for the most part set-

Bermuda [so] I granted him a third to make warr upon the
French," etc.

"This Tew appeared to me not only a man of courage and activity, but of the greatest sence and remembrance of what he had
seen, of any seaman I had mett. He was allso what they call a
very pleasnt man, so that at some times when the labours of my
day were over it was some divertisment as well as information to
me, to heare him talke. I wish'd in my mind to make him a
sober man, and in particular to reclaime him from a vile habit of
swearing. I gave him a booke to that purpose ; and to gain the
more upon him a gunn of some value. In returne hereof he made
me also a present which was a curiosity and in value not much ;
and this is the sum of all the kindness I am chged with," etc.
[Dec. 24, 1698, Col. Benj. Fletcher's answer to charges. *N. Y.
Col. Docs.* vol. iv, p. 446.]

"Preparations [have] some while [been] mak'g of sending a
squadron of ships of Warr to suppress them [the pirates] there
[at Madagascar] and at Sta Maria." [Jan. 5, 1698–99, Lords of
Trade to Bellomont. *N. Y. Col. Docs.* vol. iv, p. 454.]

"Jos. Bradish born at Cambridge near Boston. Ran away with
ship Adventure an interloper to East Indies. Came to East end
of Nassau Isl [Long Island] & sunk the ship between that &
Block Isl — a ship of abt 400 tons. B. left money with Lt Col.
Peirson £942,19,3 — gave govr of R. I. notice where the money
concealed, which I heare he has since secured, Block Isl being in
his government. Some of the men who ran away with the ship
went out with Tew." [New York, May 3, 1699, Bellomont to
Lords of Trade. *N. Y. Col. Docs.* vol. iv, p. 512.]

"I send you the speech of Mr Cranston Gov of R. I. to the Assembly there about a fortnight since, wich you may please show
to the Lds of Trade as a specimen of the Temper of the people.
'Tis an original for Insolence and Nonsense. I do not mention it
in any of my letters to their Ldships, etc. But that I know that
Govmt and People to be the most piraticall in the Kings Domin-
ions." [Boston, Sept. 15, 1699, Bellomont to Sec. Popple. *N. Y.
Col. Docs.* vol. iv, p. 586.]

tled down to the practice of legitimate privateering; henceforth pirates, when caught, were hanged.
In Queen Anne's War the most distinguished
privateersmen were the Newport Wantons. The
founder of this family was Edward Wanton, a
Massachusetts man converted to Quakerism by
sight of the stark bodies of Quakers dangling on
Boston Common. Two of Edward's sons, William
and John, removed to Newport and established
themselves in ship-building. They were hardy and
resourceful, with a natural aptitude for the sea,
and just before the Peace of Ryswick, which ended
King William's War, performed with a volunteer
crew the daring feat of getting alongside a twenty-
gun French privateer which had been harrying the
coast and boarding and capturing her. For this
service, and for the capture (in 1702) of three
armed French vessels in the Gulf of St. Lawrence,
the brothers were summoned to England and
made the recipients of flattering attention by the
court.

The Wantons were valiant, yet in the family
character there evidently lurked something of the
spirit of mischievous perversity. It was brother

"I formerly acquainted your Ldships that Nassaw Isl alias
Long Isl was become a great Receptacle for Pirates; I am since
more confirm'd that 'tis so. Gillam a notorious pirate was suffered
to escape thither from R. I. and tis believed he is still there. . . .
I take that Isl especially the East End of it to exceed R. I."
[Oct. 20, 1699, Bellomont to Lords of Trade. *N. Y. Col. Docs.*
vol. iv, p. 591.]

John, magistrate, that in 1719 arbitrarily imprisoned Nathaniel Kay, the king's collector, in the
royal custom-house. It was brother John, deputy-
governor, that in 1731 reconvened the General
Assembly to discuss Governor Jenckes's veto of
the paper money bill after the governor himself
had declined to act. Ultimately the unpredictable
John — following his father's example — turned
Quaker; but not a whit the less for that did he
continue a fighting servant of the crown. As governor from 1734 to 1740 he issued commissions to
privateers, with a chuckle at the scandal thus
created. Admonition he met with the dry remark,
that "in all concerns he had listened to the still
small voice of divine emanation, and been obedient
thereto."

Queen Anne's War was brought to a close in
1713 with the signing of the Peace of Utrecht.
In 1714 the queen herself died. The next year
she was followed to the grave by the great Louis,
her own long-time enemy and the ancient enemy
of King William and of Marlborough. Until 1739
there was unwonted repose among the nations.
Then, under George II, there broke forth against
Spain the War of Jenkins' Ear. In 1744 France
went to the aid of Spain. Thereupon the conflict
became known as the War of the Austrian Succession, or King George's War, and the Rhode
Island privateers, which meanwhile had been do-

ing service merely as trading craft, renewed their
armaments and put to sea. But as this war in a
naval way had an important official as well as
privateering phase, it will be well to consider the
official phase of it first.

It is an interesting circumstance that the first
lord of the admiralty under the Walpole government — the government responsible for the Spanish War — was Sir Charles Wager, for as a lad
Wager had lived in Newport with John Hull.
While with Hull the youth had shown such remarkable talent for the sea that he had been taken
into the royal navy. Here he had risen through
the grades of captain and of rear- and vice-admiral.
In 1718 he had passed into civil office as a lord of
the admiralty. In 1733 he had been made first
lord, — a position which he held at the outbreak of
the hostilities now under review. Sir Charles was
much regarded by Rhode Islanders. His brilliant
career served to fire their seafaring natures with
restless zeal against both Spain and France.

The chief naval provision now (1740) made by
the colony was the construction of the Tartar, a
twenty-six gun sloop capable of berthing a hundred men. This vessel, sometimes alone and at
other times in company with the Connecticut colony sloop Defence, patrolled the coasts from Long
Island to Martha's Vineyard and effected a number of captures. The Tartar served as convoy in
the fruitless Cuban expedition of 1741, but its

principal service was performed in 1745, under Captain Daniel Fones, against Louisburg.

Rhode Island was of the opinion that the Louisburg expedition — the project of Governor William Shirley of Massachusetts — was a piece of reckless folly. As Governor Gideon Wanton said, "The scheme [which was carried by but a single vote at Boston] supposed the concurrence of many accidents, the consequences of any one of which failing would be fatal; the pretense to surprise such a town at such a distance with such a fleet and army appear'd to us . . . a most vain expectation. . . . As there was not to be one experienced officer or soldier . . . nor one engineer in the whole army, we could not avoid reflecting on the fatal miscarriages at Augustine and Carthagena." Shirley had a faith which Rhode Island lacked, and the following thrust by him in a letter to Governor William Greene is not wanting in keenness: "I must acknowledge, Sir, when I consider'd what frequent and very large emissions of paper bills of credit your assembly has of late made for the conveniency of the inhabitants of your colony, . . . I could not entertain the least doubt but that it would have made one emission for his majesty's service."

Although somewhat retarded by convoy duty, the Tartar reached Louisburg on April 25, 1745. On the way the sloop had fallen in with his Catholic Majesty's ship Renommée of thirty-six guns,

bringing dispatches from France, and Fones had
been compelled to run the gauntlet of four broadsides in order to avoid capture. In June the plucky
captain was sent with the Tartar and two consorts
to intercept a body of French and Indians which,
to the number of some twelve hundred, were
approaching in a fleet of sloops, schooners, and
canoes to the relief of the fortress. He met his
enemy in Femme Goose Bay and beat them pre-
cipitately back.

The next year (1746) the Tartar was held in
readiness to convoy Rhode Island's quota in the
third great expedition planned by the colonies
against Canada; but to such a design the French,
by a dramatic and wholly unforeseen movement,
put an end.

On the 6th of September, the Kinsale, one of
Vice-Admiral Townsend's fleet off Louisburg,
brought into port a prize — La Judith. The master, Antony Rodinguez, stated that on the 22d of
June he had left Rochelle in company with a fleet
of seventy sail, men-of-war and transports; that
the former consisted of fourteen ships of the line
of from fifty to seventy-four guns each; that the
transports carried eight thousand troops; and that
the entire force was under the command of the Duc
d'Anville. The news was at once forwarded to
Governor Shirley, and by him in turn, on September 22, to Governor William Greene at Newport.
Shirley's message was accompanied by a declaration

by René Het (a merchant of New York) that it
had been learned from the captain of a French
prize that Admiral Conflans, while at Petit Gouave
in Hispaniola, had taken from a fleet of merchantmen under convoy by him all the masters and pilots
acquainted with North American waters, and that,
putting others in their room, he had sailed away.
What the two statements — Rodinguez's and Het's
— meant was that D'Anville and Conflans were to
rendezvous somewhere to the north, and, united, to
make a descent upon Louisburg.

In the midst of the excitement resulting from
this disclosure Fones and the Tartar were sent out,
at the request of Governor Shirley, to meet if possible Admiral Lestock, who was daily expected at
Louisburg from Spithead with a body of troops,
and to warn him of D'Anville's approach. Orders
were that until October 25 Fones was to cruise
to the southward of Nova Scotia with sealed dispatches for the admiral. If the Tartar should be
taken by the French, Fones was to destroy his dispatches, "by no means suffering them to fall into
the enemy's hands." But the plans of French and
English alike came all to naught. As it chanced,
Conflans had reached Halifax (the stipulated rendezvous) early in September. Not finding D'Anville, he had sailed for home. A terrible gale had
arisen and the fleet of D'Anville had been badly
shattered. To complicate things still more, D'Anville had been stricken down with apoplexy and

had died. His second in command, D'Estournel, overcome with horror at the situation, had literally fallen upon his sword, and the third officer, La Jonquière, had conducted the fleet, battered and pestilence ridden, back to France. The Tartar, meanwhile, sought in vain for Lestock; that officer was yet upon the English coast.

In 1748, upon the conclusion of peace at Aix, the Tartar — the Old Ironsides of Rhode Island — was put up at auction (that melancholy limbo of so much that is historic) and sold to the highest bidder.

The privateering phase of King George's War was brilliant in the extreme. After twenty-six years of quiet the king had authorized Rhode Island to issue letters of marque and reprisal. The streets of Newport, therefore, were thronged with seamen in quest of adventures and prize money. Shirley complained roundly that the Boston sailors all fled to Newport to avoid impressment for Cape Breton, and the complaint was in great part just. Rhode Island, too, was highly cautious about restraining the practice, for privateering was a principal source of wealth to its people. The Malbones, the Browns, the Wantons, the Ayraults, the Freebodys — Newport merchants who had gained wealth in the West India trade — converted their fast sailing ships into armed cruisers, or built ships especially for cruising, and sent them out (brigantines and

brigs), a dozen or fifteen in a year, to prey upon
Spanish and French commerce.

There were the Triton, the Victory, the Defiance,
the Cæsar, the Mary, the King George, the Young
Godfrey, the Prince Frederic, the Prince Charles
of Lorraine, and a host more. Each had its own
favorite ground of operations. Silently, beautifully,
yet withal grimly, they dropped one by one out of
the harbor : some for the shrouding fogs of the
Newfoundland Banks ; some for the straits and
channels of the Leeward Islands ; some for Madagascar and the Red Sea. If to watch the departure
was interesting, it was thrilling to watch the return. Within hulls scarred in fight and beaten by
weather there lurked one knew not what treasures
of silks or " Kirman " wool, of gold, wines, or ivory.
In 1746, 22,500 pieces-of-eight were brought back
by the Defiance — John Dennis, captain. As early
as 1744, wealth had been garnered by the Prince
Charles under Captain Simeon Potter. In the latter case it took the form to some extent of sacred
plate rifled from churches along the Spanish Main.
The tale of the despoiling of one of these churches
— that of Oyapoc — has been told by a Jesuit missionary, Father Fauque, in a letter to his superior.
The good priest (he was of exceptional charity)
finds excuse for the avariciousness of his Yankee
enemy in the fact that " Rodelon [as he calls
Rhode Island] was a kind of little republic which
did not pay tribute to the King of England, which

elected its governor every year and which had *not even any silver money but only notes for daily commerce*."

Sometimes privateers went forth and did not return. In 1745, on the day before Christmas, there sailed from Newport for the Spanish Main two large vessels owned in part by Godfrey Malbone and manned by four hundred men. They were met by a fierce " northeaster " accompanied by snow, were never heard of afterwards, and nearly two hundred Newport women were left disconsolate. Then there often was stiff resistance to be encountered. Captain John Dennis was the chief hero in such affairs. In January, 1746, he, while cruising in the West Indies with the Defiance, came up with a French ship of twenty guns, attended by two lesser craft. He boarded the ship, losing fifteen killed and fifteen wounded in the operation, but was rewarded with five hundred hogsheads of sugar and fifty-seven of indigo. It was Dennis who, at this period, got the Rhode Island government into trouble with the governor of Havana by carrying to Newport and selling into slavery (because of their mulatto complexions) twenty - two free Spaniards. In retaliation the Spanish governor, securing one of Dennis's prize crews, shut them up; treating them, as they indignantly wrote, with more brutality than any slaves. An exchange was soon happily effected. The deeply insulted freemen of Spain were bought

back from their Yankee subjection by the owners
of the Defiance and of the Duke of Marlboro' (a
privateer involved with the Defiance), and sent to
Cuba in a flag of truce.

Dennis's crowning exploit was performed in
1747 near the island of Martinique. His name
had become a terror to French traders, and the officials at Fort de France sent out a vessel of fourteen guns and one hundred and forty men to make
an end of him. After a four hours' conflict, in
which Dennis himself was slightly wounded, he
took his would-be captor captive and sailed with
her proudly to St. Kitts.

Rhode Island, after the Bellomont and Dudley
period, was guilty of little that could be called
piracy. Nevertheless that ingrained spirit of individualism which showed itself on land in the
policy (persistently maintained) of an irredeema-
ble paper currency, and of which the colony's
marked freebooting tendencies may also be considered an indication, was not easily tamed. During King George's War, flags of truce (vessels
bearing to the French islands French prisoners to
be exchanged for English ones) were systematically made use of to carry not alone prisoners
but provisions, thus giving direct aid and comfort
to the enemy. In 1748, no less than twenty such
fraudulent "flags" left Newport. Colonel Robert
Rogers, the celebrated scout of the French and
Indian wars, boldly declares that the Rhode

Islanders would divide a company of prisoners among a whole fleet of flags of truce, and then with official connivance send to the enemy articles more welcome than all the prisoners, or than would have been the ship and cargo originally taken.

In the war with France that began in 1754 (technically 1756) — the Old French, or Seven Years, War — Rhode Island did nothing at sea as a colony. On land its quotas were kept well filled, and at Lake George, Fort William Henry, Ticonderoga, and Fort Frontenac (as also in 1762 at Havana) it gave a good account of itself. But while at this juncture putting in commission no Tartar, the colony, besides furnishing seamen to the royal navy, commissioned over sixty privateers carrying fifteen hundred men, and repeated the triumphs of former years. Now, though, by reason of the growth of commerce, the losses in merchantmen were heavy. Providence (which since 1740 had come rapidly forward) lost nearly fifty vessels, and Newport more than one hundred. Possibly the greatest loss of all was not that of any merchantmen but of the privateer Foy with bold John Dennis in command. Whether this loss was by tempest or by the enemy was never known. Neither ship nor commander was heard of after August, 1756. In the war of the Revolution William Dennis, a son of John, commanded successively thirteen privateers. Stronger proof there could not well be that the wonderful privateering of Rhode Island led (among other things) to an American navy, — to a Talbot, to a Whipple, to a Hopkins, to the Decaturs, and to the Perrys.

CHAPTER V

THE GOLDEN AGE OF NEWPORT

(*Commerce*)

Sugar and Molasses — The Slave Trade — Merchant Magnates — Slaveholding — The Jews as Merchants.

A MORE immediate result of the sea power of Rhode Island was the rise into commercial, social, and intellectual importance of the town of Newport.

By 1675 the exportation from Rhode Island (from Newport especially) of lumber, horses, pork, butter, and cheese had become considerable. At Barbadoes and Nevis these commodities were exchanged for sugar and molasses; and in sugar and molasses the future of Newport became bound up. That is to say, the future of this mart became thus bound up for all of the seventeenth century and for a part of the eighteenth. With the waxing of the eighteenth century the slave trade arose, and thereupon Newport's future became bound up with it.

By means of the reports of the colony governors to the Lords of Trade the evolution of the island of Rhode Island from the agricultural stage into

the commercial may be readily traced. In a report
made by Peleg Sanford in 1680 we are told that
there were then in the colony no merchants nor
" men of considerable estates ; " that there was
" no shippinge " save a few sloops ; and that no
customs duties were imposed. Twenty-eight years
later the story is quite a different one. In 1708,
Governor Samuel Cranston made report that the
colony within a decade had built one hundred and
three vessels. Of these it possessed twenty-nine
itself, and by means of them a brisk trade was carried on with Jamaica, Barbadoes, and Nevis ; with
the Bermudas and the Bahamas ; with Madeira and
Curaçoa ; and with the American settlements from
Massachusetts to South Carolina. The articles imported were sugar, molasses, cotton, indigo, woolens, linens, salt, rum, wines, cocoa, rigging, and
iron. A naval officer had been regularly appointed
by the governor since 1681. At the date of the
Cranston report the population of the colony was
7181. Newport led with 2203, of whom 220 were
negroes ; Providence came next with 1446, of whom
seven were negroes ; and third came Kingstown
(the Narragansett country) with 1200, of whom
the negroes were 85.

As regards Newport, the most significant statement by Cranston is that now for a considerable
period the land of the island had all been " taken
up and improved in small farms," a condition
which had compelled later generations to betake

themselves to the sea. It was from this cause that
ship-building had been developed. From this cause,
too, there were beginning to appear those "merchants," those "men of considerable estates" the
lack of whom in 1680 was dolefully recorded by
Peleg Sanford. The sugar and molasses which
ever since 1660 had been coming into Newport
were distilled there into New England rum, and
this article (together with candles made from tallow
or oil substances) found a market throughout the
West Indies. By 1731, when Governor Joseph
Jenckes made his report to the Lords of Trade,
it is evident that sugar and molasses on the one
hand, and rum on the other, were the staples of
Newport, and so of Rhode Island, prosperity.

Newport consisted now of four hundred houses.
It had passed beyond the time (1707) when, as
the town records inform us, the streets were at the
mercy of filth precipitated from stables and sinks to
"ye spoyling and damnifying of peoples Apparill."
In 1731 the centre of life was "the parade"
(Washington Square), at the head of which stood
the Colony House. Into the parade Thames Street
opened, and from it there projected westwardly
into the old town cove a wharf — Long Wharf.
The principal dwellings were about the parade and
on Thames Street. Along the wharves were warehouses and sailors' boarding-houses, together with
the shops of venders of anchors and cordage and
of sail-makers, caulkers, and shipwrights. Long

Wharf was largely the scene of the activities of
Newport's four hundred seamen. From this station
there passed out to sea the colony's ten or twelve
sail that each year visited Surinam, St. Eustatia,
and St. Thomas ; and the one or two that ranged
as far as Genoa, Leghorn, Holland, or the British
Isles. At this station there were unloaded the
duck, cordage, broadcloths, serges, hollands, thread,
laces, needles, pins, tape, scythes, and iron-ware
brought in coasters from Boston.

The prosperity thus indicated, and a like prosperity indicated by the crowded wharves of Boston
— all based on sugar and molasses — was by no
means relished by the English sugar planters of
the West Indies — of Jamaica, Barbadoes, Antigua, and Nevis. These planters were desirous of
exclusively supplying the northern colonial market; and when they found themselves (as in 1731
they constantly did) anticipated by the Dutch of
Surinam and St. Eustatia, they complained loudly
to the Lords of Trade. By the latter, in 1731,
steps began to be taken toward the imposition of
a sugar duty. The agent for Rhode Island in
London was Richard Partridge (a successor to
William Penn and, like him, a Quaker), and, between 1731 and 1733, he did what he could by
representation and petition to defeat the projected
measure. It was, he pointed out, the profits of the
trade in sugar and molasses that enabled Rhode
Island merchants to purchase English manufac-

tured goods. All, however, was to no avail, and in 1733 a law went into effect imposing 9d. per gallon on rum and 5s. per hundredweight on sugar. This law was continued without modification down to 1764.

It was while the Sugar Act was pending that Governor Jenckes submitted his query regarding the veto power (if any) which pertained to his office, and Partridge was highly concerned lest the query should complicate Rhode Island's position toward the act. But when at length the act was about to pass, the agent — a man evidently of conviction as well as of circumspection — prophetically wrote: " I am of opinion if such a Law take place (besides the present Injury it will do), it will be rather worse in the consequence of it than the Bill of prohibition last year, because of the levying a subsidy upon a Free People without their knowledge agst their consent, who have the libertys and Immunitys granted them of Natural born Subjects, and when they have enough to do to raise Taxes for their own Support; besides it may be drawn into a President for the future, for by the same Rule that a British Parliamt imposes a duty on the King's Subjects abroad, who have no Representatives in the state here, they may from 4/ advance to 20/ — to £100, on different things, and so ad infinitum, which is an Infringement on Liberty and Property and as I apprehend a violation of the Right of the Subject."

The law against human slavery, passed by the mainland towns of Rhode Island in 1652, expressed the sentiment of the northern part of the colony. It may be doubted whether it expressed the sentiment of the southern part then under an independent government. Whether it did or not, it did not do so after that part had (about 1700) begun to exchange agriculture for commerce. Yet even the slave trade was divisible into varieties. There was the respectable or, as it has been called, "genteel" variety lasting throughout the period when the traffic was legal — the first three quarters of the eighteenth century. There also was the outlawed and piratical variety lasting to the middle of the nineteenth century. Newport was concerned with both varieties, but it was the "genteel" variety that built up its fortunes.

By the Treaty of Utrecht, concluded between Queen Anne and Louis XIV on April 11, 1713, England obtained the Hudson Bay territory, Acadia, Newfoundland, and Gibraltar. Further, there was obtained an assignment of the *Assiento* — a contract with Spain on the part of a French corporation, called the French Guinea Company, whereby forty-eight hundred African slaves were to be landed each year in Spanish America for thirty years. The execution of the contract was intrusted by England to a company, called the Royal African, which, besides paying a large sum to Spain in cash, was to divide one half its

profits annually between the Spanish and British
kings. But so much fault was found with this
monopoly by Parliament that it was deemed advisable to continue the former practice of admitting private persons to the benefits of the trade,
on the payment of a duty of ten per cent on all
goods sent by them to Africa to be exchanged for
negroes.

The overthrow of the Assiento monopoly was
followed by an immense expansion in the slave business. Prior to 1708 Rhode Island had imported
but one human cargo from Africa. It came in 1696,
and the negroes were disposed of at between £30
and £35 per head. Between 1698 and 1707 negroes to the number of twenty or thirty a year were
imported from Barbadoes. They sold at from £30
to £40 per head, but were in no great demand. By
1700, however, Rhode Island had begun to perceive
where lay the path to fortune. In that year, instead
of importing negroes for itself, it sent (under the
tutelage of two Barbadian merchants) three vessels
to Africa to obtain a cargo of slaves to be sold in
Barbadoes.

Henceforth it was not seldom that advantage
was taken of the West India market to cover the
so-called triangular course: from Newport (with
rum manufactured from West India sugar and
molasses) to Africa; from Africa (with slaves
purchased with this rum) to the West Indies; and,
finally, from the West Indies (with more sugar and

molasses purchased with the proceeds of the slaves) back again to Newport. Yet the business of home importation was not neglected, for out of the avails of a £3 duty levied in 1708 upon each negro imported from Barbadoes, provision was made for paving and renovating those Newport streets along which people had not yet ceased to fare to "ye spoyling and damnifying of [their] Apparill."

But to resume from 1739. Between that date and about 1760 the trade in slaves was at its height; and as by means of the trade in question there was amassed the wealth which formed the foundation of Newport society and of Newport culture, an account of it will be of use.

In 1740 the colony, according to Governor Richard Ward, possessed 120 sail, "some on the coast of Africa." By 1763 the number of sail had increased to 184, exclusive of coasters, which were 352. In navigating the various craft there were employed 2200 seamen. Eighteen hundred hogsheads of rum had for a long period been carried annually to Africa and exchanged for negroes, gold dust, and ivory. To supply the rum there were operated in Newport between twenty and thirty "distill houses." In a word, between 1750 and 1760 Newport was the great slave mart for America, as London and Bristol were for England. Its wharves — in the multiplicity of which Long Wharf could barely be distinguished — were so crowded "with vessel lading for Guinea" that often, we are told, it was impracticable " to get one hogshead of rum for the cash."

A coterie of Newport merchants, let us suppose, are about to send out two or three slavers in the year 1750. One of the vessels will be a new one built for the occasion. The work of building probably will be done at Newport, but it may be done at Warren or Bristol — towns among those acquired in 1747 from Massachusetts, and both eager traders in slaves. In freeboard dimensions the new vessel (according to the naval writer Mr. John R. Spears) will compare with the largest " cup defenders " constructed to-day at Bristol by the Herreshoffs. Her register will be not far from fifty tons ; she will be rigged as a sloop or brigantine ; and her approximate cost will be £1350.

Our three craft (now ready for their cargo) will be laden each with 120 or 150 hogsheads of rum, a quantity of provisions, muskets, and powder, and an assortment of shackles. There will still remain insurance to be effected, and this — secured at a rate of eighteen or twenty per cent — will be found to justify its cost by the indemnity afforded against such hazards (besides fire) as " men-of-war, enemies, pyrates, rovers, thieves, jettisons, letters of mart and countermart, sorprizals, taking at sea, barratry of the master and marines," etc. Then the little fleet will sail " bound," as the bill of lading will piously declare, " by God's grace for the coast of

Africa." Even yet there may be no sailing if the
horoscope has not been cast; or if, on being cast,
it has not been found favorable; for the captains
of the day are nothing if not superstitious, and will
as soon think of quitting port without a clearance
as without warrant from a soothsayer.

Once on the coast (at Anamaboe let us say), the
captains will summon the native chiefs or head-
men to a collation well spiced with rum and gifts,
and in return the chiefs will supply to the captains
slaves : men, women, and children made captive in
war, or otherwise reduced to subjection. As fast
as received the slaves will be paid for at an average price (per head of sound adults) of a hundred
gallons of rum, and stowed in the between-decks
space, — a space three feet and ten inches in
height. Here the women and children will be
given their freedom, — a freedom to sit or lie down.
The men will be stretched upon their backs feet
out-board, and in this position will be ironed fast
by chains or rods. When a cargo of one hundred
or one hundred and twenty negroes for each ship
has been collected, the return voyage or, as it was
technically called, the " middle passage " will be
begun. It will consume from six to ten weeks and
terminate at Barbadoes, where the cargo will be
sold at a profit of from £12 to £25 per head. Our
little coterie of Newport merchants will (as a
coterie) reap a profit, per ship, on their venture
of from £1800 to £2000; all, too, in six or eight

months' time, and without taking into the account the cargo of ten thousand gallons, or more, of molasses with which they will load at Barbadoes for Newport.

In spite of soothsayers and horoscopes, ill luck occasionally beset a voyage. It was in view of an unusual bit of ill luck that David Lindsay of Newport, captain of the brigantine Sanderson, wrote from Anamaboe and Barbadoes, in 1753, those delightfully misspelled letters which proclaim him (along with Mrs. Benjamin Franklin) a true child of the eighteenth century. "I have Gott 13 or 14 hhds of rum yet Left aboard," wrote the captain from Anamaboe, "and God noes when I shall Gett clear of it." "Ye traid is so dull it is actually a noof to make a man creasey. . . on the whole I never had so much Trouble in all my voiges." Nevertheless from Barbadoes he could write : "My slaves is not landed yet: they are 56 in number for owners, all in helth & fatt. I lost one small gall." Not so bad this, after all. And that Captain Lindsay got his cargo through "in helth & Fatt," only "one small gall" having been so inconsiderate as to die on his hands, shows that he was a worthy servant of those Newport magnates who, as James Fenimore Cooper tersely phrases it, in becoming slave-dealers had become gentlemen.[1]

[1] "Sales of Forty Seven Negroes, & a parcel of Lumber & Water Casks imported in the Brigg'a. *Sanderson*, & put into my hands by Captain David Lindsay, on the proper account and

The magnates at Newport between 1730 and 1770 — while the town was advancing in population from five to nine thousand souls — who were they ?

There had just died (1727) one of the most risque of Messrs. William Johnston & Peter Brown, of Rhode Island, owners of said Brigg'a.

Date. 1753	Men.	Women.	Men Boys.	Small Boys.	Girls.	Small Girls.	Feet of Boards.	Staves.	Shingles.	Water Casks.	Prices	£ s. d.
June 18	10	4	11	–	–	–	–	–	–	–	£35 ..	875 0 0
	–	1	–	–	–	–	–	–	–	–	.. .. ..	30 0 0
	–	–	–	–	–	1	–	–	–	–	.. .. ..	25 0 0
	–	–	2	–	–	–	–	–	–	–	£29	58 0 0
	–	–	–	1	–	–	–	–	–	–	.. .. ..	28 0 0
	1	–	–	–	–	–	–	–	–	–	.. .. ..	30 0 0
	–	–	–	–	–	1	–	–	–	–	.. .. ..	22 10 0
	–	–	–	1	–	–	–	–	–	–	.. .. ..	22 10 0
	–	–	–	1	–	–	–	–	–	–	.. .. ..	22 10 0
	–	1	–	–	–	–	–	–	–	–	.. .. ..	29 0 0
	–	–	–	1	–	–	–	–	–	–	.. .. ..	24 2 6
	–	–	–	–	–	1	–	–	–	–	.. .. ..	21 0 0
	–	–	–	–	1	–	–	–	–	–	.. .. ..	30 0 0
	2	1	–	1	–	–	–	–	–	–	Ord'ry £25	100 0 0
	1	2	–	1	–	–	–	–	–	–	do. do.	100 0 0
	–	–	–	1	–	–	–	–	–	–	.. .. ..	15 0 0
	14	9	11	8	2	3	–	–	–	–	.. .. ..	£1432 12 6
	–	–	–	–	–	–	4256	1353	–	–	@ £4 per m.	22 13 6
	–	–	–	–	–	–	–	–	8500	20	@ 15s. & 5s.	11 7 6

                                                   £1466 13 6

CHARGES DEDUCED, VIZ.

		£ s. d.	
To cash paid for Permit to Land the Slaves	£00 5 0	
" Duty on 47 Slaves @ 5s.	11 15 0	
" for Drummer attending the Sales	0 5 0	
" paid for carrying Notes into the Country, for Liquor at the Sales & for Wherry hire	1 19 5	
To the Captain's Coast Commission on £1432 12 6	55 2 2	
To Commissions on £1466 13 6 @ 5 p. ct.	73 6 8	142 15 3

                                                   £1324 0 3

Nett Proceeds carried to the credit of
    Messrs. William Johnston & Peter Brown,
        Rhode Island ; Their Acct. Curt.
           Barbados July 10th 1753
                Errors excepted

                                    ELIAS MERIVIELLE."

Am. Hist. Record, vol. i, p. 339.

notable Newport magnates of the old or landed
order — the order of William Harris, William
'Coddington, and William Brenton — namely,
Samuel Cranston. Thirty successive times had he
been elected governor of the colony. Within the
period of his incumbency there had fallen the ex-
citing decade of piracy, perplexing years of the
endless disputes over money and boundaries, and
one war — Queen Anne's. At no time had he
failed to inspire public confidence by the exercise
of that rare faculty which he possessed of sympa-
thetically reflecting public feeling ; a faculty exercised no less in the admitting of pirates to bail
than in a careful avoidance of acts offensive to
either the advocates of soft money or hard.

Of the new or mercantile class — the class of
genuine sea-lords — the first in point of date and
consequence were undoubtedly our acquaintances
William and John Wanton. With them ship-
building, privateering, and mercantile adventuring
were interchangeable occupations.

A later group of merchants (and upon the
whole the group most characteristic of eighteenth
century Rhode Island) embraced in large part
men already known to us through their protests to
the king against paper money. These men (Newporters all) were Abraham Redwood, William
Ellery, Henry Collins, John Brown, Peleg Brown,
Daniel Ayrault, John Freebody, Samuel Freebody,
Godfrey Malbone, John Malbone, Sueton Grant,

John Channing, Gideon Wanton, Joseph Wanton,
Samuel Vernon, Thomas Hazard, Solomon Townsend, and Abraham Whipple. And not only were
these men merchants; they in the main were merchants of magnanimous minds. They belonged to
the class that in the Italy of the fifteenth century
delighted to adorn the State with palaces, and to
fill these palaces with beautiful and costly objects
of art. It of course was at a humble distance that
the Newport dealer in sugar, rum, and slaves trod
in the steps of the Venetian or Florentine who had
trafficked in silks, tapestries, precious stones,
aromatic woods, and ivory, but none the less he
trod there; so obviously, indeed, that in one instance (that of Henry Collins) the appellation bestowed is that of the Lorenzo de Medici of Newport.

The dwellings of the mercantile group before us
consisted in spacious wooden houses of two and a half
or three stories, with gambrel or hip roofs. The doorways were ornamented by fluted posts and scrolled
pediments. The halls were central and wide, and
the principal chambers were wainscoted nearly to
the ceiling. Moreover, there were not wanting (to
those possessed of the wealth or humor for them)
country places — suburban villas. The latter were
approached by roads (none too good) over the
undulous and, in that day, tree-clad surface of the
island; and, when gained by the visitor, were
found surrounded by gardens somewhat formally

laid out but made bright by flowers and sweet by
scented shrubs. The country abode of Abraham
Redwood was in Portsmouth, and, under the name
of " Redwood," was widely known for its unusual
botanical specimens.

According to tradition, the rural mansion and
estate which, between 1744 and 1766, outranked
all others near Newport was that of Godfrey Malbone. There is little in the way of information
about Malbone that is trustworthy ; but we know
that he was a rough and ready seafaring man of
Virginia birth, a bold trader in slaves, fond of
privateering enterprises, and a stanch churchman,
in short a Byronic character. In 1744, just after
the Spanish War had merged into that of King
George, and just after a handsome return had begun to be realized from the sale of condemned
Spanish and French prizes, Malbone purchased at
the foot of Miantonomy Hill a tract of six hundred acres sloping full to the bay on the west.
Here he built of Connecticut stone a large house
which he surmounted with a cupola and surrounded
with grounds embellished by hedges, terraces, par-
terres of flowers, and ponds of glinting fish. A
famous *bon vivant* was our nabob in the style of
the day — the Georgian style — one rather heavy
and coarse when the company consisted of men.
And of men we may be assured that it frequently
did consist with a host who relished exceedingly
his turtle, his joint, his punch brewed of rum, sugar,

lime-juice, and arrack, and above all, his oath and
his broad jest.

As early as 1740 Newport was cosmopolitan.
The Redwoods were there from Antigua; the De
Courcys from Ireland; the Grants and Edward
Scott (grand-uncle of Sir Walter) from Scotland;
and the Bretts from Germany. Huguenot families,
too, from the Carolinas, driven away by the Indian wars, had to some extent made the place a
refuge with their slaves. Society possessed strong
elements of attraction. Clubs, or what were the
equivalent of clubs, soon appeared in such organi-
zations as the Newport Artillery, formed in 1741,
and the Fellowship Club (a mariners' society),
formed in 1752. In 1761 the town was visited by
a theatrical troup. For two months renditions of
plays were given; of Shakespearian plays sometimes, but oftener of " The Spectre Bridegroom,"
" The Conscious Lover " (by Richard Steele),
" The Lying Valet," and " The Devil to Pay."
The same company afterwards went to Providence,
but the colder temper of that locality proved inhospitable, and the next year theatrical exhibitions
were prohibited throughout the colony.

At this time, as during the Revolution, the
young women of Newport were charming for color
of cheeks, lightness of foot, and grace of deport-
ment; and the fact that many of them were from
Quaker families did not interfere with their participation in the gayeties that prevailed. Besides the

theatre and the prim "teas," there were parties to
Fort George at which dainties were served and sets
formed to dance the "Faithful Shepherd" and
"Arcadian Nuptials." Then, too, the shops held
forth a constant lure in fabrics and curiosities from
both Europe and the Indies; and if naught else
offered, a young woman could join a spinning
match at Dr. Ezra Stiles's, buy a lottery ticket for
a charity, or invest her pin-money in spermaceti
candles to be carried abroad and converted into
Irish linen for her future domestic establishment.

Newport life was ministered to by slavery as a
traffic. It also to some degree was ministered to
by slavery as an institution. In 1708 the town
possessed 220 negroes, and even in 1680 Governor
Peleg Sanford had reported the presence of
"blacks" as a distinct element. By 1730 there
were in the town 649 "blacks." In the entire
colony at this date the negroes were 1648. Eighteen years later the total for the colony, including
those belonging to the recently acquired towns on
the east of the bay, was 3077; and by 1756 this
number had been increased to 4697 — the maxi-
mum before the Revolution.

It was no unusual sight at a Newport wharf,
that of some slaver discharging its human cargo;
"the sellers and buyers of men, women, and children
thronging the market place." The fact that a man
was a Quaker did not as yet much restrain him as

a buyer. Joseph Wanton, son of Governor William Wanton, and last colonial governor of Rhode Island, made affirmation that "in 1758 he had sailed from Newport in the snow King of Prussia, with a cargo of 124 hogsheads of rum," etc., and that "while at anchor at Annamibo, having on board fifty-four slaves," he was taken by a French privateer, etc. Yet this same Joseph was careful to record at the beginning of his statement that "he was one of the people called Quakers and conscientiously scrupulous about taking an oath." Every Newport family of pretensions owned slaves. They were kept as domestic servants and not treated harshly. Upon one occasion the Newport "Mercury" printed an advertisement as follows: "Wanted: a negro from sixteen to twenty-five, free from bad smell, strait limbed, active, healthy, good-tempered, honest, sober, quick at apprehension, and not used to run away." If the advertiser got what he sought he was fortunate.

On the whole, the negro slave at Newport was more a nuisance than a benefit. There was little work there for him to do that could not be done better by a white man, and the climate gave him no superiority in point of endurance. He had three distinct failings: he was fond of rum, he would steal, and he would run away. The offenses of theft and absconding were usually combined. In the Newport "Mercury" there may be found notices not a few of the escape of Pomp "very artful and insinu-

ating ; " of the escape of Cæsar " who plays well
the violin ; " or of the escape of Sarah, " a lusty
mulatto, polite and ingenious at needlework " —
each and all the bearers of some purloined article.
To place the slave under better control, various
laws were passed. In 1704 negroes were forbidden
to be abroad after nine at night. In 1714 ferry-
men were forbidden to transport them without a
certificate from their masters. In 1743 (and of
special significance is this law) a punishment by
branding and scourging was provided for " negroes
that shall attempt to commit rape on any white
woman." Between 1728 and 1770 acts also were
passed regulating manumission and against the
keeping by free negroes of " disorderly houses."

Among the free negroes of Newport the most
celebrated was Newport Gardner. He is described
as " tall, straight, and dignified ; " and his attain-
ments (for one of his race) were remarkable. He
taught himself much of the science and art of
music, composed tunes, conducted a successful
singing school, and founded a colored church. In
addition to being able to read and write English,
he could speak French. His weakness was an
appetite for rum.

Two classes of the Newport merchant magnate
have been considered : the class that was as much
privateersman as merchant (of which the Wanton
family in its earlier representatives is an apt illus-

tration) and the class that though engaged in privateering were not so engaged personally and that
depended more and more for emolument upon the
slave trade.

But there was a third class. It consisted of the
Newport Jew, and it differed from the others in
that, besides the rum and slave trade, its members
followed general commerce, reaching out for the
commodities of the Mediterranean and the Le-
vant.

Jews are heard of in Newport in 1658 — the
Campannalls, the Packeckoes, the Levis, and others.
Then in 1694 a number of families arrived from
the West Indies (Curaçoa). It was natural that
Jews should seek Rhode Island. In enumerating
the persecuted races and classes for the benefit of
whom the "livelie experiment" was designed,
Roger Williams had specifically spoken of the
Children of Abraham. " By the merciful assistance
of the Most High," Williams had said, " I have
desired to labor in Europe, in America, with English, with Barbarians, yea, and also I have longed
after some trading with Jews themselves, for
whose hard measure, I fear the nations and England have yet a score to pay." " All these consciences (yea the very consciences of the papists,
Jews &c.,) . . . ought freely and impartially to be
permitted their several respective worships." Yet
even in Rhode Island the lot of the Jew was not
always happy. As early as 1684, Simon Medus,

David Brown, and other Jews found it expedient
to secure from the Rhode Island General Assembly
a declaration that they " might expect as good protection as any stranger . . . residing amongst us,
. . . being obedient to his Majesty's laws."

The Jews who became Newport magnates were
of the eighteenth century — Aaron Lopez, Abraham Rodriguez Rivera, and Myer Pollock. They
arrived from Portugal and Spain, by way of New
York, between 1740 and 1760. Aaron Lopez was
the most prominent of them, and he had fled from
Portugal to escape the Inquisition. Associated with
Aaron Lopez was his brother Moses. This firm
and Myer Pollock gave attention to the trade in
molasses and slaves. The Lopez Brothers — who
owned no less than twenty-five or thirty different
craft — encouraged also a movement (seriously begun in 1733) for the participation of Rhode Islanders in whale-catching, extending the " catch," it is
said, as far as the Falkland Islands. It was Rivera
who more particularly devoted his energies to commerce with France and the East. But his activities
were not limited to commerce. Superior methods
for the production of sperm oil were introduced by
him. Indeed, so successful were his methods that
by 1761 there were in existence at Newport seventeen oil and candle establishments. Largely at the
instance of the Jewish merchants in the various
colonies, there had come to be formed an intercolo-
nial combination or trust for the maintenance of

prices by an apportionment of material and regulation of output.

"We had yesterday," wrote Richard Partridge from London on November 25, 1755, "advice via France of the dreadful Earth Quake and Fire at Lisbon on 1st Novr. wherein were destroyed as its judged 100,000 People and the greatest part of the City." As a sequel to this catastrophe, the number of Portuguese Jews in Newport was increased. Just prior to the Revolution there were there in all perhaps two hundred Hebrew families.

By the early trade in molasses and rum ; by the privateering of the Wantons ; by the slave trade of the Malbones ; and finally, by the wider and more princely commercial ventures of the families of Lopez and Rivera, Newport so waxed in wealth that although between 1750 and 1770 still behind Boston, "a bold prophet was he who said then that New York one day might equal Newport."

CHAPTER VI

THE GOLDEN AGE OF NEWPORT — *continued*

(*Letters, Art, Science*)

Dean Berkeley — The Redwood Library, Gilbert Stuart, the Jewish Synagogue — Dr. Ezra Stiles — Newport *vs.* Boston.

THE individualism of Rhode Island — based, as it
was, on that which was spiritual — on the Soul
Liberty of Roger Williams and the " inner light "
of the Antinomians, Anabaptists, and Quakers —
could not, under favoring conditions, but flower
forth in idealism. Beginning with 1729, these
conditions were supplied at Newport by the development there of wealth through commerce, and by
the presence there, for a time, of the greatest idealist among English philosophers — George Berkeley,
Dean of Derry.

It was early in the year when Dean Berkeley
reached Newport. He brought with him his wife
(daughter of Chief Justice Forster), whom he had
just married, and the portrait painter Smibert, of
whom Walpole makes mention in his "Anecdotes
of Painting." Dr. Thomas Moffatt, a learned Scot-
tish physician, was also to have been of the party,
but was detained by illness. " The Dean," said the

" New England Weekly Journal," announcing his
arrival, " is a gentleman of middle stature, of an
agreeable, pleasant, and erect aspect." The object
of Berkeley in coming to Rhode Island was to await
the remittance by Sir Robert Walpole of £20,000
for the founding of a college in the Bermudas for
the Christianization and education of Indian youth;
but the coming was not significant for Newport because of this. It was significant because of something altogether different; because, in a word, of
what Berkeley himself was in mind, spirit, and
training.

The advent of the dean in Newport was like that
of Petrarch in Parma or Avignon; it was the advent of a renaissance. Along with him there came
not alone great intellectual independence and
abounding human charity, but there came culture
— the atmosphere of intimate association with men
of letters : with Richard Steele, with Dean Swift
(to whom our visitor was indebted for presentation
at Queen Anne's court), with " Young Mr. Pope,"
and finally with Addison, whose " Cato " he had
witnessed on its first night in the company of the
author, the latter a bit nervous but fortified for the
occasion by two or three flasks of burgundy and
champagne. Nor was the culture which came with
him by any means purely insular. It breathed of
the Continent and of travel : of France and Gothic
cathedrals; of North Italy and dim fugitive ma-
donnas ; of Naples pulsing with life ; of Vesuvius ;

of Capri; of Cumæ and Misenum and the spirit of Virgil.

As has been intimated, there was at Newport a considerable preparedness for the influences emanating from Berkeley. In what, specifically, did this preparedness consist?

Throughout the colony there was little in the way of means of public education. Despite the earnest plea of Master William Turpin, preferred in impeccable script in 1685, Providence maintained no public school, nor was to do so for many years to come. Conditions were somewhat better, though not much, in Portsmouth and Warwick. In that part of Rhode Island which in 1729 was still claimed by Massachusetts things were promising. At Barrington and Bristol there were schools — schools that since 1673 and 1682 had taught such formidable branches as "Grammar, Rhetoric, Lattin, Greek, and Hebrew." Newport, in respect to schools, might not compare with Barrington or Bristol, but it had not fared ill. There was a schoolhouse there in 1685, and by 1710 permission had been granted for "a Latin school in the two little rooms" in the town schoolhouse.

The press — a further means of education — had no place in the colony at large; but in 1727 James Franklin (brother of the progressive Benjamin) had removed from Boston to Newport, and now was printing books. In a short while (1732) he was to begin the publication of Rhode Island's

first newspaper, the "Gazette," and in 1758 his
son was to found the "Mercury."

But if — even at Newport — public education
was in no very forward stage,[1] a measurable substitute for it existed in an active sectarianism.
There was, it is true, no longer manifest that
feverishness which had provoked sorrow in Winthrop and ire in Cotton Mather. The theological
mixture no longer seethed in its tiny caldron.
Precipitation, indeed, was well advanced, for,
where once there had been Gortonism and Antinomianism and Anabaptism and Quakerism and
Seekerism, there now were only Baptism and
Quakerism; and instability in these elements was
checked by Episcopalianism and Congregationalism.

At the time of Berkeley's coming there were in
flourishing condition in Providence the original,
or Roger Williams, Baptist Church and one
Congregational and one Episcopal body; the
Congregational body ministered to by the Rev.
Josiah Cotton, a great-grandson of John Cotton,
the early antagonist of Williams in public controversy. In Westerly the Seventh Day Baptists
held strong sway. In Narragansett — scene of the

[1] Down to 1904 Rhode Island was without a uniform system of
education. Until 1902 children could be withdrawn from school
at the age of twelve. They still may so be withdrawn at thirteen.
Attendance up to thirteen is unsatisfactory, as local sentiment
(especially among the foreign-born) sanctions the employment of
young children in factories. — R. I. School Reports, 1903, 1904.

devotional labors of both Roger Williams and
William Blackstone — Episcopalianism was established. In Newport itself there were no less than
seven churches, four of them Baptist — one a
Seventh Day church organized in 1671. Of the
others, one was Congregational, one Episcopal,
and one Quaker; the latter, of course, very large.
The men — the more prominent of them — at the
head of these bodies were the Rev. Nathaniel
Clap (Congregationalist), the Rev. John Comer
(Baptist), and the Rev. James Honyman (Episcopalian). Moreover, in the case of Honyman, a
handsome church edifice with ample interior and
lofty steeple was at command; as, withal, a tower-
ing pulpit from which the visiting dean might, as
he often did, deliver his chastened message to the
flock below.

The preparedness of Newport for Berkeley,
however, is made evident not so much by the
existence of varied and active church circles as
by the fact, first, that these circles were mutually
tolerant; and by the fact, second, that in the case of
such among them as had wealth, that wealth had
been used in the cultivation of a taste for books,
pictures, and architecture.

On April 24, 1729, the dean wrote to his friend
" Tom Prior " at Dublin : " Here are four sorts
of Anabaptists, besides Presbyterians, Quakers,
Independents, and many of no profession at all.
Notwithstanding so many differences, here are

fewer quarrels about religion than elsewhere, the people living peaceably with their neighbors of whatsoever persuasion." Of the intellectuality of the Newporters the writer was fast making proof through his acquaintances: William Wanton, churchman and governor of the colony; Daniel Updike of Narragansett, attorney-general and lover of history; William Ellery, father of the William Ellery who one day was to be a signer of the Declaration of Independence; the munificent Henry Collins, soon to be accounted a patron of Smibert; and Samuel Johnson, future president of King's, afterwards Columbia College, New York. It is altogether likely that the plan which now was conceived by a number of these men for forming a society for literary and philosophical discussion — the Philosophical Society so-called, precursor of the Redwood Library — was an outcome of the presence at Newport of Berkeley. At all events, it was in 1730 that this body was organized.

Less than three short years the dean remained in Rhode Island, — an interval which he improved by building a country home (Whitehall) near the Hanging Rocks and the sea, and by composing his Plato-like "Alciphron,"— but the radiance with which his coming had been attended did not vanish away at his departure. When, in the autumn of 1731, assured at length of the recreancy of Walpole in the matter of the Bermuda College, he

took ship for England, he left behind him a
stimulus that lasted far into the century.

With the unique figure of Berkeley removed —
that figure the forerunner of Hume, who was the
forerunner of Immanuel Kant — things of intellectual and artistic consequence in the little harbor
town were cared for down to the Revolution by
various individuals, worthy successors to the phi-
losopher and man of artistic appreciation. As
patrons of art and public improvements, there
were Henry Collins and Abraham Redwood ; as
architects, there were Richard Munday and Peter
Harrison ; as painters, there were John Smibert,
Robert Feke, Gilbert Stuart, Cosmo Alexander
(Stuart's teacher), and Samuel King ; as scholars
and theologians, there were Nathaniel Clap, James
Honyman, John Comer, John Callender, Isaac
Touro, Ezra Stiles, and Samuel Hopkins ; as printers and publishers, there were the Franklins and
Solomon Southwick ; as men of science, there were
Dr. Thomas Moffatt, Dr. Thomas Brett (Leyden
graduate), and Dr. William Hunter, distinguished
lecturer upon anatomy.

Upon the achievements of these men a glance
only may here be bestowed. Redwood in 1747 furnished the nucleus of a book fund. Collins the
same year donated a site for the construction of a
building to be called the Redwood Library ; and,
from the plans of Harrison, who had received his

training under Sir John Vanbrugh, architect of
Blenheim House, the structure was completed in
1750. Harrison, later, was to design the City Hall
and Jewish Synagogue. Already Munday had
wrought the elegant proportions of Trinity Church
and the dignified proportions of the Colony Cap-
itol. Smibert, Feke, and King (portrait painters
in oils) are known from their works preserved in
many collections in New England; while of Gilbert Stuart as a painter it is in no wise necessary
to speak. Apropos of him (a snuff grinder's son,
born in Narragansett on December 3, 1755, in
a house remote, lonesome, and looking into the
depths of what not inaptly may be called the dark
tarn of Auber), one can but marvel at the sources
and haunts of genius.

Of exceptional interest are the theologians of
the Newport golden age. Gathered in one small
community — one at the best of not over nine
thousand souls — there were not merely Baptists,
Quakers, Congregationalists, and Episcopalians,
but Jews; and (after 1758) Moravians.

In the case of the Jews, the position of huzan
or reader was filled by Isaac Touro, a refugee from
Portugal after the great earthquake. It was during
Touro's incumbency that the synagogue was dedicated. December 2, 1763, was the date, and the
ceremony was stately and impressive. There now
were some seventy or eighty Jews resident in Newport, and the Books of the Law (three copies of the

Pentateuch executed on tanned calfskin, one a copy from Amsterdam two centuries old) were carried by them in solemn procession to be deposited (symbolically) in the Ark of the Covenant. Dr. Ezra Stiles was present on the occasion, and he describes the reading of Scripture by the huzan and the intoning of the service by huzan and people as profoundly impressive. The impressiveness in no small degree was due to the synagogue itself, spacious, and with a deep gallery supported on Ionic columns which in turn were surmounted by Corinthian pillars sustaining the roof. Says Dr. Stiles: "The order and decorum, the harmony and solemnity of the musick, together with a handsome assembly of people, in an edifice the most perfect of the Temple kind perhaps in America, and splendidly illuminated, could not but raise in the mind a faint idea of the majesty and grandeur of the ancient Jewish worship." Nor, in this connection, should it be overlooked that to Abraham and Judah Touro, sons of the huzan of 1763, Newport stands indebted for its noble Jewish cemetery, fenced from the street by granite and iron, and kept ever beautiful with flowers, — a cemetery the land for which was in part purchased in 1677.

Not a little strange must it have seemed to the Rev. Dr. Stiles and to the Rev. Dr. Hopkins — Congregationalists of the strictest sect — to find themselves in such religious company as obtained

in Newport. Episcopalianism even was less exotic
in Rhode Island than was Congregationalism.
Trinity Church had been founded since 1699; and
St. Paul's, Narragansett, since 1707; and it had
been an observation of Berkeley's that the Anabaptists and Quakers each agreed that the Church
of England was "the second best." Stiles and
Hopkins were in a highly undogmatic atmosphere;
and though upon Hopkins (disciple of the relentless Edwards) the effect was limited, upon Stiles
it unquestionably was far-reaching.

The latter, indeed, despite the *brusquerie* of his
memorable consignment to hell of the unregenerate
Ethan Allen of Vermont, was a man of astonish-
ing breadth. He was broad enough to make a close
companion of Touro, and of a visiting Rabbi, Haym
Isaac Karigal. He was broad enough to seek out
Albertus Ludolphus Rusmeyer, the pastor of the
Moravians, and to make a companion of him. He
was broad enough to converse tolerantly with a visiting Romish priest, a knight of St. John. He was
broad enough to read the Philosophical Dictionary
of Voltaire, and to finish it with the comment:
"He [Voltaire] has some instructive remarks."
He was broad enough (and perhaps this was a cru-
cial test) to take an intelligent interest in Roger
Williams and Samuel Gorton, making a pilgrimage
to the grave of the one, and seeking throughout
Warwick for incidents in the life of the other.[1]

[1] Nowhere, possibly, is the catholicity of Stiles more clearly

Not only did Stiles have breadth, he possessed
(and in this no doubt lay much of the secret of his
breadth) a scholarship and an intellectual curiosity
that were splendidly varied. His interest ranged
easily from "Jeremiah" to comets. Little that
was human was alien to him. The result was
that instead of degenerating into a pedant, he became one of the most useful men in Newport. He
was librarian of the Redwood Library. When
George II died, he preached the commemorative
sermon. When Dr. Franklin's experiments in elec-
tricity were published, he at once procured the
quarto. When, on June 3, 1769, there occurred
the transit of Venus, he was ready for it. For days
in advance he had been "taking equal altitudes ; "
"getting made an astronomical sextant ; " "regulating two clocks by the meridian." On the event-
ful day itself the record stands thus : " Fine serene
day. . . . The transit of Venus will not happen

shown than in his lament (June 8, 1782) upon the death of his
friend Aaron Lopez, the Jewish Newport merchant. He writes :
" He was a Merchant of the first eminence ; for Honor & extent
of commerce probably surpassed by no Mercht in America. . . .
Without a single enemy & the most universally beloved by an extensive Acquaintance of any man I ever knew. . . . The amiable
and excellent Characters of a Lopez, of a Manasseh Ben Israel,
of a Socrates, & a Gangenelli, would almost persuade us to hope
that their Excellency was infused by Heaven, and that the virtu-
ous & Good of all nations & religions, notwithstandg their Delu-
sions, may be bro't together in Paradise on the Xtian System,
finding Grace with the all benevolent & adorable Emmanuel who
with his expiring breath & in his deepest agonies, prayed for those
who knew not what they did." — *Literary Diary*, vol. iii, p. 24.

again in above an hundred years at either node;
and at this descending node again, not in 236 years
or before A. D. 2004. . . . There were three ob-
servers at the same time looking at the sun. . . .
I was the first that espied Venus's entrance. . . .
At sunset Venus had passed the middle of the
transit and sat in the Sun's disk." Among Stiles's
assistants at the observation were William Vernon,
William Ellery, and William Marchant — a merchant and two lawyers. In this fact there was
nothing strange in the Newport of 1769.

It would be interesting to emphasize the catholicity of Stiles by noting the promptitude with
which everybody with anything on his mind or in
his heart sought him out; from a French fencing-
master to the young daughter of Myer Pollock and
her Hebrew lover who wished to become Christians.
A better way, perhaps, will be by noting the approach which the Newport pastor made to Berkeley
in power of prevision. Looking westward, before
1729, the dean had sung: —

"Westward the course of Empire takes its way."

Looking westward in 1770, Ezra Stiles wrote:
"[When] English America is fully settled from
the Atlantic to the Mississippi, the English of the
present idiom may be spoken by one hundred million. . . . Probably the English will become the
vernacular tongue of more people than any one
tongue ever was on earth except the Chinese."

Toward one only of the great humanities was
Stiles in his catholicity indifferent, not to say hostile, and that was music. Herein he but reflected
contemporary Newport. Berkeley, on his return to
England, had sent an organ to Trinity Church;
but none was admitted to any other Newport house
of worship, and in fact it was not until 1770 that
Providence so far became progressive as to tolerate
an instrument. In that year the First Congregational Church of Providence erected an organ of
two hundred pipes. This departure King's Church
(the Episcopal body) imitated by importing an
instrument from Boston — one, as Dr. Stiles sar-
castically records, from "Concert Hall where it has
been improved in promoting festivity, merriment,
effeminacy, luxury and midnight revellings." In
1739 the organist of the Berkeley gift had written:
"The Want of Instruments together with the Nig-
gardliness of the People of this Place, and their
not having a Taste for Musick, render it impossible for any one of my Profession to get a competent maintenance here; and their Feuds and
Animosities are so great concerning their Government, that a Man can take but little Satisfaction
in being among them."

But while Newport in the middle eighteenth
century was to most things strikingly alive — alive
to letters, alive to art, and alive to science [1] — Bos-

[1] "Is it truth, or am I blinded by partiality," wrote Dr. Ben-

ton at the same period was, intellectually considered, in a state bordering on deadness. What
for Newport was a golden age, for Boston, and indeed for Massachusetts at large, was an age little
short of glacial. In point of pure pedagogics,
Massachusetts was altogether in advance of Rhode
Island; but until in Massachusetts history there is
reached the period just preceding the Revolution,
— the period of the Otises and the Adamses, —
Massachusetts life, Boston life, was manacled and
numbed by theology.[1]

At a time when at Newport and in Narragansett

jamin Waterhouse to Thomas Jefferson on September 14, 1822,
" when I say that this small State of Rhode Island has been fer-
tile in events, and by no means destitute of distinguished characters. . . . It was the Redwood Library that rendered reading
fashionable throughout the little community of Rh. Island during
70, or 80 years, w^c advantage was not then enjoyed in Mass$^{ts.}$ New
Hampshire or Connecticut. It diffused a knowledge of general
and particular history, geography, ethics & poetry & polite literature. . . . It sowed the seeds of that science and rendered the
inhabitants of Newport, if not a learned yet a better read, & [more]
inquisitive people than any other town in New England." — *Pub.
R. I. Hist. Soc.* vol. ii, pp. 175, 176.

[1] " The Magnalia," says Mr. Charles Francis Adams, " stands
to-day the one single literary landmark in a century and a half
of colonial and provincial life, — a geological relic of a glacial
period,— a period which in pure letters produced, so far as Massachusetts was concerned, absolutely nothing else, — not a poem,
nor an essay, nor a memoir, nor a work of fancy or fiction of
which the world has cared to take note." — *Massachusetts: its
Historians and its History*, p. 67.

" The remarkable literary revival of Queen Anne's reign was
little observed or felt here [in Boston]." Delano A. Goddard,
Memorial History of Boston, vol. ii, p. 413.

private libraries (as we are reminded by Mr. William E. Foster) contained books such as the "Faerie Queene," "Hudibras," "Samson Agonistes," the plays of Ben Jonson, Pope's Homer, and the plays of Molière, none of these was to be found in the library of Harvard College, the largest library in the Bay colony. Nor did Harvard possess a line of Addison, Steele, or Swift, writers with whom (through Berkeley) Rhode Islanders were intimately acquainted, and whose works were among those earliest secured for the Redwood collection. Or, to put the matter otherwise, at a time when in Rhode Island religious feeling was not permitted to become tense, in Massachusetts the tension, religiously, was such that men, maddened by the thought of impending perdition, not only carped at Baptist, Quaker, and Episcopalian, but daily groveled before their Maker as before a Moloch. Hours upon their knees did the Mathers, the Sewalls, and the Edwardses wrestle with Jehovah, as wrestled Jacob of old; imploring, beseeching, aye, even demanding of God mercy as promised in his Holy Word.[1]

And the culmination — what was it? Instead of an intellectual renaissance, it was an hysteria, a mania, — the great religious awakening of 1740

[1] On Christmas Day, 1696, Samuel Sewall, as he relates in his interesting diary, made a solemn ceremonial visit to the family tomb, where he rearranged the coffins and found the exercise "an awful yet pleasing Treat." — *5th Mass. Hist. Coll.* vol. v, p. 443.

under Edwards and Whitefield. In certain of the
American colonies, as for instance Virginia, the
Great Awakening wrought undoubted good. It set
man and God, hitherto far apart, face to face.
But in Massachusetts it produced excess. Still,
for us the noteworthy fact in connection with
it is that it failed to react with any power upon
Rhode Island. Here, as in North Carolina, the in-
ward serenity of the Quaker, backed by the outward serenity of the churchman, gave it little
quarter, and it fell back substantially a broken
wave.

The Newport golden age, — the age of the commercial, social, and intellectual preëminence of
Rhode Island, — the age which, beginning with
the Wantons in the realm of seamanship and trade
and with Berkeley in the realm of ideas, counts
upon the rosary of its years so many names that
are inspiring, passed away with the Revolution.
Since the Revolution, Massachusetts (largely under
the individualizing influence of Unitarianism) has
realized its golden age. To-day, perchance, it is the
dream of Massachusetts hardly less than of Rhode
Island that

"Time will run back and fetch the age of gold." [1]

[1] In 1891 Mr. Henry Cabot Lodge contributed to the *Century
Magazine* for September a paper on the distribution of ability in
the United States. According to Mr. Lodge (whose basis of estimate was Appleton's *Encyclopedia of American Biography*), the
United States had produced 14,243 persons of more than average
talent. Of those Massachusetts was to be credited with 2686 and

Rhode Island with 291. In 1890, by the Federal Census, the population of Massachusetts was 2,238,943, and that of Rhode Island 345,506. In Massachusetts, therefore, the men of ability (up to 1891) had been about one in eighty-four of the total population, and in Rhode Island about one in one hundred and eighteen.

CHAPTER VII

OLD NARRAGANSETT

Huguenot Refugees — English Planters — The Torrey Lawsuit — Dr. James MacSparran — Plantation Life.

THE Narragansett country (called in 1665 the King's Province and in 1686 Rochester) embraced that part of Rhode Island lying west of Narragansett Bay and south of the Warwick line. In 1660 the southwestern corner of this region had been preëmpted by Rhode Island, as against Connecticut, under the name of Misquamicutt, — a name changed in 1669 to Westerly; and in 1677 the northeastern corner had been preëmpted under the name of East Greenwich.

The settlement of East Greenwich derives interest from the case of Dr. Pierre Ayrault and his compatriots.

In 1686 the Atherton Land Company, which, under the mortgage to it in 1660 by the sachems, assumed to control the unoccupied parts of Narragansett, sold to forty-five French families (driven from home by the revocation of the Edict of Nantes) betweeen four and five thousand acres within the limits of East Greenwich. These lands were duly taken into possession and improved.

Moreover, when in 1690 war broke out between England and France, the settlers cheerfully bound themselves to good behavior by an oath of allegiance to the English sovereign. But as time passed the English occupants of lands in the vicinity of the French — lands obtained under grants from the colony of Rhode Island, and which, prior to the coming of the refugees, had been platted into lots and highways — began to assert themselves by seeking to extend the highways through the property of the newcomers. The outcome was trouble to such a degree that in 1692 the entire French settlement, save two families, removed to New York or Boston.

Of the two families that remained, Dr. Ayrault's was one. The doctor had built a substantial house, planted an orchard and a vineyard, and, failing altogether (through unfamiliarity with the English tongue) to comprehend the question of title involved between the Atherton Company and Rhode Island, saw no reason why he should abandon his homestead. He not only did not abandon it, but obstructed such of the highways as were sought to be opened through it. At length, in July, 1700, a warrant of arrest was issued against him by the assistants of the town of Warwick sitting in East Greenwich. He and his son Daniel were dragged with cruel severity before these officials by an excited mob, and forced to give bonds for their appearance for trial. The trial resulted in an order for the extension of the highways, but the outrages perpetrated upon the Ayrault family were recorded in affidavits, and formed not the least substantial part of the plea against Rhode Island submitted to the Lords of Trade by Dudley in 1705.[1]

Of the many things of interest in the history of Narragansett the Huguenotic settlement and dispersion constitute but one. Others are the rise of a class of large landholders and the contemporaneous rise and spread of Quakerism and Anglicanism.

The settlement of the Narragansett country was effected by land companies, — especially by the Pettiquamscutt Company of 1657 and the Atherton Company of 1659. These companies, along with the Misquamicutt settlers on the Pawcatuck River, controlled between them that great strip, two to four miles wide, which extends westwardly along the bay and seacoast from Wickford, — a strip remarkable for fertility in a region otherwise stony and barren. And not only was the land controlled by companies. The companies were composed of few members, so individual estates were large. Such estates, too, for many years were kept large. They were favored by the English custom and law

---

[1] A Huguenot prominent in Rhode Island and identified with Newport, Narragansett, and Providence, was Gabriel Bernon. He came from Boston, and, like the Huguenots from Massachusetts to South Carolina, was a stanch friend to the Church of England. He was instrumental in founding Trinity Church, Newport (1699–1700), St. Paul's, Narragansett (1707), and St. John's, Providence (1722).

of primogeniture (not finally abrogated in Rhode Island until 1770) and by a law prohibiting attachment for debt in the case of a resident landowner. Neither Providence, Portsmouth, Warwick, nor Newport was settled exactly as was Narragansett. None of them was settled by a few men of large means, · although in this respect Newport more closely resembled Narragansett than did Providence, Portsmouth, or Warwick. The peculiarity of large, not to say enormous, estates in the King's Province was remarked upon in 1670 by Major Mason of Connecticut, who described the holdings as " five, six and ten miles square."

Of the Pettiquamscutt Company the members originally were in part Episcopalian and in part Congregationalist. John Hull, the Boston member, was clearly Congregationalist; Wilbor, Mumford, and Brenton were probably Episcopalian; Arnold, Wilson, and Porter were nondescript. In 1668 the company donated for ministerial support in Pettiquamscutt three hundred acres, specifying that the minister was to be "orthodox," but failing to declare wherein orthodoxy consisted. In 1679 the three-hundred-acre grant for the support of a minister was confirmed; but so completely was it still left in the dark as to what the principles of the minister were to be that in 1692, when the land was being platted, Jahleel Brenton (then a member of the company) advised that no attempt be made to settle the point, but that it be left open

to dispute. Accordingly a very pretty dispute was
waged between the Congregationalists under the
Rev. Joseph Torrey and the Episcopalians under
MacSparran until 1752. In that year the king in
council, moved by the fact that Brenton, Wilbor,
and Hull all had at some time been members of
the First Church of Boston, rendered a decision
in favor of Congregationalism as the "orthodoxy"
meant to be subsidized in the grant of 1668.[1]

It was the Quakers and Episcopalians who in
Narragansett created the religious atmosphere.
At the same time it should be borne in mind that
in Westerly Quakers and Episcopalians alike were
outnumbered by the Seventh Day and other Baptists. The Seventh Day Society was an offshoot
from the early Seventh Day Church at Newport,
and was organized in 1708. Among the other

[1] In 1695, 1696, and 1702, Samuel Sewall, who was a son-in-law
of John Hull, and who succeeded him as a proprietor in Pettiquamscutt, made gifts of land there for school and ministerial
purposes as follows : five hundred acres (near Yagoo Pond) for a
local school, five hundred acres (adjoining) to Harvard College,
and three hundred acres on Tower Hill for a meeting-house. The
lands for the support of a local school were sold in 1825, and
the income from the proceeds (about $350 a year) is used to sup-
port a teacher. The Harvard College land also has been sold,
and the income from the proceeds supports two scholarships
worth, each, two hundred dollars a year. The ministerial land
(of which Sewall was in reality but one of the proprietors) was
the tract over which there was waged the lawsuit *Torrey vs.
Gardner*. The proceeds of this land (which in 1878 amounted to
nearly $6000) are devoted to the support of a Congregational
minister in Narragansett. — *Pub. R. I. Hist. Soc.* vol. ii, p. 117.

Baptists were the New Lights, a society which came into existence about 1742 with the White-field revival. It served as the medium for so much of the Whitefield influence as found scope in Rhode Island. As determined by conditions purely economic, Narragansett life was favorable to the Episcopalians. That life, too, had the fortune to be blessed, during a considerable part of the eighteenth century, with the ministrations, religiously, of a man who fitted into these conditions with remarkable nicety, — the Rev. James MacSparran. The witty and genial personality of the doctor may well serve as a centre about which to group the life in question.

On arriving in Rhode Island in April, 1721, MacSparran (a Scotch-Irish bachelor and missionary twenty-eight years old) found awaiting him a tasteful church building (St. Paul's) and seven or less communicants. As a first important step the young missionary proceeded (May 22, 1722) to get rid of his bachelorhood by marrying a handsome lass of seventeen summers — Hannah Gardiner. This step at once brought the husband into the select circle of the Gardiners, the Hazards, the Robinsons, and the Updikes ; withal it soon increased the number of his communicants. Just who the Gardiners, the Hazards, the Robinsons, and the Updikes were it becomes for us of interest to inquire.

Beginning with the Updikes, these families

were the present owners of the Wickford (Caw-camsqussick) and Boston and Point Judith Neck lands, and they had as landed neighbors the Champlins, the Stantons, and the Babcocks. The lands in question opened upon the old Pequod Path (Post Road) and embraced, per owner, anywhere from two to twelve thousand acres. The Smiths (to whom the Updikes succeeded) were proprietors at one period of a tract nine miles long by three wide; and Thomas Stanton lorded it over a tract measuring four and one half by two miles. Upon such estates the dwelling-houses were large, with gambrel roofs, low beam-traversed ceilings, and of course great fireplaces. Negro slaves were the servants, and quarters for them were provided in the spacious attics or else in a special wing attached to the dwellings after the plan of a Maryland manor. The primary products of a Narragansett farm were sheep and cattle. From these animals there were derived wool, butter, and cheese — the latter a reproduction of the famous Cheshire article, the recipe for which had been brought from England by the wife of Richard Smith. There were produced also horses, the Narragansett pacer, an animal (whether Spanish or native in origin) proverbially easy of gait and so fleet that, according to MacSparran, it could pace a mile in little more than two minutes.

The social customs to which the economic conditions in Narragansett gave rise were, despite the fact that there was produced no single staple like tobacco, almost exactly those of Virginia. The men were large-hearted, hospitable, and commanding; the women dignified and courteous. As in the Old Dominion, dwellings were widely separated and visiting was made an institution. Taverns hardly existed, for strangers were expected to bring with them letters of introduction, which would admit them to the family and neighborhood circle. With strangers as guests, various were the forms of entertainment resorted to. If the visitor were fond of shooting, the innumerable coverts abounded in partridges and quail. If he were a devotee of the chase, hounds and horns and hunters were at his disposal, with if anything rather a superfluity of walls and ditches to test the sureness of his seat. Berkeley's "Alciphron," which reflects closely the Rhode Island environment of the writer, depicts in the fifth dialogue a fox hunt, with the noise of the opening of hounds, the winding of horns, and the clamoring of country gentry in frocks, short wigs, and jockey boots. Or, if the visiting stranger were a Virginian, as readily he might be (for a similarity of tastes led to an exchange of civilities between the two sections) horse-racing for silver tankards was a favorite pastime.

Nor were the gentry of Narragansett indifferent to the higher forms of pleasure. A good many private libraries existed among them. Daniel Up-

dike, the Kingstown representative in the Newport Philosophical Society, owned Pope's Iliad, the
works of Hesiod, Virgil's poems, the "Colloquies
of Erasmus," dialogues from Molière, and other
books ; while Smibert, fresh from the Madonna
del Granduca and the glories of all Tuscany,
found patrons in Pettiquamscutt as well as in
Newport. There were no schools, but the Virginia
plan of private tutors obtained, and both young
men and damsels were trained with care in polite
learning. Dr. MacSparran instructed young men.
Peter Simons, a Newport teacher of music and
belles lettres, instructed young women. Hannah
Robinson, the Narragansett beauty of her day,
fell madly in love with Simons, — so madly, and
withal unfortunately, that a mere historical pen
must despair of doing justice to the romance.

In the midst of the life described, James Mac-
Sparran (made a Doctor of Sacred Theology by
Oxford University in 1737) moved ever, as at first,
a leading figure. Before he was forty he had grown
portly, — "a full-bodied fat fellow," he calls himself ; and in his broad wig he not a little reminds
one (as the editor of his diary, Dr. Daniel Goodwin, truly observes) of a clerical Dr. Samuel Johnson. Scotch-Irishman that he was, his tongue was
sharp. He said of Rhode Island two memorable
things : one, that "liberty of conscience there was
carried to an irreligious extreme ; " and the other,
that "the Rhode Islanders [apropos of their paper

money delusion] were perhaps the only people on
earth who had hit on the art of enriching themselves by running in debt." His tartness, and, too,
a certain air of superiority which no doubt he carried, led the vigorous Ezra Stiles to brand him in
his diary as a " vainglorious, turbulent, haughty,
domineering priest." The MacSparran rectory was
located on the brow of the hill which to-day bears
the name MacSparran, and the outlook from it was
(and is) one of the most comprehensive in Rhode
Island. To the north and left was Pettiquamscutt
Pond, with the mill of Stuart the snuff grinder at
the head of it; in front flowed the Pettiquamscutt
River; beyond (across the shores of Conanicut)
rose the Colony House and spire of Trinity Church,
Newport; to the south and right stretched miles
of bay and sea line lost in the ultima thule of
Block Island.

Like every one about him, MacSparran was a
slaveholder, and he occasionally deemed it wholesome to administer the lash. In June, 1745, he
notes that he gave " Moroca one or two Lashes
for receiving presents from Mingo. I think it was
my duty to correct her," he says, and then adds:
" W^{t}ever Passion passed between my wife and
me on y^s occasion Good L^d for give it." Hannah
MacSparran evidently was possessed of a mind
and temper of her own, for elsewhere the doctor
alludes to her as " my poor passionate dear."

In subsequent years in Narragansett the tender-

ness of the rector's wife for the maid Moroca was
to be justified in the growth toward the negro
(under the fostering care of " College Tom " Hazard) of a sentiment so compassionate that slaveholding little by little was undermined. In 1745
small was the thought of such a thing. At that
period the very existence of local society seemed
to be, and probably was, dependent upon slavery.
In contrast with Newport, Narragansett had real
work for the negro to perform ; and unless performed by him, it is difficult to see by whom it
would or could have been. The great farms needed
to be manned ; and white laborers found on the
sea a life too profitable and too full of freedom to
be abandoned for dairy tasks.

By 1750, Narragansett, in respect to the number
of its slaves and hence in respect to its material
prosperity, was at its zenith. It contained within
its limits about one thousand negroes — a proportion (in South Kingstown) of one negro to every
two or three white men. In Newport the negroes
were 1105. Together, therefore, the two localities
contained almost exactly two thirds of the negro
population of the colony.[1]

---

[1] On April 14, 1751, Dr. MacSparran preached on Tower Hill
a sermon of high admonition before Thomas Carter of Newport
who had been condemned to death for the murder (near Pettiquamscutt Pond) of William Jackson, a Virginia trader. Carter
was hanged on the 10th of May, and his execution was witnessed
by a great throng. So many came from Newport that, it is said,
fear was felt there lest the negro slaves, taking advantage of the

The sports of the negro in the sometime King's
Province were in the main the dancing and frolics
of Virginia; but corn huskings took the place of
'coon and 'possum hunts, and one sport was thoroughly unique — the negro election. It was held
on the third Saturday in June in each year, and
was conducted for the purpose of choosing a negro
town leader called the governor. Electioneering,
styled "parmenteering," was rife for weeks in advance, and the result was determined by a count of
heads taken after the voters (resplendent in pow-
dered queues and monster cocked-hats and swords)
had been drawn up in double rank under the supervision of a grand marshal.

It is now nearly one hundred and fifty years since
Old Narragansett began to fade and pass. To-day,
as the pedestrian wends his way by the home of
Gilbert Stuart, up MacSparran Hill, and back three
miles into the country to the site of St. Paul's
Church, he finds it hard to convince himself that
any life at all, save that of wild creatures, ever pul-
sated in the solitude about him. Everywhere the
paths are invaded and overarched by thickets; the
meadows and ponds darkened and made eerie by
surrounding woods; the old-time mansions either
wholly gone or lapsed into melancholy ruin. St.

absence of their masters, should rise in insurrection. MacSparran's
sermon, which covers eighteen pages of print, may be found in
the *Narr. Hist. Reg.* vol. i.

Paul's itself — under which in 1757 MacSparran
was tenderly laid to rest, and on the site of which
his monument now stands — has bodily disappeared
(object apparently of aerial witchery), and may
only be found by a visit to Wickford.   Dr. Edward
Channing has suggestively remarked that Old Narragansett even in its own day was anomalous in
Rhode Island.   Based upon agriculture, the agriculture was not of the ordinary limiting and particu-
laristic sort.   It rather was part of that eighteenth
century coöperative and commercial movement of
which Newport (though less wealthy than South
Kingstown) was at once the inlet, the outlet, and
the heart.

CHAPTER VIII

GROWTH OF PROVIDENCE : STEPHEN HOPKINS AND
MOSES BROWN

The Old Town — Brown University — Polly Olney — Limitation
of Slavery — Hopkins-Ward.

PROVIDENCE in the eighteenth century is interesting in a special sense. It began the century as the centre of the agricultural and separatist influences of northern and northwestern Rhode Island. It ended it (or rather the first three quarters of it) as the commercial peer of Newport.

Inordinately slow was the town in taking the first step. Down to 1740 or 1742 it was still, as in the seventeenth century, but a long, straggling street by the water front, where on summer evenings the inhabitants sat in their doorways, smoked their clay pipes, and fought the swarms of mosquitoes that rose from the marsh opposite. The close corporation of (now) one hundred and one proprietors into which the astuteness of William Harris and Thomas Olney had converted the free gift of Roger Williams stood out resolutely against progress as represented by the newer freemen. The town was agricultural, and agricultural the proprietors were determined that it should remain.

As late as July, 1704, it was resolved in town meeting that no more " warehouse lots by the salt water side " should be granted, as the space was needed as a common for the landing of cattle on their return from the Weybosset pastures.

Yet the fact that some lots for warehouses and wharves had been granted (as to Pardon Tillinghast in 1680) shows a commercial tendency; and by 1711 Nathaniel Brown, a Plymouth shipwright forced out of Massachusetts because of his Episcopalianism, began to ply his trade in Weybosset Neck. There was a further sign of progress in the fact that in 1731 the old town or district of Providence Plantations (now with a population of 3916) was divided into the four towns, — Providence, Smithfield, Scituate, and Glocester.

Among the earliest Providence merchants were the Crawfords, Gideon and William. Between 1685 and 1720 they traded largely to the West Indies and were the means of affording the slow-going burghers on the Mooshassuc a glimpse of the great world through a display of wares including periwigs, looking-glasses, bird-cages, flutes, wine-glasses, gold-headed canes, etc. What Providence had to give in exchange for commodities of any sort was chiefly lumber and horses, but its resources were supplemented by those of western Massachusetts. Privateering (after 1739) helped Providence much, and the slave trade (in which the town never was very ardent) helped it a little.

It was with the rise to manhood of the sons of William Hopkins and James Brown that Providence received its greatest impulse. William Hopkins was descended from Thomas, who was at Providence in 1638; and James Brown was the great-grandson of Chad Brown, the associate of Roger Williams. Of the several sons of William Hopkins, one (William) became a celebrated merchant; another (Esek) became commander of the first American fleet; and a third (Stephen) became the greatest statesman of Rhode Island. Of the sons of James Brown — Nicholas, Joseph, John, and Moses — all gained eminence as merchants. By 1760 the family were operating no less than eighty-four sloops, schooners, and brigantines. Each member, too, had severally an avocation — the public service, science, or philanthropy.

Stephen Hopkins was born in the town of Providence [Cranston] on March 7, 1707. He removed to the "compact part of the town" in 1742. Here, as his biographer, Mr. William E. Foster, has pointed out, he won prominence as a man, master, among other things, of the art of evoking public improvements. Commerce, however, engaged his principal thought, and as early as 1746 we hear of "Stephen Hopkins & Co."

It perhaps was about 1757 that Moses Brown, then just twenty years old, began to assume with Stephen Hopkins, his senior by thirty-one years, that place of intimate friend and trusted colleague

which he ever afterwards held. Brown as a boy had
been highly observing and alert. He had made it
a practice to haunt the wharves of Providence,
where casks of molasses were constantly being discharged, with the laudable design of catching the
drippings. " What casks are your best? " asked a
would-be buyer of an importer on one occasion.
" I don't know," the latter replied. " Ask that
little molasses-faced Moses ; he will tell you."
By 1763 Moses was so far a judge of molasses that
he was taken into partnership by his brothers.
Soon we find him, in connection with Hopkins and
such other public-spirited men outside his own
family as Daniel Abbott, John Jenckes, Samuel
Nightingale, Nicholas Cooke, Darius Sessions, and
Jabez Bowen, striving to stir Providence to do
something for education.

With Stephen Hopkins knowledge had long
been an absorbing pursuit. In 1732 he had begun
making trips to Newport, where, gravitating to the
Berkeley group as iron to its lode, he had been admitted (along with Daniel Updike of Narragansett
and Samuel Johnson of Connecticut) among the
out-of-town members of the Philosophical Society.
By 1750 he had got together books with which to
start in Providence a public library : full sets of
Pope, Swift, and Addison ; together with sets of
Shakespeare, Milton, and Bacon ; selections from
the Greek and Latin classics ; and the standard
works of the day on politics, law, and medicine.

By 1762 he with others had established the Providence "Gazette," the early publishers of which were William Goddard and John Carter.

But just now (1763) there was to be taken in Rhode Island a step in the direction of light and learning that for boldness was far to exceed anything of which, as yet, Moses Brown or Stephen Hopkins could have dreamed. Rhode Island College (afterwards Brown University) was to be founded.

As early as 1761 a college after the model of Yale, though less sectarian, had been projected by Dr. Ezra Stiles. Little progress with it had been made, when, in October, 1762, the Philadelphia Baptist Association decided to establish a college in Rhode Island — the point in America where the Baptists wielded most power. Accordingly in 1763 James Manning — a College of New Jersey (Princeton) graduate — set out for Newport. On arriving, he summoned a meeting of Baptist leaders and submitted to them a "rough draft" of a charter for "a seminary of polite literature." The seminary was to be "subject to the government of the Baptists," but was to admit to its boards of control representatives of other religious bodies. Manning went away, and Dr. Stiles as a man of "learning and catholicism" was asked to put the "rough draft" in final form. He did it in such a manner as to divide the control of the proposed

institution between the Baptists and Congregationalists. To the latter he in fact gave a preponder-
ance on the Board of Fellows. The charter, as
drawn, was introduced in the lower house of the
General Assembly, but on objection, followed by
loss of the instrument, failed of passage. In 1764
a new charter, so drawn as to give complete control to the Baptists but allowing representation to
the Quakers, Congregationalists, and Episcopalians,
was introduced and passed. The Congregationalists, because of their forwardness as displayed in
the Stiles charter were accorded one less representative than either the Quakers or Episcopalians.[1]

The charter adopted was broad-minded to an
extraordinary degree. The college was denominated " liberal and catholic." No religious tests
were ever to be admitted. All offices, except the
office of president (which must be filled by a Baptist), and all professorships were to be open to
the adherents of any Protestant communion. The
public teaching " was to respect the sciences."
Sectarian views were not to be taught, but " all
religious controversies might be studied freely."
Upon this foundation, Stephen Hopkins, in 1764,

[1] As regards Dr. Stiles's own views in this connection, they are
set forth in a draft of a letter by him dated August 26, 1768.
He says : " We had lately a catholic plan for a college in Rhode
Island but it turned out Supremacy & Monopoly in the hands of
the Baptists, whose Influence in our Assembly was such that they
obtained a most ample charter to their purpose." — *Literary
Diary*, vol. i, p. 22, n. ; Rider, *Book Notes*, vol. vi, p. 153.

and James Manning, in 1765, were chosen respectively chancellor and president. In 1769, at Warren, where Manning was conducting a grammar school, the first college class (seven in number) was graduated. Among the graduates was James M. Varnum the defender, in 1786, of sound money in *Trevett vs. Weeden.*

The young institution, it is hardly necessary to say, was beset with financial difficulties. Dr. Morgan Edwards of Philadelphia (long remembered as forecasting the day of his death and as surviving that day to his own confusion) was early sent to England to solicit aid, but accomplished little. At this time in Rhode Island, as for seventy-five years thereafter, lotteries were the accepted mode of liquidating hard debts. So President Manning, whose own church had in 1767 been granted the privilege of a lottery, broached to one of his English correspondents a lottery project in aid of the college. The reply which he received was remarkable for the day. " As to raising money by a lottery," runs the letter, " I dislike it from the bottom of my heart. 'T is a scheme dishonorable to the supreme head of all worlds and of every true church. We have our fill of these cursed gambling lotteries in London every year. They are big with ten thousand evils. Let the devil's children have them all to themselves. Let us not touch or taste."

The next thing thought of was to make the college (for which as yet no building had been secured) an object of competition among the five counties, into which, ere this, Rhode Island had been divided. Between Providence and Newport — the principal centres — the contest was close and sharp. At length, on February 7, 1770, a decision (somewhat constructively reached) was announced in favor of Providence. There, on the old home lot of Chad Brown, the corner-stone of the first building (University Hall) was laid, on March 27, by John Brown, a lineal descendant of the original lot owner. Strong claims had the name " Brown " upon the new institution before Nicholas Brown, Jr., made to it in 1804 a donation of five thousand dollars. Especially strong were these claims in view of the fact that it was no less a person than Moses Brown who, as a member of the General Assembly, first brought forward Providence as a competitor for the college against Newport.

In 1761, when the college question was broached, Stephen Hopkins was fifty-four years old and had been twice married. Moses Brown, his friend, was but twenty-three years old, and as yet had not been married at all. Moses, consequently, was an eligible bachelor ; and his connection with a Providence-Boston romance of the day — a romance preserved in old letters among the papers of the Rhode Island Historical Society — will serve to admit us to a glimpse of mid-eighteenth-century philandering.

Brown was a Free Mason. So also was one of his friends — William Palfrey of Boston. Early in 1761 Palfrey visited in Providence, where he was cordially entertained by Brown, and where he met several damsels. Among them was Polly Olney, a daughter of the wealthy innkeeper, Joseph Olney, in whose yard the Providence " liberty tree " was soon to be dedicated. On returning to Boston, Palfrey found that his heart had been lost to Polly, and he concluded to make a clean breast of the fact to his friend Brown, then, as ever, a man notable for discretion. So, on March 26, he wrote asking that his " compliments " be conveyed to " the dear Polly," toward whom he felt altogether more than he was able " to express."

By August 17 complications began to arise. Palfrey had heard that Polly was " being courted " by others ; especially by one other — Moses Brown himself. With some spirit he laid the rumor before Brown, professing " thankfulness " that he had " not as yet advanced so far but that he could Retreat with Honour." At the same time, he demanded " the true state of the case by the Return of the Post without fail." It was now Brown's turn to show spirit. He did so by giving a Roland for an Oliver. Disclaiming on his part any designs upon Polly, he plainly told Palfrey that rumor had it that he, Palfrey, was paying his addresses " to a young Lady in Boston," — a course of conduct by which (if it were being practiced) he could but consider both Polly and himself " Very Ungenteely Us'd." In reply Palfrey explained that the young Boston lady in question was a Miss Cazneau with whose brother he was acquainted. The extent of his intimacy with her had been that (and

that only) implied in sometimes taking a walk with her
and her sisters, or in occasionally "Carrying her and
her sisters with some other Ladies to a play."

There now ensued on the part of Palfrey a silence
long and ominous. In fact, he did not again write
to Brown until February 20, 1762. What pangs he
meanwhile had suffered are then disclosed in detail. He
went, it would seem, to Providence in August, 1761,
but found Polly gone from home. She was at Newport. In desperation he wrote to her making a full
avowal of his passion. He got no reply. He resolved on
another journey to Providence, whither he "sett out
with Mrs. Eustis who was going there to see the plays"
[evidently those noted in chapter v, which led to the
suppression of the theatre in Rhode Island], but Polly
was still at Newport. Thereupon the much disappointed
Palfrey himself went to Newport, where he found Polly,
but where "something or other," as he plaintively
records, "Continually happened which hindered our
being in private." Polly then returned to Providence.
Palfrey attended her, but found himself "as bad off as
before," because of "the great number of Travellers
upon the Road." What was he to do? He contrived, by
the aid of Polly's brother "Jo," a neat stratagem. A
certain Miss Paget was to invite Polly and himself to her
home "in the Evening & take an oppor'y of Leaving
us together." "This scheme," he relates, "took." With
what result? With the result only that the ardent
and laborious Palfrey was coolly rejected by Polly,
with the approved admonition "to think no more of
her."

So comes to an end the first chapter in this Provi-

dence-Boston love tale of a century and a half ago. The
second chapter transfers the characters to Boston.

Palfrey, rejected of Polly, bethought himself straightway of Miss Cazneau. Toward her now his attentions
became marked. At this critical juncture — just as
" Miss Cazneau " was quietly being substituted for the
once "dear Polly " — what should occur but that a
long-delayed, and hence unexpected, letter from Moses
Brown, dealing with the Polly affair, should fall into
the hands of the Boston damsel and be by her ("from
Curiosity Natural to her Sex," as Palfrey put it to
Brown) opened and read. The escape was narrow. It,
however, was an escape, for no harm followed. Soon
Palfrey was ready to inform Brown that " Miss Cazneau was a fine young Lady & every way Calculated to
render the marriage State agreeable." Polly meanwhile
(for of her we are not to lose sight) had taken a journey
to Boston.

On April 16, 1762, Palfrey wrote in some excitement to Brown : " Polly is this minute gone out of
the Store, having come in with another young Lady to
buy some Silks. . . . She did not seem to be quite so
much upon the Reserve as usual." On April 27, Palfrey
again wrote : " Polly told my friend Flagg Last Evening
that she thought it would have looked odd for a young
Lady to say Yes so soon and that if there was any mis-
understanding between us she was very sorry for it."
Alas, Polly ! Palfrey, to his honor be it said, adhered
to his engagement to Miss Cazneau, merely remarking
to Brown his confidant : " I am sorry I was not acquainted with her [Polly's] temper and disposition before, as it would have prevented all that has happened."

The third chapter in our love tale consists of a single item in the columns of the Providence "Gazette." On August 25, 1764, there was published the following: "Tuesday evening last, Mr. Thomas Greene of Boston, merchant, was married to Miss Polly Olney of this town, a young lady who has real merit, added to a beautiful person, to grace the connubial state and perpetuate its felicity." After all it was not in vain that Polly had journeyed to Boston.

The year 1764 — that of Polly's marriage — was also the year of the marriage of Moses Brown. He took to wife his cousin Anna. Thenceforth business claimed him until 1773, when he retired and devoted himself to securing the abolition of slavery in Rhode Island and the curtailment of the slave trade. Anna Brown died in February, 1773, and one day her husband, speaking of his bereavement to a friend, said: "I saw my slaves with my spiritual eyes as plainly as I see thee now, and it was given me as clearly to understand that the sacrifice that was called for of my hand was to give them their liberty." In December he manumitted ten slaves.

Next to Brown the individual chiefly concerned in securing effective action against slavery in Rhode Island was Stephen Hopkins. In 1774 the General Assembly passed an act prohibiting the importation of slaves into Rhode Island. To this act Hopkins dictated the preamble, which recited that "those who are desirous of enjoying all the advantages of liberty themselves should be willing to extend personal liberty to others." Yet Hopkins, despite his preamble, was a slave owner; one, moreover, that had withstood admonition from the Quakers, a society to which, since 1755, he had himself belonged. Something led him to promote the Act of 1774; what was it? Presumably it was the course of the Providence town meeting. In May the town had resolved that " it is unbecoming the character of freemen to enslave . . . negroes." The deputies of the town, of whom Hopkins was one, had then been " directed to use their endeavors to obtain an act prohibiting the importation of negroes into this colony and providing that all negroes born in the colony are to be free after attaining a certain age."

The influences (interblending and cumulative) to which the conversion of Moses Brown on the slavery question is to be attributed, and to which also is to be attributed the conversion (or rather re-conversion) on the same question of the Providence town meeting, were at least four: The letters and exhortations of the Quakers, the sermons and pastoral ministrations of the Church of England; the preaching of Dr. Samuel Hopkins; and the unprofitableness in Rhode Island (outside of Narragansett) of slavery itself.

The earliest influence was exerted by the Quakers. It was perceptible in 1729, and by 1748 (through the efforts of John Woolman) was strongly felt.

It culminated in 1770 with the condemnation by
the Rhode Island Yearly Meeting of ownership of
any negro " of an age, capacity, and ability suitable for freedom." Participation by the Church of
England in the local anti-slavery movement was
effective though indirect. Berkeley, Honyman,
MacSparran, and the Rev. John Usher of Bristol,
all, between 1730 and 1743, sought by catechetical
exercises to awaken the consciences of the slaves
and to lead them to baptism and communion.
These efforts were supplemented by the Rev. Marmaduke Brown, — a successor to Honyman, — who
in 1763, at Newport, opened a school for the in-
struction of negroes; and by Mrs. Mary Brett, —
widow of Dr. John Brett, — who in the same town
opened a similar school ten years later.

If the anti-slavery efforts of the Episcopalians
were indirect, such were not the efforts of Samuel
Hopkins. The doctor, stanch Puritan that he was,
gathered headway slowly; but when in full career
about 1770 he came little short of the mark set
later by the illustrious company of Massachusetts abolitionists. His church contained many
slaveholders and slave traders, but the doctor spake
right on. He said : " Newport has been built up
and has flourished . . . at the expense of the blood,
the liberty and happiness of the poor Africans."
Nor did he labor altogether in vain. At length his
church was brought to resolve, that " the slave
trade and the slavery of Africans, as it has existed

among us, is a gross violation of the righteousness and benevolence which are so much inculcated in the gospel, and therefore we will not tolerate it in this church." [1]

Indeed to such lengths did Hopkins go that in 1773 he tried to persuade Dr. Stiles to join with him in sending back to Africa, as missionaries, two of his colored communicants — Quamine and Yamma. And here an amusing element enters. Stiles began fearsomely to suspect that the real object of his brother minister in seeking to send out these men was the "Christianizing of the Africans on Principles to his Mind" — on principles not so much evangelical as Edwardsian and Hopkinsian. Nothing, unless it were an allegory on the banks of the Nile, could be more ineffectively headstrong than the Edwards-Hopkins theology on the coast of Guinea, and that the broad-minded Ezra Stiles failed to perceive it argues him as sadly deficient in a sense of humor as was good John Winthrop himself.

Of the four influences at work in Rhode Island against slavery, the influence which most of all

[1] In Mr. F. B. Sanborn's *Life and Letters of John Brown of Osawatomie*, 1881, there is printed a statement made by Owen Brown, father of John, as to what led him to embrace Abolitionism. "The Rev. Samuel Hopkins of Newport, Rhode Island," said the father, " came to visit the Rev. Jeremiah Hallock, with whom I lived, and I heard him talking with Mr. Hallock about slavery in Rhode Island, which he denounced as a great sin. From this time I was anti-slavery."

must be regarded as a determining one was the unprofitableness of the institution. Of the truth of this assertion the law of 1774 itself is proof. That law forbade the importation of slaves into Rhode Island, but it took noteworthy pains to protect and even encourage slave importations by Rhode Islanders into the West Indies, — the place chiefly where a handsome profit upon such merchandise was yet to be expected.

The course of the Narragansett Bay commonwealth in relation to negro slavery is not, upon the whole, one that invites applause; yet neither is it one from which there should be withheld all commendation. The General Assembly did not declare for emancipation till 1784, nor against participation in the foreign slave trade till 1787; but in 1788 it was agitation by Rhode Island Quakers (an agitation reinforced by the action of the General Assembly) that led to legislation in Connecticut and Massachusetts; and of all the States that between 1787 and 1790 deliberated upon the Federal Constitution, Rhode Island alone (by a majority of one in its convention) proposed an amendment directing Congress to " promote and establish such laws and regulations as may effectually prevent the importation of slaves of every description into the United States." That the commonwealth did not do more against African bondage than it did, and that it did not do it earlier, is no small indication of the extent to which the individualism of the seventeenth century — an individualism capable of originating the famous anti-slavery law of 1652 — had been encroached upon by the commercialism of the eighteenth.

But go back a little. By 1750 Providence had grown greatly in wealth and importance. Its population now, after the separation from it of Smithfield, Scituate, and Glocester, was nearly 3500. It was become a standing challenge to the political as well as the commercial supremacy of Newport. Just where and when, had it not been for Stephen Hopkins, this attitude of challenge would have found a champion, it is impossible to tell. As it was, the championship fell naturally, and at once, to Hopkins himself. The latter, since his abandonment of rural life in 1742, had (up to 1751) filled the positions of justice of the Providence Court of Common Pleas, member of the eastern boundary commission, speaker of the General Assembly, commissioner to the Colonial Congress of 1746, member of the northern boundary commission,[1]

---

[1] By both the Massachusetts charters, that of 1628 and that of 1691, the southern boundary of Massachusetts was fixed at " three English miles on the south part of Charles River or of any part thereof." In 1642 Massachusetts laid down the line but in so doing placed it " seven miles and fifty-six poles " south of the Charles River. In 1719 Rhode Island, in ignorance of the error în the Massachusetts survey, accepted the line as laid down. In 1769, upon petition of Moses Brown, correction was sought by the Rhode Island Assembly, and Brown and Stephen Hopkins were made members of a northern boundary commission. The

and justice and chief justice of the Superior Court.
Still further was he to minister to the aspirations
of Providence by entering, in 1755, upon a successful contest for the governorship.

First, however, there met the famous Albany
Congress, — that of 1754, — and to it Hopkins was
sent as a delegate. Beginning with 1684 there had
been held in English America nine several con-
gresses anent the French and Indians, and. Rhode
Island had kept aloof from most of them. We
have seen in chapter iii, how, in 1693, a certain
Albany Congress and its requirements were ingen-
iously evaded; and in 1722 the colony met a plea
from Massachusetts for help against the eastern
Indians by asking: " Who knows but that his
Majesty in his great wisdom may find out and prescribe ways to make these wild and inaccessible
subjects of his come in and tamely submit to his
government without the melancholy prospect we
now have of shedding much blood? " When, therefore, Hopkins not merely attended the Congress
of 1754, but, along with his colleague, Martin
Howard, Jr., of Newport, voted in its sessions for
Franklin's plan of colonial union, with its Presi-
dent-General to be appointed by the crown and
its Grand Council of Representatives to be chosen
on the basis of population, Rhode Island was a
good deal stirred.

matter was not then disposed of but recurred in 1791, and later.
In 1847–48 a " conventional line " was established, and in 1883
this line was made the legal boundary.

It was in the face of no little detraction that in May, 1755, Stephen Hopkins was duly elected governor in the stead of Greene. With the election referred to, the spell of a practically uninterrupted succession of Newport gubernatorial magistrates was broken. In 1727 a Providence man, Joseph Jenckes, had been chosen governor, but upon election he had found it advisable to remove to Newport. Greene himself, though from Warwick, was one with Newport in interest and sympathy. Hopkins was like neither Jenckes nor Greene. He was the representative — the champion in fact — of Providence in a long pending and now irrepressible conflict between the new and the old. The case was one not of country against town, as in the contest over paper money, but rather (for still another time) of upstart democratic Florence against staid aristocratic Pisa; and the bitterness engendered (the bitterness of jealousy) was largely without rational foundation.

Newport sent forth into the lists, as its representative, Samuel Ward, — a young man of parts and education, son of Governor Richard Ward, and owner of a large estate at Westerly in the Narragansett country. In 1757 Samuel Ward aided in defeating Governor Hopkins for reëlection, and at the same time subjected himself to a suit for libel. Thenceforth, until 1768, Rhode Island politics were little else than an annual propounding and answering of one question: Shall Stephen Hopkins or

Samuel Ward be governor of the colony ? in other
words, shall Newport or Providence — the rising
North or the risen South — wield a preponderant
local influence ? In England it still was the day
politically of Sir Robert Walpole, — the day of
bribery elevated into an art, — and neither Hopkins
nor Ward scrupled to pay to the example of the
dead premier the sincere tribute of imitation. A
large purchasable vote would seem to have been
found in King's County, for the efforts put forth
to carry that county have been described as com-
mensurate relatively with those later put forth, in
a different field, " to carry Indiana." Of course
the animosity aroused by political warfare of the
kind described — like that of the tribal feud — was
implacable ; and when, in 1768, an arrangement
was at length concluded by which Hopkins and
Ward each yielded his pretensions to first place,
it was cause for hearty rejoicing. The ten years
of Hopkins against Ward may be taken to have
thoroughly demonstrated the weight and growing
importance of Providence. During the entire
period Ward — in every way a fit counterpoise to
Hopkins [1] — obtained the governorship but three
times.

[1] " I well knew Gov. Hopkins. He was a man of a penetrating
astutious Genius, full of Subtlety, deep Cunning, intriguing and
enterprizing. He read much esp^y in History & Government ;
& by read^s Conoversa & Observa acquired a great Fund of
political Knowledge. He was rather a Quaker, hav^g a seat in
the meeting, but it has been said these thirty years by his most

intimate Acquainta that he was a Deist, and of this I made no doubt from my own frequent Conversa with him. He was a man of a noble fortitude & Resolution. He was a glorious Patriot! — [but Jesus will say unto him *I know you not*]." — Stiles, *Literary Diary*, vol. iii, p. 172.

CHAPTER IX

CONSTITUTIONAL DEVELOPMENT

Soul Liberty — The Suffrage — The Function of Legislation —
Legislature-Judiciary.

In both the seventeenth and eighteenth centuries
the main feature of Rhode Island constitutional
development was distrust of delegated power. In
the seventeenth century distrust showed itself in
the political system. Local communities — the
towns — were independent to a great degree of the
central authority to which nominally they were
subordinate. In the eighteenth century — after
town subordination had been effected — distrust
was shown in the administrative system. Executive
and judicial departments were kept subject to the
immediate will of the freemen through an omnipotent legislature semiannually renewed.

But first a word apropos of Soul Liberty, the
suffrage, and the exercise of the function of legislation in eighteenth century Rhode Island.

I

At Newport, upon one occasion after 1700, the
Jews were accorded illiberal treatment. In 1762
Aaron Lopez and Isaac Elizar applied for natu-

ralization under the English statute the 13th of George II, and were denied by the Superior Court on two grounds: on the ground, first (divertingly transparent), that the colony was already " so full of people that many of his Majesty's good subjects, born within the same, have removed and settled in Nova Scotia; " [1] on the ground, second, that by the charter " the propagating of the Christian religion " was one of the chief ends of the founding of Rhode Island, and that the General Assembly, in 1663, had enacted that " no person who does not profess the Christian religion can be admitted free of this colony." [2]

It is with difficulty that one can be persuaded that words such as these were ever uttered by the highest judicial body in the commonwealth

[1] The Nova Scotia movement is described in detail by Mr. R. G. Huling in the *Narr. Hist. Reg.* vol. vii. A good many were concerned in it — over one hundred persons. If the colony was crowded (its total population in 1762 did not exceed 43,000 souls), the removal of the Nova Scotia contingent certainly made room enough for a few families of Hebrews.

[2] The statement that the colony in 1663 had passed a law restricting the freemanship or elective franchise to Christians was presumably based upon the fact that the Charter of 1663 (after the style of royal charters of the day) abounded in expressions of pious regard for the furtherance of the Christian religion. Such expressions possibly may have been understood by some as carrying the force of legislation. Between the Patent of 1644 (which was displaced by the Charter of 1663) and the charter itself, the difference in respect to pious ascriptions and avowals is marked. In the patent there is no allusion to Christ or Christianity, and only a passing allusion to the Deity.

established by Roger Williams, — a commonwealth where " a permission of the most Paganish, Jewish, Turkish, and Antichristian consciences and worships " was, under no circumstances, to be abridged.

Is it, indeed (we are led to ask), true as averred by the court that in 1663 Rhode Island passed an act limiting the freemanship to Christians? It is not true that such an act was passed in 1663, or that such an act ever was passed in the usual mode and upon debate. It is true that in 1719 an act of the year 1665 was so modified by the interpolation of words, " professing Christianity," as to read: " All men professing Christianity, . . . though of different judgments in religion, . . . shall be admitted freemen," etc. The act as modified had its origin with a revising committee of the General Assembly. It appeared first in the digest of 1719, — a digest that so far as known never was adopted by the Assembly. By subsequent revising committees it was permitted to pass into the digests of 1730, 1744, and 1767, which were adopted.

The court, therefore, illiberal though it were in denying freemanship to Lopez and Elizar, must be allowed the benefit of the plea that it was within an act of the colony; an act repugnant to the statute of George II, but one which the court nevertheless may not have felt itself at liberty to disregard.

There is yet a further phase to the act of 1665.

Not only was it radically modified by the interpolation of the words, "professing Christianity;" it was modified still more radically by the interpolation of the words, "Roman Catholics only excepted." In Rhode Island after 1730 not only were none but Christians eligible by local law to the freemanship, but of Christians themselves only a certain sort were eligible, namely, such as were not Roman Catholics. In the case of the Catholics, however, if not in that of the Jews, the local law was purely a dead letter. To furnish an example: Stephen Decatur, a Catholic and a Genoese, — the grandfather of the illustrious commodore of that name, — was made a freeman in 1735.

It was not until 1783 that the altogether un-Rhode Island-like statute in question was abrogated. But despite this fact one thing may be said of it. The feeling that inspired it was confined to so few that had the law not found its way into the statute book in the covert way that it did, it probably never would have found its way there at all. A colony which had not hesitated to withstand as contrary to its charter the command of the crown to subject its militia to the control of Sir William Phips; a colony, moreover, which in 1735 had empowered its Superior Court to restrain by injunction his Majesty's Court of Admiralty; such a colony would in the first instance hardly have hesitated to reject as contrary to its charter a proposition by which it was to be cut off, through the most

odious of tests (a religious one), from ever electing
to the smallest office, or even permitting to cast a
single vote, a Jew like Lopez, a Catholic like Decatur, or any one of the Deistical thinkers in which
it abounded and had abounded from the days of
the English Commonwealth.[1]

Concerning the suffrage in Rhode Island, two
observations by distinguished Rhode Islanders of
the past (Mr. Henry C. Dorr and Mr. Samuel G.
Arnold) will furnish us with what probably is the
clue to it. Says Mr. Dorr: "Solvency has at all
times held the same place in Rhode Island which

---

[1] While neither Mr. S. G. Arnold nor Mr. S. S. Rider expresses
approval of the interpolation which burdened the laws of Rhode
Island with a religious test for the freemanship, both writers offer
a plea in extenuation. They say (*Hist. R. I.* vol. ii, p. 494; *Hist.
Tract* (2d ser.) *No. 1*): Neither Jews, Catholics, nor any other
communion had ever been guaranteed political privileges by
Rhode Island, so when denied such privileges there they could not
logically complain. But in this plea there would seem to be lost
to view what the Rhode Island idea, as a working doctrine, really
was. According to that idea no man, however much he might be
discriminated against for other causes, ought to be discriminated
against merely for cause of religion. Had the colony in the seventeenth century assumed ground different from this, it would have
puzzled seekers after Soul Liberty to distinguish between what
was offered them in Rhode Island and what, for instance, was
offered them in the proprietary and royal province of North Carolina, where Soul Liberty (including the privilege of voting) was
to be obtained for a price, for the yielding up of money in the
form of a tax. The circumstance that in Rhode Island the anti-
Jewish and anti-Catholic statute was systematically ignored, shows
that instinctively the people realized the incompatibility between
it and the Rhode Island idea.

Puritan orthodoxy once held in Massachusetts;"
therefore (to pass now to Mr. Arnold), "the colony was a close corporation and has ever remained
so." In other words: while Plymouth, Massachusetts, Connecticut, and New Haven were each a
close corporation from religious motives, Rhode
Island was such from the highly secular motive of
acquisitiveness.

To this conclusion ample support is lent by the
facts.

Massachusetts throughout the entire period of its
first charter (1628–1684) kept religion foremost as
the touchstone for the freemanship or right to vote.
At the time of the adoption of the Cambridge Plat-
form (1648), "orthodoxy in eighty-nine [two] different articles" (according to Mr. John A. Doyle)
was needful for the franchise. Even upon the demand of the royal commissioners for a pure property qualification in 1664, the law was so contrived
that, as the commissioners said, "he that is a church-
member, though he be a servant and pay not two
pence, may be a freeman." It was not until the
conversion of Massachusetts into a royal province in
1691 that a pure property qualification — a freehold
worth £2 a year or personalty worth £40 — brought
with it the franchise. New Haven, too, never based
the freemanship on property; while, as for Plymouth and Connecticut, both (as Professor Herbert
L. Osgood has recently shown) made religion the
practical, if not uniformly the statutory, test.

In Rhode Island it was otherwise. There, at the outset (under town rule), the freeman was the freeholder.[1] It is true that in 1665, in connection with the visit of the royal commissioners, an act was passed providing for the admission of colony freemen upon proof of their being merely " of competent estates;" but this act was deemed by Rhode Islanders at once too undiscriminating and too centralistic. In 1724 a law went into effect by which the colony fixed the property qualification for colony freemen at £100 freehold (approximately $134), or at £2 freehold income, yet gave back into local hands (the towns) something of their original power over the colony franchise. Persons who had been made free of a town, even though

---

[1] " Landholding was closely associated with the right to exercise the franchise. Providence, on May 15, 1658, ' Ordered yt all those that injoy land in ye jurisdiction of this Towne are freemen.' " — George G. Wilson, " The Political Development of the Towns," Field's *R. I. at the End of the Century*, vol. iii, chap. i. See also H. K. Stokes, " The Finances and Administration of Providence," *J. H. U. Studies*, extra vol. xxv, p. 33 and n.

" That rule [democracy] was perfectly consistent, at the foundation of the State, and long after, with a landed qualification. It was then in this State, as it is now in our newly settled western States; — he who did not own land owned nothing. . . . But the condition of things has changed," etc. — Thomas W. Dorr, *Address to the People of Rhode Island*, 1834.

" There was no need [in 1665] of formally requiring the ownership of real estate as a qualification for the franchise, for at that period nearly all the permanent inhabitants of Rhode Island were freeholders." — Francis Bowen, " The Recent Contest in Rhode Island," *North Am. Rev.* vol. lviii.

they had not been made free of the colony, were permitted to vote for deputies to the General Assembly. At the same time, by an adaptation from the waning custom of primogeniture, the eldest son of a freeman was permitted to vote in right of the freehold of his father.[1]

Upon these two acts — the act expressly attaching the suffrage to the freehold yet reserving the selection of the particular suffragist to the local unit or town, and the act enfranchising a freeman's eldest son (both of them the acts not only of a close corporation but of one based upon Mr. Dorr's principle of solvency or acquisition) — there hung in Rhode Island, until late in the nineteenth century, all of the law and the prophets in respect to voting.

With regard now to the exercise of the legislative function. By the Rhode Island charter the deputies or immediate representatives of the people were, as will be remembered, a locally chosen body composed of six from Newport, four from Providence, Portsmouth, and Warwick, and two from each town additional. The assistants, or council, on the other hand, were an unvarying body of ten chosen by general vote. In 1696 the deputies and assistants became permanently separated into distinct branches. In 1722 the town of Kingstown

[1] In England the heir apparent of a peer, or of a freeman, was allowed to vote. — Statutes of Anne, chap. v; 3d George II, chap. xv.

was divided into the towns of North Kingstown
and South Kingstown, and to each there was
allowed an assistant or member of the upper
branch of the Assembly. By this act, which made
the number of towns equal to the number of assistants (ten), there was established a precedent
for the practice of introducing a member into the
house of assistants for each new town organized,
and so virtually of converting the Rhode Island
upper house into what it is to-day — a body of
representatives more intensely local than the house
of deputies.

II.

The dominance in Rhode Island of the legislature over the executive and judiciary — a dominance at present as great as ever in the case of the
executive, and only in 1860 finally gotten rid of
in the case of the judiciary — was at its height in
the eighteenth century.

In none of the New England colonies was the
governor by and of himself a chief executive. This
function was reserved to the governor and assistants. When, therefore, in 1731 Governor Jenckes
raised the question of the right of veto as pertain-
ing to his position, it was easy for the crown, by
a citation of the colonial charter, to answer him.
Only royal governors might veto ; not even a John
Winthrop or a John Endicott could do it, governors as they were purely by grace of charter. So

Rhode Island was not peculiar in that during its nonage its governor was largely a figurehead. What perhaps is peculiar is that Rhode Island as a State should, along with Delaware, North Carolina, and Ohio, have withheld from its governor the veto power. The peculiarity, though, disappears when it is remembered that by means of such power the immediate will of the town freemen (as, for instance, on a question like that of paper money) might be given a check.

But while the governor as against the General Assembly was (and still is) helpless, it was different with the judiciary. In Rhode Island, as in the rest of New England, the principal early judicial body was the Court of Assistants, or General Court of Trials, consisting of the assistants themselves (to the number of not less than six) reinforced by the governor and deputy-governor. This court under the Charter of 1663 exercised jurisdiction both appellate and original ; but its action was subject to review by the General Assembly, called also the General Court of the colony. The ground of the right of review claimed and exercised by the Assembly was set forth substantially under the first charter. In 1647 it was enacted that " in case a man sues for justice and he cannot be heard, or is heard and cannot be righted by any Law extant among us, then shall the partie grieved petition to the Generall or Law making Assemblie, and shall be relieved." What here the Assembly asserted

was not the competency of a court of law but a
general competency to do justice — a chancery
competency; accordingly when in later days matters were brought before it from the courts, they
were spoken of as brought to be "chancerized."
At first, too, the distinction was more or less regarded, for in 1678 the Assembly expressed im-
patience at an appeal which it was asked to entertain. By 1680, however, its appellate duty, as well
as authority, was formally recognized.

Nor in all this did Rhode Island act very differ-
ently from Massachusetts or Connecticut. In both
of these colonies the General Assembly entertained
appeals and served as a court of chancery; though
in Massachusetts the practice ceased with the seventeenth century, and in Connecticut with the second
decade of the nineteenth. The longer continuance
of the practice in Rhode Island, coupled with the
bitter struggle waged there between legislature and
judiciary, makes evident the more intense distrust
of delegated power felt in the Roger Williams
colony.

The four legislative acts to which were due the
existence of a Rhode Island judiciary separate and
distinct from the upper house of the legislature
were those of 1703, 1729, 1741, and 1747; and the
earliest and latest of them were attended by the
creation of counties, an indication of how purely a
contrivance for judicial purposes the Rhode Island
county is. The Act of 1703 divided the colony into

two counties — the county of Providence (the mainland) and that of Rhode Island (the islands), and provided for two civil courts (inferior courts of common pleas) in each. The Act of 1729 provided for a criminal court (a court of general sessions of the peace) in each county, and changed the name of the Court of Trials to that of Superior Court of Judicature. The Act of 1741 created an equity court of five judges to hear appeals in lieu of the General Assembly, but this act was repealed in 1743. In 1747 (when, in connection with the settlement of the eastern boundary with Massachusetts, the county of Bristol was created) the courts of common pleas were reorganized, and the Superior Court was made to consist, with enlarged powers, of one chief justice and four associates annually to be chosen by the General Assembly. Complete formal separation of judiciary from legislature had thus by 1747 been secured. Still, in 1780, it was found expedient to enact that no member of either branch of the General Assembly should be eligible to the office of justice of the Superior Court.

The extreme jealousy of judicial power felt by Rhode Islanders before the final establishment among them of the Superior Court of Judicature was not soon modified. In 1708 an appellee, grieved at the action of the General Assembly in a particular case, had appealed to the crown, and the queen in council had sustained the appeal, refusing to sanction the exercise of chancery power by a legislative body. Upon this the wily assembly had merely provided for a procedure before it by " petition," and had continued to entertain appeals as aforetime. Such appeals after 1747, despite the enlarged jurisdiction of the Superior Court, the Assembly still welcomed. It also seemingly encouraged a practice by which three jury trials of the same issue might be obtained : one to secure a verdict ; another to secure a different verdict ; and a third to secure a verdict in confirmation of one of the other two ; all, moreover, as mayhap but preliminary to a prayer for legislative interposition.

In yet two other ways did Rhode Islanders of the eighteenth century manifest their distrust of a separate judiciary : by permitting the appointment of very few lawyers to positions upon the bench (albeit among the appointees are some illustrious names — Hopkins, Ward, Ellery, Howell) and by arrogating to themselves, through the General Assembly, the power not merely of commuting sentences but of entirely abrogating them. A striking instance of abrogation is that in which the privateersman Simeon Potter, who had retired to Bristol in 1750, was in 1761 cleared of a conviction and heavy fine meted out to him for assaulting the Rev. John Usher.

Slow was the development of Rhode Island judicial power, but development nevertheless there was. In 1768 the Superior Court (in *Randall vs. Robinson*) took sharp issue with the legislature, and in

1786 (in *Trevett vs. Weeden*) it maintained resolutely the responsibility of its members to God
alone for their conscientious judgments.

From a point of view distinctively economic and
social, the eighteenth century in Rhode Island was
a period of coöperation due to commerce. From a
point of view distinctively political and constitutional, it was, as the present chapter has shown,
a period marked by the old particularism. One
influence may be noted (constitutional as well as
economic) which made for coöperation, and that
was the influence arising from the incorporation
with the commonwealth in 1747 of the Plymouth-
Massachusetts towns. " When," says Mr. William
E. Foster, speaking of Cumberland, Warren, Bristol, Tiverton, and Little Compton, "the stress of
British hostilities, of [post-Revolutionary] paper
money madness, and of opposition to the constitution, called for the best energies, and the best
intelligence of Rhode Island men, no towns were
more steadfast in the defense of correct principles
than these."

NOTE by Dr. Frank G. Bates on local government in Rhode
Island : —

The Rhode Island town to-day conforms externally to the New
England type, but is socially less firmly knitted than elsewhere
in New England.

The process of town formation, even at first, was scarcely organic. No new centre was deliberately selected. There was no
village green, no common meeting-house or school, no dominant

ecclesiastical bond, nothing about which society could organize. When towns of large area were subdivided, there being no centres, it was done by a purely arbitrary process, more suggestive in its somewhat rectangular product of New York or the Middle West than of New England.

The result of such a course of development has been a lack of common interests, of common action, and of civic pride. In spite of unfavorable environment instances have occurred where chance centres have sought but failed to give expression by the formation of a new town to an acquired sense of unity.

Though population has become dense, town subdivision is the exception; towns have long deferred becoming cities; and no intermediate form exists, save a rudimentary organization called a " fire district." This institution of narrow powers recalls conditions in England before the recent reforms in local government.

From the beginning the town councils exercised probate jurisdiction. A recent attempt to transfer this power to circuit judges of probate chosen by the General Assembly has been defeated by the rural vote, as an invasion of local privilege.

PART III

UNIFICATION AND MANUFACTURES

1764–1905

CHAPTER X

PORTENTS OF REVOLUTION

Causes of Resistance — Affair of the Gaspee — Loyalism at Newport —'Creation of a United States Navy.

By slow degrees two convictions have gained the
minds of writers of American history : one, that
the American Revolution was not the outcome of
causes suddenly arising at the close of the Seven
Years' War, — causes converting into rebels a people hitherto fundamentally loyal and content; the
other, that the causes of the Revolution, whatever
they were, varied considerably with the locality.

In the case of Massachusetts, the leading cause
of revolt was Puritanism itself with its inbred fear
of curtailment and even of ultimate suppression
at the hands of the established church. A strong
secondary cause was the renewal and enforcement,
in and after 1764, of the Sugar Act of 1733. In
the case of Virginia and South Carolina, alienation matured step by step out of the assertion
and counter assertion, on the part alike of popular
assembly and royal governor, of many sorts of
" rights."

But to say these things is to say naught else than
that the American colonies (both northern and

southern) had from the first resented almost every
kind of interposition by the mother country, and,
finally, were brought to rebellion because of such
interposition. What form the interposition took
mattered little. Orders and measures salutary and
constitutional — such as those suppressing piracy
and paper money and providing for appeals to the
king in council, or such as the Navigation Act
of the 14th of Charles II, which actually stimulated New England ship-building — were abhorred
equally with measures like the Sugar Act and the
Stamp Act, which, whether constitutional or not,
were blundering. As Adam Smith put the matter
with regard to the Acts of Trade: "These measures (barring the Sugar Act), while not cramp-
ing American industry, or restraining it from any
employment to which it would have gone of its own
accord, are impertinent badges of slavery." It was
the "impertinence" of unacceptable interposition
that led at length to hostilities.

But how had this interposition been shown toward Rhode Island? What, there, had the English
government all along been doing, which, because
of its "impertinence" (real and so-called), gave
rise to the spirit of resistance?

Down to the days of the *quo warranto* against its
charter (1686), Rhode Island had had no quarrel
with the crown, and for a threefold reason: because, in its long contest with Massachusetts and
Connecticut it had had only the crown to look to

for support; because, having no state religion it
had put no affront upon Episcopalians, Baptists,
or Quakers; and because, having no royal governor its acts and temper had never much been
inquired into. Indeed, so loyal and obedient to the
crown had the colony always proved to be, that,
upon the return of the king's commissioners in
1666, it had been especially named and commended
by Charles II as an example to the rest of New
England. Nor did this loyalty and obedience suffer
diminution from the *quo warranto* itself. Upon
the issuing of the writ, the General Assembly at
once resolved "not to stand suit with his Majesty"
— a resolution happy in its effect, for when Sir
Edmund Andros in the discharge of his duty found
it incumbent upon him to ask for the actual surrender of the charter, he did so in words that
broached on regret.

Rhode Island's troubles began with the determined efforts against piracy put forth under Bellomont in 1699; were continued by the executive
and Parliamentary measures against paper money
taken between 1720 and 1751; were heightened
by the passage of the Sugar Act in 1733; were
still further heightened by an attempt of the crown
to control the naval office at Newport in 1743;
and were brought to a climax by the renewal of
the Sugar Act and proposal of a Stamp Act in
1764. These, in short, were the items of unacceptable, and hence of "impertinent," interposition

which gave rise to the spirit of resistance in Rhode Island.

On October 11, 1763, the Lords of Trade wrote to the governor of Rhode Island that it was his Majesty's command that he "make the suppression of the clandestine trade with foreign nations and the improvement of the revenue the constant and immediate object of his care." On October 22, Admiral Colvill wrote from Halifax that he had thought it necessary, "for the encouragement of fair trade by the prevention of smuggling, to station his Majesty's ship the Squirrel for the approaching winter at Newport." Thus confronted, it behooved the colony to take action promptly if it meant to do so at all, and in January, 1764, Governor Stephen Hopkins, responding to a resolution by the General Assembly, forwarded to Joseph Sherwood, agent for Rhode Island in London since 1759 (the year of the death of faithful Richard Partridge), a letter stoutly protesting against the renewal of the Sugar Act on the ground taken in 1733 by Partridge himself.

Hardly had this letter been dispatched when (March, 1764) George Grenville introduced in Parliament a resolution looking toward a stamp tax to be levied in America. News was officially furnished to Rhode Island in August, and in October the General Assembly appointed a committee of seven, headed by the governor, to prepare an address to the king. In November the committee

reported an address and also a paper composed by
Stephen Hopkins, entitled "The Rights of Colonies
Examined." Both papers were ordered to be sent
to Sherwood : the first for presentation to his Majesty, and the second to be put in print and so
made of use to all the colonies.

The pamphlet by Hopkins proved to be by no
means an ordinary performance. It was philosophical but not too much so ; it was scholarly ; it was
strong ; it was dignified. In a word, it was quite
the utterance which a man ambitious of the best in
letters and bred in the traditions of Berkeley might
be expected to put forth. Its main point — one
suggested by the impending Stamp Act — was that
the direct taxation of an unconsenting people was
tyrannous and un-English, and hence unconstitutional. For the point there was, in a sense, old
Rhode Island authority. It will not have been forgotten that in 1733 Richard Partridge had written
to Governor William Wanton: "The levying a
Subsidy upon a Free People without their knowledge agst: their consent, who have the libertys
and Immunitys granted them of Natural Born Subjects—a people who have no Representatives in the
State here — . . . is as I apprehend a violation of
the Right of the Subject." This, too, was the point
on which stress had been laid in pamphlets which
James Otis and Oxenbridge Thacher had published
in Massachusetts just prior to the preparation of
the Hopkins pamphlet.

The point, however, was one not free from difficulty. It was both strong and weak : historically strong; dialectically weak. If it might be urged (as by Hopkins) that through time and usage (the basic elements of the English Constitution) self-direct taxation had become the only constitutional direct taxation for the colonies, it might also be urged that in the eye of English statute law (which took no note of time) the colonies were still, as they had been at the start, mere corporations within the realm. Nor did the weak phase escape remark in Rhode Island. At Newport a pseudonymic pen (that of " a Gentleman at Halifax," disclosed afterwards as Martin Howard, Jr.) took up the cudgels for the British government in an argument not only urbane but well-nigh unanswerable.

Meanwhile neither Rhode Island's protest against the Sugar Act, nor its petition against a Stamp Act, was producing any perceptible effect on the crown, and between 1764 and 1766 events in the colony moved toward revolution with rapid strides. At Newport trouble with the revenue vessels and (after the passage in March, 1765, of the stamp law) with the stamp officials was incessant. The schooner St. John, tender to the Squirrel, was fired on by a mob at Fort George. A boat belonging to the Maidstone — a vessel engaged in impressing seamen — was seized by a mob and burned on the parade. Augustus Johnson, attorney-general and stamp distributer for the colony, and his friends

and abetters, Dr. Thomas Moffat and Martin
Howard, Jr., were hung in effigy and their houses
pillaged. These violent manifestations of feeling
were interspersed with others less discreditable.
On August 7, 1765, the Providence town meeting
under the lead of Stephen Hopkins passed the
famous resolutions which in May Patrick Henry
had introduced in the Virginia House of Burgesses;
not excepting resolution five from which the Virginia house had shrunk. Nor was this the end. In
September of the same year the Rhode Island
Assembly made the Virginia-Providence resolutions
its own; stipulating to save harmless its officers
for not regarding the Stamp Act. Under the stipulation Samuel Ward, who had been chosen governor in May, alone of the entire corps of British
American governors refused to be sworn to execute the measure.

In October there was held in New York the
Stamp Act Congress, but Rhode Island's participation though cordial was not conspicuous, and
in 1766 the obnoxious stamp law was repealed.
The colony on Narragansett Bay went wild with
joy over the repeal, but two things remained still
a vexation. The crown refused to pay to Rhode
Island the war allotment for the year 1756 until
such time as the colony should reimburse Johnson,
Moffat, and Howard for their losses at Newport,
and the Sugar Act was being stringently enforced.

The sugar duty had been renewed at three pence

a gallon. It now was reduced to one penny; but the collection of the one penny involved interposition, and it was interposition that was the real affront. Matters waxed steadily more serious throughout the period 1767–1770, a period signalized by the tea tax; by non-importation agreements; by the quartering of troops in Boston; by the " Farmer's Letters " of Dickinson; by the ordering to England for trial, on the charge of treason, of Samuel Adams and John Hancock; by eloquent championship of America in Parliament by Burke and Barré; by the scuttling at Newport of the revenue sloop Liberty; and, finally, by the " Boston Massacre." Between 1770 and 1772 there was again quiet, but in the latter year this quiet, both for Rhode Island and America at large, was dispelled by a grave occurrence in Narragansett Bay.

One day in March, 1772, his Majesty's schooner Gaspee of eight guns, with her tender the Beaver, took station in the bay and set about the enforcement of the Sugar Act by stopping and searching all vessels, little and big, which came within reach. By this course there was caused what is known in American history as the affair of the Gaspee — the first bold, overt, organized stroke of the Revolution. The Gaspee affair, furthermore, is of interest by reason of the connection with it of Joseph Wanton, governor of Rhode Island since 1769 and the last of a distinguished line to fill that position.

The commander of the Gaspee was Lieutenant William Dudingston, and Dudingston's commander was Admiral John Montagu, stationed at Boston. By the last of March the lieutenant's searches, which under Montagu's instructions were conducted upon the assumption that the Rhode Islanders were "a set of lawless piratical people," had become vexatious in the extreme, and Governor Wanton deemed it imperative to demand sight of his commission. The lieutenant did not produce it but sent Wanton's letter to Admiral Montagu. This seaman, to whom, as may be inferred, the amenities of intercourse were somewhat foreign, at once addressed the governor, threatening to "hang as pirates" any Newporters caught attempting to "rescue any vessel from the King's schooner," and denying the governor's right to inspect Dudingston's papers. Language of this kind awoke the Wanton spirit. The admiral was reminded with merited severity that the governor of Rhode Island did not "receive instructions from the King's admiral stationed in America."

Wanton's rebuke to Montagu was administered on May 8. On June 9, a sloop called the Hannah, on her way from Newport to Providence, was chased determinedly by the Gaspee until the latter ran aground on Namquit (now Gaspee) Point, near Pawtuxet. The Hannah on arriving at Providence reported the predicament of the schooner, and John Brown — a leading merchant (albeit one not so scrupulous as his brother Moses) — resolved to seize the opportunity thus unexpectedly afforded. Brown summoned to his aid Abraham Whipple (a seasoned privateersman of the French War) and John B. Hopkins (a nephew of Stephen Hopkins), and it was planned to surprise the Gaspee toward midnight. A number of long-boats were collected, the oars carefully muffled, and soon after ten o'clock there was embarked a party of about fifty men. The small flotilla pulled steadily down the bay until the Gaspee was seen, when, with a view to avoiding her guns, the boats were so disposed as to approach the schooner on the bows. The hail of the single man on watch was answered with an oath, the crews bent to their oars, and in a few seconds the boats were alongside.

By this time Dudingston himself was on deck and had called all hands. Some pistols were fired at the boats, and the lieutenant was in the act of cutting with his hanger at one of the attacking party clambering into the starboard forechains, when he fell severely wounded by a musket-shot in the groin. All forthwith was over, and the Gaspee's crew having been set on shore, the vessel was burned to the water's edge.

Great was the excitement throughout Rhode Island and America, and in crown circles in England, on the spread of the news of the destruction of the Gaspee. Governor Wanton proclaimed a reward of £100 for the discovery of the perpetra-

tors of the deed. Edward Thurlow, his Majesty's
attorney-general, pronounced the affair of " five
times the magnitude of the Stamp Act." The
Secretary for the Colonies, Lord Dartmouth, proclaimed in the name of the crown a reward of £500
for each common perpetrator, and of £1000 for
each captain or leader. The rewards, together with
a full pardon, were to be vouchsafed to any member of the perpetrating party who would betray the
rest. Had the party consisted of hirelings or desperate characters, the unstinted offers no doubt
would have brought betrayal. But of such the
party did not consist. It was made up of substantial men, well-known citizens of Providence and
loyal subjects of the king; of men who in making
the attack wore their ruffled shirts and their hair
neatly tied behind as usual, and who reposed perfect confidence in each other. From only one quarter did danger impend. A negro, Aaron Briggs,
pretended to have been with the party, and he,
under duress from one of the king's officers, made
a so-called confession implicating John Brown.
His general veracity, however, proved to be abun-
dantly capable of impeachment.

For the purpose of eliciting actionable testimony,
the king, in September, 1772, appointed a royal
commission: Joseph Wanton, governor of Rhode
Island; Daniel Horsmanden, chief justice of New
York; Frederick Smythe, chief justice of New
Jersey; Peter Oliver, chief justice of Massachu-

setts; and Robert Auchmuty, vice-admiralty judge
of Boston. The appointment of this commission
created a stir. It was learned through the publication of a private letter from the Earl of Dartmouth to Governor Wanton that it was intended
to protect the sittings of the commissioners by
troops from Boston and to transport to England
for trial for high treason any persons arrested.

The moment these intentions became known all
chance of discovering the Gaspee culprits was at
an end. The commission began its sessions early
in January, 1773, and at about the same time the
General Assembly convened at East Greenwich.
Stephen Hopkins (now chief justice of the Superior Court) made before the Assembly the solemn
declaration that for the purpose of transportation
for trial he would neither apprehend by his own
order, nor suffer apprehension to be made by any
executive officer of the colony. It was with these
words in their ears that the commissioners bent to
their task. They gathered what evidence they could
(which was little), submitted it to the Supreme
Court for such action as might be deemed warranted,
and in June adjourned. On June 10 Dr. Ezra
Stiles, who had watched closely every move by the
commission, thus wrote in his diary : " I apprehend something severe would have been done by
the present Commissioners had not the Commission
given an extensive Alarm to all the Assemblies
upon the Continent, and occasioned the Resolutions

and Measures proposed by the Virginia Assembly
in March last, which are now circulating, and will
undoubtedly become universal, viz, forming Assembly Committees of Correspondence and enjoyning
a particular Inquiry into the Powers of this Court
of Commissioners at Rh. Island. These Assembly
Committees will finally terminate in a General
Congress. . . . A Congress had been sure if one
person had been seized & carried from Rh. Island."

But in addition to many patriots, Rhode Island
possessed among its people many loyalists.

The publication by Martin Howard, Jr., of
Newport, of a reply to Hopkins's "Rights of
Colonies Examined" made it plain that at Newport, at least, there were loyalists. Indeed, Newport
was the seat of the loyalists. Loyalism meant
simply conservatism, and conservative Newport
had always been. As founded by Coddington it
was a protest against the radicalism of Portsmouth
under Anne Hutchinson and Samuel Gorton.
Then in subsequent years Newport had amassed
wealth and acquired social prestige, and both wealth
and prestige are conservative forces. Newport
loyalism, too, was fostered in another way. The
town was filled with Quakers; it contained a good
many Baptists and not a few Episcopalians. The
Episcopalians were natural loyalists, and the Quakers contributed to loyalism by their opposition to
war. As for the Baptists, they were not opposed
to war (nearly the whole of Cromwell's army had

been Baptists), but as against the Puritans of
Massachusetts they had received succor at the
hands of the English government. It is not to be
accounted strange if, in some instances, they were
imbued with a patriotism that was but lukewarm.

Throughout 1774 events fairly crowded to an
issue. In May Providence (true to its reputation
for initiative) passed resolutions proposing a Continental Congress and instructing its deputies in
the General Assembly to strive for a " Union " of
the colonies. In June the Assembly adopted the
Providence, and by this time also the Virginia and
Massachusetts, idea, and named Stephen Hopkins
and Samuel Ward as congressional delegates. In
September Congress met in Philadelphia, passed a
Declaration of Rights and various addresses, and
signed an " Association " not to import any British
manufactures or any East India Company tea
after December 1, unless prior to that date American grievances should have been redressed. In
October, November, and December the Rhode
Island militia was reorganized and the British
frigate Rose took in Newport Harbor the place
left vacant by the Gaspee. Meanwhile, despite the
allowance of a certain amount by the General Assembly upon the claims of Augustus Johnson,
Martin Howard, Jr., and Dr. Thomas Moffat, the
money due the colony from Great Britain was
firmly withheld.

The year 1775 opened with the battle of Lexington. Rhode Island was profoundly stirred by the news, and several hundred men set forth from Providence for the scene of action, but were turned back by a message reporting the retreat of the British. At Newport there was not only excitement but terror and confusion. On April 24 Samuel Ward wrote from Westerly, counseling the " Messrs. Malbone . . . to get their vessels to sea or out of New England with all speed," and on the 26th the Stiles diary records: " Two Vessels full of Passengers sailed this morn^g for Philadelphia. The Town in great panic."

The same day a couple of flour ships bound for Providence were stopped by the commander of the Rose, Captain James Wallace; and John Brown, who owned the cargo, was detained and sent to General Gage at Boston to answer for his suspected connection with the Gaspee affair. It was no slight peril in which Brown was placed. His guilt was real, and what Gage might decide to do was doubly problematical since the day of Lexington. But at this juncture John Brown's brother Moses (from whom the fact of John's culpability had been kept a fast secret) provided himself with letters to Gage, Admiral Graves, and Chief Justice Oliver, and set out for Boston. After some parleying with sentinels he was allowed to pass the lines. He saw Oliver, was presented to Graves, and in virtue of the fact that the late royal com-

mission had been unable to elicit anything actionable against the suspect, was accorded the latter's
release. The brothers returned to Providence
mounted on one horse, John in the saddle and
Moses *en croupe*, and were welcomed with joyful
demonstrations. The General Assembly, meanwhile, had passed an act creating an army of observation of fifteen hundred men, and had suspended from office Governor Joseph Wanton for
protesting against their course.

On May 10 Congress met (the second Continental Congress) and in it Rhode Island quietly
but resolutely took an important part. Hopkins
and Ward once more were the delegates, and
Samuel and John Adams were delegates from
Massachusetts. In Stephen Hopkins Rhode Island possessed a man of the John Adams foresight
and courage. In 1757 Hopkins had asked, "What
have the King and Parliament to do with making
a law or laws to govern us by any more than the
Mohawks?" In 1772 Adams had said, "There
is no more justice left in Britain than there is in
hell." During the first Congress Hopkins had affirmed to a circle of delegates, "The gun and
bayonet alone will finish the contest in which we
are engaged." During the second Congress Adams
was writing, "Powder and artillery are the most
efficacious, sure, and infallible conciliatory measures we can adopt." Nor were these words words
merely. On June 15 John Adams nominated

George Washington commander-in-chief of the Continental forces. Already in May Rhode Island had installed as commander of its forces Nathanael Greene.

In August Rhode Island was ready for a further step. The General Assembly instructed its delegates in Congress to " use their whole influence " to secure the " building and equipping at the continental expense of an American fleet." Supremely fitting was it that the proposition for the founding of a United States Navy should emanate from Rhode Island. As declared by the Assembly to King William in 1693, the colony was " a frontier [to the rest of New England] by sea ; " and from that time forth, through the wars of Queen Anne and the Georges, under the leadership of the Wantons, of Daniel Fones, of John Dennis, and of Abraham Whipple, Rhode Island had been for Britain a nursery of seamen and of daring.

The naval proposition (after some persiflage on the part of Congress at the audacity of it) was seriously considered in October, 1775. By February, 1776, as a result of the labors of a " Marine Committee," of which Stephen Hopkins was a member, there were ready two ships, the Alfred and Columbus, the first of twenty-four and the second of thirty-six guns ; two brigs, the Andrea Doria and Cabot, each of fourteen guns ; and four sloops, the Providence, Fly, Hornet, and Wasp. Of the fleet as a whole Esek Hopkins (a mariner

of experience) was made commander-in-chief. Of
the several vessels, Abraham Whipple was made
captain of the Columbus, and John B. Hopkins
captain of the Cabot. These officers were Rhode
Islanders all, and all, be it confessed, related either
by blood or marriage to Stephen Hopkins of the
Marine Committee. In March Commander-in-
chief Hopkins was instructed to seek the enemy
along the coast. He went, however, on a cruise to
the Bahamas to capture such stores of needed
powder and guns as might there be found. The
expedition set sail from the Delaware capes on
February 17, 1776, with John Paul Jones as first
lieutenant of the Alfred. It made in due time a
descent upon the island of New Providence, and,
returning on April 8, brought some prisoners, a
little powder, and about one hundred cannon.

Ere this Rhode Island had discarded nearly
every badge of colonialism. It had issued bills of
credit for local defense; had established a local
postal system; had erected fortifications; had con-
fiscated the estates of wealthy loyalists of Newport
and Narragansett; had even at length deposed
Governor Wanton and chosen Nicholas Cooke —
a Providence man — governor in his stead. Only
one thing remained to be done to make explicit
the independence which by these acts had been
implied, and that was to pass a declaration formally absolving the people of Rhode Island from
their allegiance to the British crown. Such a de-

claration was passed on May 4, just two months before the signing of the great Declaration at Philadelphia.

Little by little, through acts of governmental interposition — several of them justifiable, some of them necessary, one of them (the Sugar Act) conspicuously a mistake — it had been brought to pass that the British American colony originally perhaps the most loyal of all to the crown was hopelessly alienated and estranged.

CHAPTER XI

RHODE ISLAND THE THEATRE OF WAR

Esek Hopkins — The British at Newport — Seizure of General
Prescott — Sullivan and D'Estaing — The Pigot Galley — Destitution — Newport and the French.

WHEN last we saw the American squadron under
Commander-in-chief Hopkins it had just returned
from the Bahamas with captured stores and ord-
nance. But the return voyage was not quite the
triumphal progress that it might have been.

On the morning of the 6th of April, about one
o'clock, there was dimly descried off Point Judith
a ship which proved to be his Majesty's ship Glasgow, of twenty guns and one hundred and fifty men,
commanded by Captain Tyringham Howe. This
vessel, since the autumn of 1775, had been serving
as consort to the Rose off Newport. By half-past
two the Cabot had got near enough to hail, and an
interchange of amenities in the form of broadsides
took place. The result was that the Cabot was
badly damaged and cut up. She lost four men
killed and eight wounded; among the latter, John
B. Hopkins her captain. Next, the Alfred came
into action. She lost her wheel-block and ropes,
was several times raked, suffered a shot through

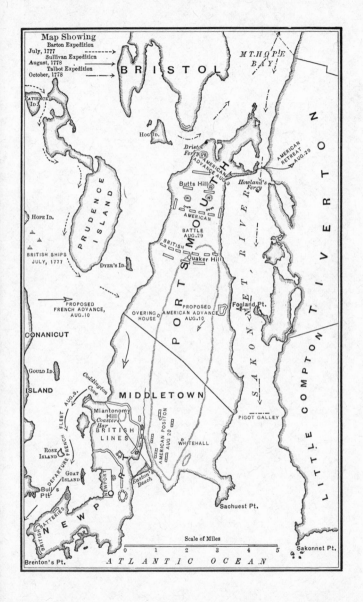

Map Showing
Barton Expedition
July, 1777 - - - ->
Sullivan Expedition
August, 1778 ---->
Talbot Expedition
October, 1778 ---->

MT. HOPE BAY

BRISTOL

PATIENCE ID.

Hog ID.

Bristol Ferry

AMERICAN ADVANCE AUG. 9

PRUDENCE ISLAND

Butts Hill

Howland's Ferry

AMERICAN RETREAT AUG. 29

HOPE ID.

AMERICAN BATTLE AUG. 29

BRITISH SHIPS JULY, 1777

DYER'S ID.

BRITISH

Quaker Hill

PORTSMOUTH

TIVERTON

SAKONNET RIVER

PROPOSED FRENCH ADVANCE, AUG. 10

PROPOSED AMERICAN ADVANCE AUG. 10

OVERING HOUSE

Fogland Pt.

CONANICUT

GOULD ID.

ISLAND

Coddington Cove

MIDDLETOWN

LITTLE COMPTON

ROSE ISLAND

DEPARTURE FRENCH FLEET AUG. 9

Miantonomy Hill Coaster's Har BRITISH LINES

AMERICAN POSITION AUG. 20

PIGOT GALLEY

WHITEHALL

GOAT ISLAND

NEWPORT

Easton's Beach

Bull's Pt.

BRITISH BATTERIES

NEWP

Sachuest Pt.

Brenton's Pt.

Scale of Miles
0   1   2   3   4   5

Sakonnet Pt.

ATLANTIC OCEAN

the mainmast, received several shot under water, and lost four killed and seven wounded. With the Columbus it fared better ; on board her there was a loss of only one wounded. The Glasgow, meanwhile, though considerably cut up aloft, had not been materially damaged. She had lost but one killed and three wounded, and had made good a retreat into Newport Harbor.

In this combat, in which there were arrayed on the side of the British not more than twenty guns and one hundred and fifty men, and on the side of the Americans at least one hundred guns and seven hundred men, the honors were decidedly with the British. The Americans showed pluck, especially the crew of the Cabot under John B. Hopkins, but of the fleet as a whole there was no adequate disposition or management.

The ill success which attended the first encounter with the enemy on the part of Esek Hopkins pursued that officer ever afterwards. In August he was ordered on a cruise off the coast of Newfoundland, but could not enlist seamen sufficient for the undertaking ; and in October, for the same cause, he was unable to carry out an order to proceed to Cape Fear, North Carolina. Finally, in December, a large British fleet appeared in Narragansett Bay, and Hopkins found himself effectually blockaded ("bottled" the late General Ulysses S. Grant would have termed it), and his usefulness as a fleet commander at an end. Hopkins's own ac-

count of his predicament at this time is little short
of pitiful. He wrote : " We are now blocked up
by the enemy's fleet, the officers and men are
uneasy, however I shall not desert the cause but I
wish with all my heart the Hon. Marine Board could
and would get a man in my room that would do
the Country more good than it is in my power to
do."

Hardly surprising is it that in August, 1776,
Congress should have censured Hopkins ; that in
March, 1777, it should have suspended him from
his command ; and that in January, 1778, it should
have dismissed him from the naval service altogether. He was described, in 1776, by Colonel
(afterwards General) Henry Knox, as " an anti-
quated figure " — a sort of belated Admiral Van
Tromp. The description was meant to apply merely
to his dress and bearing, but it really went deeper.
The " commander-in-chief " (the American navy
has had but one) was a well-meaning man, unre-
sourceful and slack ; one of those upon whom mis-
fortunes seem to descend by sheer force of natural
attraction.

It is not to be gainsaid that in seeking to re-man
his ships, after his return from New Providence,
Hopkins met with genuine perplexity. He was
forced to compete for seamen with the owners and
captains of privateering craft, and at a distinct
disadvantage. The situation was as follows: In
December, 1775, Congress, while hastily fitting out

a squadron for Hopkins, ordered the construction of thirteen vessels, — five of thirty-two guns, five of twenty-eight, and three of twenty-four. Two of the vessels — the Providence and Warren — were to be built in Rhode Island. The work was placed in the hands of a committee of the leading men of Providence : Nicholas Cooke, Nicholas Brown, Joseph Russell, Joseph Brown, John Brown, Daniel Tillinghast, John Innes Clarke, Joseph Nightingale, Jabez Bowen, and Rufus Hopkins. But, though the ships were to be finished by April, 1776, and though the committee having them in charge was thoroughly competent, the work lagged. Why ?

In March, 1776, Congress had passed an act authorizing the issuing of letters of marque against English commerce. Soon afterwards the Rhode Island General Assembly had passed an act providing for the issuing of such letters within its jurisdiction, and creating an Admiralty Court for the condemnation of prizes. The old Narragansett viking and individualistic spirit of the French and Spanish wars was at once aroused. Everything else was neglected, and privateering became the business of the day. Providence had been rebuking the unpatriotic covetousness of Newport as disclosed in a failure to observe the non-importation agreement. Now Providence itself, even to its distinguished committee of Browns, Russells, Clarkes, and Nightingales, was guilty of a

like self-seeking. In fact, to such lengths did the
committee carry its disregard of national interests,
that members of it (John Brown in particular)
were permitted to divert to their own use, in the
construction of privateers, labor and materials designed for the government work. Of this fact
Hopkins, who, weak though he may have been, was
thoroughly honest, complained bitterly to the Marine Board, and the Providence committee in high
indignation resigned its powers.

Matters did not improve. The privateers, with
their roving commissions and chances for lucrative
gains, took all the seamen; and when the sorely
beset commander-in-chief sought, through the legislature, to lay an embargo on enlistments until his
own ships should be manned, the Browns, Russells,
and others were able to circumvent him. During
a period of less than five months in the year 1776
there were commissioned from Rhode Island six-
ty-five privateers. On November 12, 1776, Dr.
Stiles records (probably with little exaggeration;
at figures and calculations the doctor was unwearied): "It has been computed that this War
by prizes by building ships of War & the Navy
has already within a year and a half brought into
Providence near Three Hundred Thousand Ster-
ling; which is double the Property of the whole
Town two years ago."

In the end — that is, by December, 1776 — an
embargo on enlistments by merchantmen and pri-

vateers fitting out in Narragansett Bay proved to
be unavoidable, and an act to that effect was accordingly placed upon the Rhode Island statute
book.

The departure from Boston, in June, 1776, of
the British force under General Sir William Howe
marked the close of the preliminary stage of the
Revolution. Down to this time the attitude of
Great Britain toward America had been that of a
mother country temporizing with rebellious de-
pendencies; particularly with that set of depend-
encies (New England) where the spirit of rebellion
was strongest. With the concentration of British
fleets and armies at New York — a concentration
which, between June and August, took place under
Admiral Lord Howe and General Howe — the British attitude changed to that of a foreign power
seeking to cut in twain (along the main artery,
the Hudson River) a hostile territory. This effort
marked the crisis of the Revolution. For Rhode
Island it was characterized by the lodgment upon
its soil and in its waters of a force advantageously
placed either for coöperating by way of Long
Island Sound with the British force at New York,
or for penetrating into New England and subduing
that section after the task of separating it from
the middle colonies had been achieved.

In March, 1776, Samuel Ward had died of
small-pox at Philadelphia, and in September of the

same year Stephen Hopkins, grown quite infirm,
had ceased to attend the sessions of the Continental Congress. In the place of Ward, and as
coadjutors of Hopkins, there now were appointed
William Ellery (*fils*) and Henry Marchant. Fear
that the British had planned a descent upon Newport began seriously to be felt in Rhode Island in
November, 1776 ; and on December 2 news was
received by way of Watch Hill in Westerly that
"eleven sail of square rigged vessels [under Sir
Peter Parker] were standing in between Block
Island and Montauk Point." On December 7,
Parker's squadron (comprising seven ships of the
line and four frigates), together with a convoy of
seventy transports carrying six thousand troops,
anchored off Middletown.

Precipitate was the withdrawal from the island
of Rhode Island of the single battalion by which it
was defended, and of a considerable part of the
inhabitants. The General Assembly met, and, in
pursuance of its measures, a convention of the New
England States was held at Providence on December 25. By this body (under the presidency of
Stephen Hopkins) it was resolved to muster from
New England six thousand men, and place them
under the direction of the Continental general commanding in Rhode Island. At about the same time
William Ellery wrote from his place in Congress
urging an attack upon the British at Newport, and
stating that Washington had appointed Generals

Benedict Arnold and Joseph Spencer to take command in New England. It had been hoped to obtain for the post either Gates or Greene.

Neither Arnold nor Spencer effected anything toward the reduction of the island. The British force there was composed of five British regiments — four of infantry and one of artillery, and four Hessian regiments of infantry, one of which was the celebrated Anspachers. The principal officers were General Sir Henry Clinton, Lieutenant General Hugh Earl Percy, and Brigadier-General Richard Prescott. Some of the Newport loyalists ere this time had suffered rustication to the mainland, but that a goodly number had not is to be inferred from the fact that an address of duty and loyalty to George III was now signed by four hundred and fifty-four freeholders of the town. A like address was signed by the freeholders and inhabitants of Jamestown, and by the Newport "society of those called Quakers."

In January, 1777, Sir Henry Clinton was recalled to England, and in May of the same year he was followed by Earl Percy. The command at Rhode Island, therefore, devolved upon General Prescott. Not long afterwards (in July) the general was made the victim of a piece of Yankee temerity which in its day caused a very great sensation indeed.

Prescott's headquarters at Newport were in the

Bannister house (still standing), but the general, as something of a high liver and *roué*, was accustomed to frequent the house of a loyalist named Overing, which was situated on the west side of the island near the Redwood villa. At this time there was stationed at Tiverton, as major of an American regiment under Colonel Joseph Stanton, a young man, the son of a hatter of Warren, William Barton. Barton was observing, reflective, full of patriotism and daring, and when, from deserters, he learned of the practice on the part of General Prescott of paying nocturnal visits to the Overing house, the news stimulated him to attempt the execution of a plan which he for some time had been maturing. The plan was to seize and make prisoner of Prescott by way of retaliation for the seizure of General Charles Lee effected a few months before by the British.

Barton confided his views to Colonel Stanton, and by him was authorized to carry them out. From a multitude eager for service he carefully selected forty men, and with them, on July 5 and 6, proceeded in five whale-boats to Bristol. The men knew nothing as to the errand on which they were embarked, but on reaching Bristol they were ordered to row out to Hog Island, where, after being sworn to secrecy, the errand was disclosed to them. Thunder-storms were now almost a daily occurrence, and it was not until the evening of July 7 that the party got to Warwick Neck, whence the expedition was to start. It was not until the night of the 9th that a start actually was made.

The boats crept stealthily between the islands of Patience and Prudence, stole as stealthily down the west shore of Prudence past Hope (near which riding at anchor was a part of the British fleet) ; rounded the large island and swept rapidly across to their destination. The men landed, marched a mile to the Overing house and secured the single sentinel on guard. They then forced the main door, found Prescott, after some search, sitting bewildered in a lower chamber on the side of his bed, and, permitting him to don merely his waistcoat, breeches, and slippers, marched him off, along with his aide, Major Barrington, and the sentinel, to the boats. " You have made a damned bold push to-night," remarked Prescott as he was being hurried along. After embarkation, as the lights of the fleet opened to view, he said: " I did not think it possible you could escape the vigilance of the water guards."

Prescott while a prisoner in Rhode Island was quartered at Providence, and it adds not a little to the picturesqueness of the episode of his capture that on his arrival he (aged coxcomb that he was) sent for Providence's learned barber, John Howland (of whom in these pages more anon), to dress his hair; and that shortly there came from Newport a flag of truce bearing the general's entire

wardrobe — his purse, his hair powder, and a plen-
tiful supply of perfumery.

To Barton and his men there was voted by the
Rhode Island General Assembly a sum of money,
and Barton himself was rewarded at the hands of
Congress by promotion and the gift of a sword.

In consonance with the British plan of separating
New England from the rest of the American Union,
General John Burgoyne had, about June 1, 1777,
been dispatched from Canada with an army of
nearly eight thousand men on a peregrination southward by way of Lake Champlain to Albany.   There
he was to be joined by Sir William Howe from New
York.   Burgoyne's orders did not permit him to
digress with his main column, but, learning that the
Americans had accumulated stores at Bennington
[Vermont], he deemed it expedient to detach Lieutenant-Colonel Baum with five hundred men (increased afterwards to a thousand) to destroy them.
Baum afterwards was to advance across the country
to Springfield, Massachusetts, a point at which he
was assured " he would be met by his Majesty's
forces from Rhode Island."   The fight led by John
Stark at Bennington on August 16 put an end to
the advance of Baum, and the surrender to Gates
on October 17 by Burgoyne himself removed all
fear of an immediate severance of New England
from the West.

So far as Rhode Island itself was concerned, the

British (in the expressive words of the General Assembly) still were lodged in its very " bowels," and an attack on Providence was apprehended. General Spencer resigned his command in December, 1777, and in February, 1778, Washington, complying with an order of Congress to name a successor, promptly named General John Sullivan. Greene, had it been felt by Washington that he then could be spared from New York, would gladly have accepted the place, and indeed had been urged by Ellery to apply for it.

It was in April that Sullivan took charge of his new department. He found Sir Robert Pigot in the stead of Prescott, and in May Pigot sent an expedition against Warren and Bristol. It was Sullivan's intention to attack the British at Newport as soon as he should succeed in assembling a sufficient force. Celerity was imparted to his movements by news received in July that a French fleet under Vice-Admiral Comte d'Estaing was upon the coast, and that Rhode Island would be the fleet's destination.

Of the three American seaports held by the British in June, 1778, — Philadelphia, New York, and Newport, — Philadelphia had now been evacuated. There therefore remained only New York and Newport for D'Estaing to choose between as objectives, and, as New York proved impracticable of approach by reason of the draught of the count's vessels, Newport became the objective from necessity.

On July 23 General Greene, with fine imaginative realization of the historic significance of what was about to take place, wrote to Sullivan from White Plains : " You are the most happy man in the world. . . . You are the first general that has ever had an opportunity of coöperating with the French forces belonging to the United States. The character of the American soldiers, as well as of their officers, will be formed from the conduct of the troops and the success of this expedition. . . . I wish most ardently to be with you. . . . *I charge you to be victorious.*" In the same letter Greene let his correspondent into the secret that Gates (more exalted than ever since the surrender of Burgoyne) had himself sought from Washington the distinction of being the first American general to coöperate with the French.

In the movement against Newport Washington sent to Sullivan's aid (under the Marquis de Lafayette) the Continental brigades, some two thousand strong, of John Glover and James M. Varnum. He gave to General Greene and to Colonel John Laurens (the dashing son of Henry Laurens, President of Congress) leave to participate, and by August 4 men and officers were in the vicinity of Providence. As for the French fleet, — composed of twelve ships of the line and four frigates, — it had arrived off Newport on July 29.

The position of the British on the island of

Rhode Island (a position held now by about six thousand men) was exceedingly strong. It constituted a right angle of which Newport formed the apex, the sea on either hand the sides, and of which the mouth from side to side was completely subtended by two lines of works, one a mile within the other. As supplementary, moveover, to the main position, there was Butts Hill at the north end of the island. It commanded both Bristol and Howland's ferries and had been carefully fortified. So strong was the British position that successfully to attack it by land alone was, for a force not markedly superior to the garrison, difficult in the extreme. Any column of moderate strength which should leave Butts Hill in its rear would be likely to have its communications severed. Any such column that should pause to capture the hill was likely to be taken in rear by a relieving force from Newport.

All these difficulties at once vanished if the attacking army held command of the sea. To command the sea was to command the British rear, and it was with a view to the advantages of a rear as well as front attack that D'Estaing on July 29 (the day of his arrival) urged preparations for immediate action. But at this time the American general had with him practically no troops at all. Lafayette did not arrive with the Continental brigades until August 4, and the militia were mustering slowly. Had an attack been made forthwith,

it must have been made almost wholly by the
French force of about twenty-eight hundred marines, the inadequacy of which was obvious for
operations in rear alone.

In any event, the task first to be performed was
to clear the bay of British war-vessels. It proved
not difficult, for on the appearance of ships from
the French fleet in the west, middle, and east
passages, the British ships (ten in number) were
burned or blown up. Next it was decided that on
August 10 — a date satisfactory to Sullivan —
there should be effected, simultaneously, a landing
by the French marines on the west side of the
island of Rhode Island, and by the Americans on
the east side. The garrison on Butts Hill would
thus be cut off, and the way to Newport would be
cleared. On August 8 D'Estaing ran the batteries
at the entrance to Newport Harbor. But by the
morning of the 9th the Butts Hill garrison had
been withdrawn; so Sullivan at once transferred
his force — now by the influx of the New England
militia raised to ten thousand men — to the island.
The same day D'Estaing began disembarking his
marines on Conanicut to move to Sullivan's support. The British were completely trapped. Their
front and flanks were menaced by the Americans
and the marines; their rear was at the mercy of
the French fleet.

Before the disembarking of the marines was
completed, however, Admiral Lord Howe, with

thirteen ships of the line and seven frigates, came in sight off Point Judith. D'Estaing, in order himself not to be trapped in turn, put to sea to meet Howe. A storm of wind and rain arose, and though upon the subsidence of the elements some bloody ship duels took place, both fleets (on August 20) were forced into harbor: the British at New York, and the French at Newport.

Sullivan, meanwhile, in daily expectation of the return of D'Estaing, had advanced his army down the east side of the island, and from Honyman's Hill was assailing the British works with an effective cannonade. He was thus engaged on the 20th of the month when the French fleet, battered and in part dismantled, reached port. What was his astonishment to be told that D'Estaing, instead of returning to give aid, had done so to announce his determination to go to Boston to refit. Nothing remained to be done save vehemently to protest at the course of the French admiral (a proceeding in which Lafayette would not join, and which it afterwards took no little diplomacy to smooth over), and either to storm the British lines or retreat. To storm, with the militia deserting in shoals as now was the case, was manifestly out of the question. Retreat began on August 28, and the so-called battle of Rhode Island, which occurred on August 29 in the depression between Quaker and Butts hills, was simply a spirited repulse by the Americans of the pursuing British; a repulse dur-

ing the infliction of which Lafayette, with fiery
zeal, was riding a-gallop to Boston to make a last
vain appeal to D'Estaing for the return of the
fleet; and at the end of which the American army,
under cover of night and without loss, was conveyed over Howland's Ferry to the heights of
Tiverton.[1]

The departure of D'Estaing — by reason of the
loss of the command of the sea thereby entailed,
and so of access to the British rear — had brought
failure to the Sullivan expedition : an expedition
the first fruit of the Franco-American alliance ;
one the success of which would have rivaled that
of the capture of Burgoyne ; one, therefore, that
might have led to an acknowledgment of American
independence. No wonder that Greene, in his July
letter to Sullivan, had said : " *I charge you to be
victorious.*"

To Rhode Islanders in general the withdrawal
from before Newport was a step full of dishearten-
ment. The discriminating refused to blame Sullivan, but there were those that were not so con-
siderate. Such an one was our acquaintance John

[1] In February, 1778, the General Assembly passed an act permitting the enlistment in Rhode Island of "negro, mulatto, or
Indian man slaves." Under this act two battalions of negroes
(slave and free together) were forthwith raised, and they participated in the battle of Rhode Island. It has been customary to
ascribe prowess to these battalions, but the investigations of Mr.
S. S. Rider (*Hist. Tract. No. 10*) have proved that the negroes
acquitted themselves with little distinction. Indeed, in July, 1780,
the Assembly forbade any further enlistments of negroes.

Brown — John Brown, author of the destruction of
the Gaspee, postponer of government to private
advantage, source of solicitude upon all occasions
to his brother Moses. And what, in his disgust at
still being forced to run his privateers past British batteries, John Brown did, was to write a letter to General Greene, in which he pronounced the
late expedition " the worst concerted and the most
disgracefully executed of any during the war." It
is gratifying to know that Greene's reply, after a
careful review of events, was this: " I cannot help
feeling mortified that those that have been at home
making their fortune, and living in the lap of luxury, and enjoying all the pleasures of domestic
life, should be the first to sport with the feelings
of officers who have stood as a barrier between
them and ruin."

By far the most brilliant local naval exploit of
the year 1778 was the opening of the east passage
of Narragansett Bay through the capture, by Major Silas Talbot, of the Pigot galley.

In 1776 Talbot, a Bristol youth residing at
Providence, had performed on the Hudson River
the daring feat of piloting a fire-ship against the
Asia, a British sixty-four gun vessel. Ever since
that time Henry Marchant (to whom very likely
there was familiar also the thrilling story of the
fire-ships of Antwerp) had been a zealous advocate
of the use of such craft against the blockaders near

Newport. But while, in deference to Marchant, it had been arranged in August, 1777, to send out six large fire-vessels from Providence, Talbot in October, 1778, conceived a surer plan.

With the consent of General Sullivan, he fitted out with two three-pounders and sixty men a coasting sloop (the Hawk) in which to make an attack on the Pigot galley by night. In order to reach the galley, it was necessary to pass two British batteries: one on the south side of Bristol Ferry, and the other on the west side of Fogland Ferry. The first battery was passed without damage, though not without discovery, and refuge was taken in Taunton River. Here Talbot found himself obliged to await a change of wind, and he improved the interval by riding down the east coast to a point in Little Compton opposite the galley, where, with a glass, he was able to make a study of that craft. She was a stout brig of two hundred tons, from which the upper deck had been removed, and upon the lower deck of which there had been mounted eight twelve-pounders and ten swivels. Furthermore, she was protected all around by a boarding net of unusual height.

As a result of his survey, Talbot asked for and obtained a reinforcement of fifteen men under Lieutenant John Helme. On the night of October 28 he slipped silently past the battery at Fogland Ferry, and then made all sail. Fearing after some time that he might have missed the galley in the darkness, he anchored and sought the blockader in a boat. She soon loomed up massively ahead, and Talbot, carefully noting her position, returned to the Hawk. The latter was then directed at full speed against her antagonist. The oncoming sloop was loudly hailed from the galley, and then greeted with a volley of musketry; but soon the jib-boom of the Hawk, which had been armed with a kedge anchor, tore a wide hole in the galley's net, and Talbot and his men were enabled to leap on board.

There was little or no struggle. The crew of the Pigot all fled below. Only the young commander, Lieutenant Dunlop, made a serious show of fight, and he, like Dudingston of the Gaspee, was quickly overpowered. When he found that he had been vanquished by a sloop armed with three-pounders and with but two of these, he threw himself in tears upon the deck, lamenting the loss of his chances of promotion, — an exhibition of natural feeling with which Talbot was altogether too generous not to sympathize.

Elation in Rhode Island over the capture of the Pigot galley was quickly followed by most intense anxiety regarding the means of subsistence. Already in July, 1777, at a convention of the New England States held at Springfield, resolutions had been passed on the money question, — the resolutions referred to in chapter iii. Others were passed against State embargoes on food stuffs, and against the practice of " forestalling " or " cornering" the market. So far, however, as embargoes were concerned, the action taken had accomplished little, and in January, 1779, William Greene — governor in succession to Nicholas Cooke and a son of the William Greene who had served as governor in the days of the land banks — found it incumbent upon him to write a letter of earnest appeal to Connecticut.

The winter was one of appalling severity. More than a thousand refugees from Newport were on the mainland in a condition of almost complete destitution. " Our situation," wrote Governor Greene, " is perhaps somewhat similar to that of the good old patriarch Jacob and his numerous family (a little republic) when he sent into Egypt to buy a supply of corn, saving in this that he found no embargo to prevent his purpose." Connecticut was then solemnly adjured to remember that "whoso stoppeth his ears at the cry of the poor, he also shall cry himself, but shall not be heard." Be it said at once that Connecticut did not prove recreant. At an early session of its General Assembly it granted generous relief. And not only in this way was Rhode Island helped. In the following summer General Gates, who had been appointed to succeed Sullivan in the eastern department, sent Talbot, in the sloop Argo, to clear Long Island Sound of loyalist privateers, which in great numbers were hindering the importation of grain, and never was task of the kind more effectively performed.

D'Estaing, after a long sojourn at Boston — a sojourn enlivened by the unwearied hospitalities of John Hancock — set sail in November, 1778, with his fleet for the West Indies. In January, 1779, Lafayette sailed for France. From the West Indies D'Estaing went to Savannah, and thence home. Never again did he behold America. In France he, like others of the period, sought to secure reforms while avoiding revolution, and his fate was what might have been expected. He died by the guillotine in 1794. As for Lafayette, his heart and mind were absorbed in the American cause, and it was through him chiefly that the French government was induced to send to America, in the spring of 1780, an earnest of substantial succor in the form of fifty-five hundred regular troops, commanded by Lieutenant-General Comte de Rochambeau, and convoyed by six ships of the line under Admiral Chevalier de Ternay.

Newport was evacuated by the British in October, 1779. When, therefore, in July, 1780, De Ternay[1] (whose orders, inspired by Lafayette, were to land in Rhode Island) came to anchor off

[1] Admiral de Ternay died at Newport in December, 1780. His monument lends to-day a contemplative interest to the interior of Trinity Church.

Brenton's Point, there was no enemy to gainsay him.

It was a brilliant and distinguished group of Frenchmen that for a year graced the social circle of Newport. There was first of all Rochambeau himself quartered in the stately William Vernon house ; a man not striking of stature but keen-visaged and able to discuss in creditable Latin with Dr. Ezra Stiles (now President of Yale College) the capture of André. Next there were Rochambeau's three *maréchaux-de-camp*, with quarters at Mr. Joseph Wanton's, — the two Vioménils, fair haired and tall, and the Chevalier de Chastellux, member of the Academy, and pronounced by those with a taste for letters " the glory of the army." Aides, too, and officers of varied rank (among them the Duc de Lauzun, famed for his amours) were domiciled with the Levis, the Malbones, the Redwoods, the Wards, the Hazards, the Freebodys, the Riveras, and the Coggeshalls. And what was more, these men (as William Channing noted upon their arrival) were found to be not at all " the effeminate Beings we were heretofore taught to believe them, but as large & as likely as can be produced by any nation."

Nor, in turn, did the social resources of Newport prove inadequate to the unusual demands thus made upon them. The beauty and grace of the women — always notable — more than ever were notable now; so much so, in fact, that the French

gentlemen who met Polly Lawton the Quakeress,
or Margaret and Mary Champlin, or Mehetable
Redwood, or the Misses Hunter, or the Misses
Ellery, were apt quite to forego words of soberness
in describing their impressions. A certain fashionable Newport diversion, however, — that of copious
tea-drinking, — gave pause even to Gallic politeness.
Not only was the practice amiably satirized by
Abbé Robin, but the story was told how a French
officer, after heroically imbibing what seemed to
him quarts of the insipid beverage, burst forth
to his hostess : " I shall veesh to send zat servante
to helle for breenging me so much hot vater to
dreenk."

The pleasure of the French occupation of Rhode
Island was not confined to Newport. A share fell
to Providence. Many a gallant Gaul yielded hom-
age in the old home of Polly Olney to the charms
of that coquettish damsel's worthy successors, — the
Misses Bowen, Miss Waity Arnold, and Miss Sally
Church. The erudite Chastellux alone waxed cen-
sorious. He wrote : " The hair of the feminine
American head is raised and supported upon cush-
ions to an extravagant height, somewhat resem-
bling the manner in which French ladies wore
their hair some years ago."

In March, 1781, Washington (not in the best
of humors, it is said) came to Newport to confer
with Rochambeau, and the honors vouchsafed to
him by the French were of the most elaborate

kind — those, in a word, as Dr. Stiles observed at the time, accorded only to a marshal of France. The fleet thundered a salute; the general, with Rochambeau unbonneted on his left, walked from Long Wharf between a double line of soldiers to the State House, and thence to the count's head-quarters in the Vernon house. In the evening there was an illumination of the town. Later a great ball was given, and Washington, choosing for a partner the radiant Margaret Champlin, asked her to select the dance. That lady, with a tact that threw the French officers present into an ecstasy of delight, selected "A Successful Campaign." And a successful campaign it proved. Washington, departing westward, ere long was followed by the army of Rochambeau; and, on October 14, 1781, Yorktown (into which the distinguished Rhode Islander, Nathanael Greene, had edged Cornwallis from the Carolinas) was taken by assault, with Stephen Olney of Rhode Island commanding a detachment at the head of the storming column.

CHAPTER XII

THE FEDERAL CONSTITUTION

The Articles of Confederation — David Howell and the Impost
Measures — Ratification of the Great Instrument.

To the Articles of Confederation, submitted by
Congress to the States for ratification in November, 1777, Rhode Island had acceded in February,
1778. Such promptitude in the adoption of a
scheme of joint political action on the part of a
commonwealth opposed traditionally to any scheme
of the kind was due to the necessities of war, but it
was due also to saving clauses of the articles in
question. Not only did the articles expressly reserve to each State its " sovereignty, freedom, and
independence ; " they made the reservation effective by inhibiting Congress from regulating the
commerce of a State with other States or with foreign countries, and from levying upon a State or
its people either direct or indirect taxation. How
completely the Articles of Confederation (which
could be amended only with the consent of all the
States) marked the extreme limit of willing approach by Rhode Island to a system of Federal
control was to be strikingly demonstrated in the
period embraced between the years 1781 and 1791.

On February 3, 1781, while the French still
were in occupation of Newport, Congress advised
the States that it was absolutely indispensable, to
the end of meeting the public obligations, that it
be vested with power to impose a duty of five per
cent ad valorem on all goods (with enumerated
exceptions) to be imported into the United States
after the first of May. Robert Morris was then
chosen Superintendent of Finance, and the course
of events anxiously awaited. Among the congressional delegates from Rhode Island was James M.
Varnum. Born in Massachusetts, he was so little
of a Rhode Islander in spirit that, writing to Governor Greene in April, 1781, he conceived it no
impropriety to suggest that a national "convention" ought to be called "to revise and reform
the Articles of Confederation, to define the aggregate powers of the United States in Congress assembled, to fix the executive departments and
ascertain their authorities." Indeed, so little of
a Rhode Islander was he that, writing again in
August, he said: "We are at a loss to conjecture
the rumors which have induced the State of Rhode
Island to delay complying with the requisition of
Congress, respecting the five per cent duty."

At the close of 1781, when Varnum returned
home, his perplexity over the "delay" by Rhode
Island in authorizing the five per cent duty was
removed. In January, 1782, the pen of "Dixit
Senex" declared in the columns of the Providence

" Gazette " that while " Congress may call on us for money, it cannot prescribe to us methods of raising it." In this statement there was condensed the whole Rhode Island doctrine. The Narragansett Bay commonwealth had withheld its approval of the proposed tariff for the reason that it perceived in it a limitation upon its autonomy. Even in colonial days — the days of its nonage — Rhode Island had been the most restive of all the colonies under the regulations of British commercial policy. Why, therefore, after it had just freed itself from the plague of outside tariffs and outside collectors, should it, through an authorization to Congress of a five per cent duty, re-subject itself to tyranny? So argued " Dixit Senex."

To " Senex " Varnum replied forcibly, but with the result of calling into the field of debate the keenest and best equipped champion of the peculiar political ideas of Rhode Island which that commonwealth has ever possessed — David Howell. Both Varnum and Howell have come within our ken as they stood a few years later — the one a powerful advocate at the bar, and the other a courageous and discriminating judge upon the bench; but at the moment Howell was a young lawyer of Providence unknown to fame. Upon his graduation from Princeton in 1766 he had come to town at the earnest request of James Manning, and had since filled the chair of natural philosophy in Brown University. His literary style

was fluent, flexible, and trenchant, and at the end
of his controversy with Varnum he became widely
enough known to be elected to Congress.

The conditions which confronted him in that
body were not encouraging. Eleven States had
signified their more or less cordial approval of the
projected tariff or impost. Only Georgia and
Rhode Island were holding back, and of these
Georgia was not fixed in resolution. In order to
bring matters to a head, Congress appointed a committee to inquire of the two States why they had
not pursued the course of the other States. At the
sessions of this committee Robert Morris attended
and Howell appeared for Rhode Island. The ob-
jections by Howell to the impost were four in number : (1) that the revenue raised by it would go
to the United States, whereas in the case of Rhode
Island (a maritime community) any such revenue
ought to go to the State alone; (2) that the war
had so wasted the shores of Narragansett Bay that
it was needful for Rhode Island to conserve every
source of income ; (3) that a sovereign State should
itself collect all taxes levied within its borders ;
and (4) that the duration of the proposed impost
was indefinite and might be made perpetual. In
modification of the measure as it stood, Howell
suggested clauses providing for the deduction of the
proceeds of the impost from the annual quota of
Continental requisitions upon a State and for collection by officers locally chosen.

A careful reply to Howell was submitted by Robert Morris to Governor William Greene on August 2, but without result; and in October Congress, under the leadership of Alexander Hamilton and James Madison, passed a resolution demanding from both Georgia and Rhode Island an explicit avowal as to whether they would or would not approve the impost.

The crisis drew from Howell one of his most telling appeals to his constituency. It bore date October 15 and began thus: "The object of a seven years' war has been to preserve the liberties of this country. . . . It has been on our part a contest for freedom — not for power! . . . We know your early, continued, and persevering zeal in your country's cause. We cannot doubt your firmness. To quicken your memory, awaken your feelings, and to fix your attention, is the object of this letter." The abiding arguments of particularism against authority were then lucidly rehearsed, and the State was abjured not to take the irrevocable step of sanctioning the impost if it had "a single remaining doubt." With Howell's plea before it, the Rhode Island General Assembly met at East Greenwich on the last Monday in October, 1782, and on November 1 voted unanimously against the impost plan.

The struggle between Rhode Island and Congress over the impost was now given a turn not a little dramatic. Howell had been in the practice of writing to John Carter, publisher of the Providence " Gazette," upon the proceedings of Congress. From one of his letters a paragraph stating that the credit of the United States abroad was such that " of late they had failed in no application for loans " had appeared in print on November 2. Indignant at the course of Howell (who was held responsible for the course of Rhode Island), Hamilton and Madison were stirred to the quick by this statement concerning the public credit — a statement designed to belittle the need of an impost — and proceedings were set on foot to discredit Howell in his own State.

On December 18 the Rhode Island delegate introduced in Congress a resolution avowing and justifying the " Gazette " paragraph and challenging criticism of himself. On December 20 Hamilton and Madison, as members of a committee of inquiry which had been appointed, recommended that Howell's resolution " be transmitted by the Secretary for Foreign Affairs to the Executive of the State of Rhode Island with an authentic copy of the several applications for foreign loans, and the result thereof." Over the recommendation a sharp struggle ensued. It was short as well as sharp, for at nearly every turn the vote of Rhode Island was left unsupported.

In undertaking, however, to influence Rhode Island by discrediting its chief delegate, it soon became apparent that Congress had erred profoundly.

In February, 1783, the General Assembly of the State passed resolutions indorsing unreservedly Howell's entire conduct. Nor did the indorsement prove to be less hearty in view of the circumstance that for six weeks the celebrated Thomas Paine, with headquarters at Providence, had been pleading eloquently the cause of Congress in the Rhode Island press.

Interest in the congressional debate of 1782 over the impost attaches in a peculiar degree to the individuals concerned. That a professor of natural philosophy should so brilliantly have withstood the embittered opposition of the superb Hamilton and astute Madison can but excite admiration. Hamilton and Madison supported each other and were both supported by Congress. Howell, save for the countenance of his colleague Jonathan Arnold, faced argument and enmity alone. The position of the Rhode Islander at this time was almost exactly that of John C. Calhoun (his intellectual compeer) in 1833, when, unsustained save by South Carolina, Calhoun threatened nullification and incurred the wrath of Andrew Jackson.

Howell was returned to Congress in 1783 and also in 1784. In the latter year, as in 1782, Rhode Island was made the object of attentions the reverse of flattering. Congress in 1783 had again proposed a five per cent duty. It was to be collected by locally appointed officers and to

continue only twenty-five years. But the haste of
Rhode Island to sanction the new proposal proved
to be no greater than it had been to sanction the
old one. Howell opposed sanction in his letters,
and what was more, some of the States formerly
receptive to the idea of an impost now (influenced
by Rhode Island's example) were of a contrary
mind. Irritated by the situation, certain of the
" young men in Congress " raised in 1784 a question
upon the technical sufficiency of the credentials of
Howell and his colleagues. After a heated debate,
Mercer of Virginia and Spaight of North Carolina
both challenged the Rhode Islander to a duel.
David Howell — man of commanding physique,
aquiline nose, and defiant chin — replied that he
meant "to chastise any insults that he might receive," and laid the communications before Congress. In 1784 Annapolis, Maryland (a town said
to have been without a single house of worship),
was the temporary seat of Continental government.
Social life there was of the gayest — a life of card-
playing, the theatre, " balls, concerts, routs, hops,
fandangoes, and fox hunting." Upon it all Howell,
as a man with New England conscience, turned
disdainfully his back.

But the uncompromising hostility of Rhode
Island to an impost was beginning to give way.
The cause was commerce. Hitherto when asked :
" How are the United States to meet their debts ? "
Rhode Island's reply had regularly been : " By the

proceeds of the public lands." Now conditions were a good deal changed. In July, 1783, Great Britain had put in operation a plan of discrimination against the extensive trade of New England with the British West Indies. English manufactured goods, too, were flooding the New England market. A tariff of some kind was demanded for self-preservation. What was to be done? Clearly one thing only, and that was to invest Congress with power to regulate commerce — in other words, to establish a uniform impost. This power Rhode Island with many qualms, but screwing its courage to the sticking point, granted in February, 1786.

There can be little doubt that the exaltation of particularism between 1782 and 1785 by David Howell laid the foundation for some of Rhode Island's extreme distrust of the Federal Constitution of 1787. The instrument would have been distrusted by Rhode Island in any event, but Howell supplied an arsenal of controversial weapons against it.

Hostility to the Constitution, though, came from a source different from that whence had come hostility to the impost. The enemies of the impost had been the merchants. They had feared its effect on trade. Toward the Constitution — an instrument largely designed to protect trade — an instrument the outcome in fact of the recommendation of a convention called in 1786, at the instance of Virginia, to deliberate upon trade — the merchants were hospitably inclined.[1]

[1] PROVIDENCE, May 11th, 1787.

Gentlemen,

Since the Legislature of this State have finally declined sending Delegates to meet you in Convention for the purposes mentioned in the Resolve of Congress of the 21st February, 1787, — the Merchants, Tradesmen, and Others of this Place, deeply Affected with the evils of the present unhappy times, have thought proper to communicate in writing their approbation of your Meeting, And their regret that it will fall short of a Compleat representation of the Federal Union. —

The failure of this State was owing to the nonconcurrence of the Upper House of Assembly with a Vote passed in the Lower House, for Appointing Delegates to attend the said Convention, at their Session Holden at Newport, on the first Wednesday of the present Month. —

It is the General Opinion here, and we believe of the well informed throughout this State, that full power for the regulation of the Commerce of the United States, both foreign and Domestick, ought to be vested in the National Council. And that Effectual Arrangements should also be made for giving operation to the present powers of Congress in their Requisitions upon the States for National purposes. —

As the object of this Letter is chiefly to prevent any impressions unfavourable to the Commercial Interest of this State, from taking place in our Sister States, from the Circumstance of our being unrepresented in the present National Convention, we shall not presume to enter into any detail of the objects we hope your deliberations will embrace and provide for, being Convinced they will be such as have a Tendency to strengthen the Union, promote Commerce, increase the power, and Establish the Credit of the United States.

The result of your deliberations, tending to these desirable purposes, we still hope may finally be approved & adopted by this State; for which we pledge our Influence & best exertions. —

This will be delivered you by the Honourable James M. Varnum, Esquire, who will communicate (with your permission) in

It was on February 21, 1787, that Congress resolved for a convention of delegates to be held on the second Monday in May, at Philadelphia, to so modify the Articles of Confederation as to render them "adequate to the exigencies of government and the preservation of the Union." In this convention by the end of June Rhode Island alone among the States was unrepresented. To Rhode Island itself the fact gave little concern. The State was under the control of the traditional separatists, the agriculturalists, and their indifference to Federal affairs had been evinced the year previous in the case of James Manning, President of Brown University, whom they had sent to Congress and then left (as Roger Williams had once been left in England) without money wherewith to hire even a barber or to keep from a debtor's prison.

But on all sides a storm of criticism was begin-

person, more particularly our Sentiments on the Subject matter of our Address.

In behalf of the Merchants, Tradesmen, &c,

We have the Honour to be, with perfect Consideration And Respect,

Your most Obedient and
Most Humble Servants,

JOHN BROWN,	JABEZ BOWEN	
JOS. NIGHTINGALE,	NICHOS. BROWN	
LEVI HALL	JOHN JENCKES	
PHILLIP ALLEN,	WELCOME ARNOLD	COMTEE.
PAUL ALLEN	WILLIAM RUSSELL	
	JEREMIAH OLNEY	
	WILLIAM BARTON	
	THOS. LLOYD HALSEY	

ning to descend. Massachusetts (true to the policy of Winthrop) was for " appropriating Rhode Island to the different States that surround her." Washington stigmatized " her public councils " as " scandalous." Madison spoke of the " wickedness and folly that reigned." Even Varnum denounced those responsible for the local apathy and obstinacy as " destitute of education and void of principle." At last, in September, 1787, after the General Assembly had thrice refused to appoint delegates and two days before the great convention at Philadelphia adjourned, the State dispatched a letter to the President of Congress in explanation of its course. Allusion was made to " our being diffident of power." But the main excuse was the shifty one that the freemen and not the General Assembly were the only body by which delegates might be appointed.

Before the month of September expired the Constitution was submitted to the several States for ratification, and Rhode Island found itself confronted by the most serious crisis in its history since the days of " boundaries." The new instrument was to go into effect upon ratification by nine States, and any State that chose not to ratify must face the prospect of an existence uncommiserated without the pale. The step first taken was to refer the instrument to the towns, and with the reference there began discussion. On January 28, 1788, a writer in the Newport " Mercury " gave warning : " If you adopt the proposed Constitution, you

will subject yourselves to a government where you
will be totally unprotected by a bill of rights. . . .
Your Federal Senate is to be in place for six
years, and senators, by reason of their importance
and of their participation in executive power, may
make themselves in effect absolute." The commu-
nication (one marked by undeniable foresight)
concluded with a statement that under the Constitution the Federal Supreme Court might issue
execution against a State in a case where a State
was a party.

To these strictures a contributor signing himself
" A Rhode Island Man " replied on February 25.
As for the exercise of absolute power by the new
government, what, he asked, could exceed for ab-
soluteness the power habitually exercised by the
Rhode Island General Assembly ? The Constitution, indeed, was like a new house built to be tenanted by a large family. Each member found
some fault with it : it was not large enough ; the
windows were upside down ; the doors were so contrived [an allusion to the purely secular character
of the instrument] that a Turk might go in and
out as freely as a Christian ; or it should have been
round, three-sided, or twelve-sided, — one side toward every State except Rhode Island. Servants,
too [representatives and senators], must be hired
for two and six years, — long periods. A better
plan would have admitted of their being hired
afresh every morning. Worse than all else, the

inmates would.be obliged to furnish their own provisions. It ought to have been so devised that they
might be supported " by manna or by quails."

The result of the reference of the Constitution
to the towns (a result intensified by abstention
from voting on the part of many) was rejection
by a great majority. Agitation then (March, 1788)
was begun for the holding of a constitutional convention. The General Assembly thrice refused to
call a convention, and by July 26 New York had
ratified and the Constitution was in effect beyond
all controversy. Where now was Rhode Island?
Along with North Carolina (the Rhode Island of
the South) it was upon its own by no means su-
perabounding resources. In November, 1789, its
isolation was made still more pronounced by ratification by North Carolina. Meanwhile the State
had four times more refused to call a convention,
and had dared even to hint at a foreign alliance.

What at length, in 1790, turned the current in
the little but resolute commonwealth in favor of
the Constitution was what in 1786 had turned the
current there in favor of a Federal impost, namely,
commerce. On the accession to the Union of New
Hampshire, the ninth State, Providence (now rather
than Newport the commercial centre) had rung its
bells, fired its cannon, and held a barbecue ; and
on the accession of New York it again had indulged
in jubilation. When, therefore, in July, 1789, the
national House of Representatives passed a tariff

act which made no exemption in favor of Rhode
Island, Providence was in a position to point to the
hurtful consequences. In September the General
Assembly indited a letter to the two houses of Congress expressing the hope that " we shall not be
altogether considered as foreigners " . . . and that
" trade and commerce, upon which the prosperity
of this State much depends, will be preserved as
free and open between this and the United States
as our different situations at present can possibly
admit." The olive branch was taken. To Rhode
Island there was granted exemption from revenue
restrictions until January, 1790.

On the 17th of January the General Assembly
by a close vote ordered the calling of a convention. The convention met on March 1 in South
Kingstown. Jabez Bowen of Providence and Henry
Marchant of Newport led the Federalists, while
the Anti-Federalists were led by John Collins and
the astute Jonathan J. Hazard of South Kingstown. The principal topic of debate would seem
to have been the Constitution and slavery. Nathan
Miller of Warren asserted that he had the Word
of God in his house, and that it contained nothing
against slavery. On the other hand, Colonel William Barton of Providence (he of the Prescott
seizure) declared that slavery was contrary to the
New Testament. A bill of rights, containing among
other things a section condemning the slave trade
as " disgraceful to liberty and humanity," was se-

cured by the Anti-Federalists, and at the same time an adjournment was taken to May 24, at Newport.

When the convention reassembled, it did so in the face of yet stronger pressure for ratification. Congress, hampered by the absence of Rhode Island representatives in its consideration of such questions as the location of the Federal capital and the assumption of the State debts, had hinted covertly at coercion. The Senate had even gone so far as to pass a resolution in favor of a bill for severing relations between the United States and Rhode Island, and for demanding of the latter a payment of money on account with the United States. Nor was it Congress alone that exerted pressure. Providence, boldly reverting to ideas current in the age of Roger Williams, threatened, under sanction from Congress, to secede from its connection with the agricultural section and to set up for itself. Wrought upon by the combined influences described, but more than by any other influence by that of fear of commercial isolation, Rhode Island on May 29 ratified the Constitution by the sufficient yet significant majority of two votes.

In his admirable monograph, " Rhode Island and the Formation of the Union," Dr. Frank G. Bates deplores the lack at this time in his native State of competent popular leaders devoted to Federalism. South Carolina had its Pinckneys and Rutledges ; Massachusetts its Ameses and Kings ; Virginia its Madisons and Marshalls ; New York its Alexander

Hamilton. Rhode Island had no one. Invaluable would have been the leadership of a Stephen Hopkins. The Nestor himself — friend of organic union in America since 1764 — had only in 1785 passed away, but no successor was at hand. James Varnum had in 1788 removed to the Northwest Territory. As for David Howell, he (had he come forward) presumably must have done so against the Union. But he did not come forward. His course in 1786 in *Trevett vs. Weeden* had alienated from him the agriculturalists, and henceforth his time and thought were devoted wholly to jurisprudence.

The stability which Rhode Island had gained under the restraints of the Revolution was augmented under the milder restraints of the Federal bond, and soon the towns began to turn their glances backward to commerce and forward to manufactures.

CHAPTER XIII

DECLINE OF COMMERCE AND ESTABLISHMENT OF MANUFACTURES

Slave Trade and Commerce at Newport and Bristol — Moses Brown and the Cotton Industry at Providence — John Brown and the East India Trade — The Barbary Corsairs — War of 1812 — Samuel Slater — Political Conditions — Visits of Talleyrand and Lafayette.

IT was Providence that directed its glances both forward and backward. Newport looked only backward.

In 1779, when the British evacuated Newport, they left it a shadow of its former self. Pigot, withdrawing within his lines before the advance of Sullivan, had burned houses and hewn down groves. The compact part of the town, too, had suffered. On May 31, 1780, Dr. Stiles wrote: " About three hundred dwelling house I judge have been destroyed. The Town is in Ruins. But with Nehemiah I could prefer the very dust of Zion to the Gardens of Persia, and the broken walls of Jerusalem to the Palaces of Sushan. I rode over the Isle and found the beautiful Rows of Trees which lined the Roads, with sundry coppices or groves & Orchards down and laid waste ; but the

natural Beauties of the Place still remain. And I
doubt not the place will be rebuilt & exceed its
former splendor." [1]

A final and irreparable piece of mischief was
worked by the departing loyalists. They carried
away with them to New York the town records.
These through the wrecking at Hell Gate of the
transporting vessel were submerged for a time in
salt water. Upon the request of Washington, they
were recovered by Sir Guy Carleton and restored;
but they were almost undecipherable, and long
remained a reddened mass ready to crumble at
the touch.

At the close of the Revolution Newport cast

[1] "I have seen not a little of other countries, but I never saw
any Island that unites finer views, rendered pleasant by variety of hill & vale, rocks, reefs, beaches, Islands & perennial ponds
than this. . . . Before the discovery of our mineral springs, Rh.
Island was in one view the Bath of the American world. . . . This
and the Redwood Library gave it both a literary & a genteel
air; and rendered it the best bred society in N. England. But
— alas! — how changed! The British destroyed, for fuel, about
900 [?] buildings, of [to] be sure the poorer sort; yet it has never
recovered the dilapidation. The town of Providence has risen
to riches & elegance from the ruins of this once beautiful spot;
while Newport resembles an old battered shield — its scars &
bruises are deep and indelible. Commerce, & all the Jews are fled.
The wharves are deserted & the lamp in the synagogue is ex-
tinct; and the people are now so poor, that there are not more
than ten, or a dozen people who would have the courage to invite a stranger to his table." — Benjamin Waterhouse, Letter to
Thomas Jefferson, September 14, 1822. *Pub. R. I. Hist. Soc.*
vol. ii. See also Brissot de Warville, *Pictures of R. I. in the Past*,
edited by Gertrude S. Kimball.

back a longing glance in particular upon the slave
trade. It was in this trade that the town had
grown rich, and to this trade that it was most attached. Difficulties, however, were accumulating
in the way of it. The Rhode Island law of 1774
prohibiting the importation of slaves gave little
concern. So did the law of ten years later providing for local emancipation. But in 1787 participation by Rhode Islanders in the foreign slave
trade was forbidden; and in 1794, 1800, and 1803
the Federal Congress passed laws amounting, when
taken together, to a prohibition of the foreign slave
trade to all American citizens, and also of the domestic trade wherever forbidden by local law.

Under these conditions embarrassment for the
slave traders was relieved by the action of South
Carolina. That State in 1788 had forbidden slave
importations. The law had failed of enforcement,
so in 1803 it was repealed. Straightway Rhode
Island began sending to Charleston great numbers
of slave ships. Between 1804 and 1807 Great Britain, France, Sweden, Massachusetts, Connecticut,
Maryland, Virginia, and South Carolina all availed
themselves of the open slave port of Charleston;
but none of them (Great Britain and South Carolina excepted) to the same extent as did Rhode
Island. Of the 202 vessels entered at Charleston
during the years indicated, three were from France,
one was from Sweden, one from Massachusetts, and
one from Connecticut; four were from Maryland,

and two from Virginia.   On the other hand, seventy were from Great Britain, sixty-one from South Carolina, and fifty-nine from Rhode Island.

The zeal of Newport in the post-Revolutionary slave trade and at the same time the comparative indifference of Providence to that trade come out clearly in the correspondence of the day.   On August, 17, 1789, Samuel Hopkins wrote from Newport to Moses Brown: "The combined opposition to a suppression of the trade in slaves is so great and strong here that I think no anti-slavery committee formed in this town would be able to do much." And in 1791 (December 5) William Ellery, himself a Newporter, wrote: "An Ethiopian could as soon change his skin as a Newport merchant could be induced to change so lucrative a trade as that in slaves for the slow profits of any manufactory."

It is true that in 1807 Congress, availing itself of a provision of the Federal Constitution, passed an act forbidding absolutely and for the whole country any further importation of slaves. But before the act went into effect (to say nothing of what took place afterwards)[1] the example of slave-

---

[1] BRISTOL, August 20th, 1816.

MR. OBADIAH BROWN

My Esteemed Friend, — The impunity with which prohibited traffic is carried on from this Place, has for some time rendered it the occasional resort of many violators of commercial law from other Places, as well as the constant residence of others. The African slave-trade is the one of this description now most

trading Newport had been followed by the energetic town of Bristol.

In 1744, when Simeon Potter was making his

successfully and extensively prosecuted. Such is the number, &
more especially the, *character* of those concerned in it, that I
should consider myself as incurring some personal hazard if I did
not know that you heartily abominate the odious trade, and would
make no disclosure to the injury of one who would only wish its
complete prevention. I do not know that it is possible to effect
this, but the facts in relation to this subject can be considered by
those capable of determining.

Cargoes suited to the American market are procured here &
taken on board vessels suited to the business and cleared for Havana [sic]. The Master there effects a nominal sale of vessels &
cargo to a Spaniard, takes on board a Spanish nominal Master
& proceeds to Africa. A power of Attorney to effect the sale is
always prepared here before sailing. When the vessel has made
one voyage she can proceed on another without returning to the
U. S. A cargo is usually sent out to her to Havana. There are
several now out that have performed several voyages since they
first sailed from here. There is one now laying here ready for sea
called " The General Peace of Providence," lately owned wholly
by Joseph Sanders of that Place, Thomas H. Russell of this Town,
Master & Attorney to effect the pretended sale. *I* wrote his
Power of Attorney. Bills of sale of parts of the vessel have been
given here : But the whole is to be covered under a Spanish name.
The [sic] even speak familiarly of their destination, & one against
whom I had a demand boldly told me I must wait till he could go
& catch some black-birds.

By such stratagems as these, hundreds of that unhappy race
are now annually torn from their homes and doomed with all
their posterity to West India Slavery. Can the Friends of humanity do nothing to prevent so outrageous an evil ?

In the number of those concerned in this business are some of
my personal Friends, and many from [sic] I derive a portion
of my business & support. My feelings revolt from the idea of
inflicting the vengeance of the law on the first, and policy (which

COMMERCE AND MANUFACTURES   263

cruise along the Spanish Main to the distress of
gentle Father Fauque of Oyapoc, there was with
him as supercargo Mark Anthony De Wolf, a young
man of Guadeloupe. De Wolf married Potter's
sister, settled at Bristol, and became the father of
a famous seafaring progeny — James, Charles, and
John De Wolf. James, who was born in 1764,
achieved in the early years of the nineteenth century great wealth in the slave trade, and in .1820
became a United States senator. Ten of the fifty-
nine slavers employed by Rhode Island between
1804 and 1807 were owned, ship and cargo, by
James De Wolf. Indeed, as between Newport and
Bristol during this interval, honors in respect to the
slave traffic were almost evenly divided. Seven
thousand nine hundred and fifty-eight negroes were
carried to Charleston in Rhode Island vessels. Of

circumstances oblige me to consult) ought to restrain me from an
open participation in the punishment of the others. I think if
you at Providence were to write and talk more on the subject, to
advertise a determination to prosecute, & thus at least evince
your knowledge of the existence of facts, you might do some
good. Humane laws, used in the spirit of humanity, ought not in
their execution to bring disgrace on any but their violators, but
such is the depraved judgment of the multitude, that to tell of
crimes is almost as odious as to commit them, & I request you
not to disclose that any of the facts herein stated come from me.
    I am Sir —
        Your Frd. &c.
                [Signature cut out].
    N. B. — Edward Mason of your Town is concerned with
Sanders.
    Pub. R. I. Hist. Soc. vol. vi, p. 226.

these nearly 3500 were carried in vessels from
Newport, and about 3900 in vessels from Bristol.
Providence vessels carried just 556.

Newport looked back with longing upon the slave
trade. It also looked back with longing, though in
less degree, upon the vanished Mediterranean and
Levantine trade of the Hebrew merchant Abraham
Rodriguez Rivera. This trade, or rather trade of a
kind akin to it, was now to be undertaken by men
who were not only residents of Newport but natives
of America — Mr. George Gibbs and Mr. Walter
Channing, constituting the firm of Gibbs & Channing, and Mr. Christopher Champlin and Mr.
George Champlin, constituting the firm of Champlin & Champlin. Between 1790 and 1812 both
houses dealt largely to Sweden and St. Petersburg
for iron ; to Java for coffee ; to Canton for teas,
nankeens, and silks ; and to Antwerp, Malaga, Bar-
celona, and Leghorn for miscellaneous commodities.
In 1810 the tonnage of Newport was 12,517, only
3347 less than that of Providence. At this period,
too, the trades of ship-building and whale-catching had been much revived. A leading position
with regard to both was taken by the town of
Warren.

For the commercial decline of Newport, as also
for that of Bristol and Warren, there may be as-
signed four general causes: foreign interference
(after 1793) with American ships; the American
Embargo Acts of the years 1807 and 1809; the

War of 1812 ; and the introduction of railroads. Providence felt the operation of the same causes, but was able to betake itself to manufactures. To Newport no such course was open. There was on the island of Rhode Island no brawling Blackstone nor swift Pawtuxet — in a word, no water-power ; and when the sea as a field of activity failed the islanders, naught was left them but to quit forever the spot of their affections, or, putting their savings at interest, to live in the memory of the stirring past.

Newport had early been the resort of wealthy English planters of the West Indies and Carolinas — the Redwoods, the Pinckneys, the Rutledges, and the Haynes. After 1840 it became increasingly the resort of the people of Charleston. Its attractions were its salubrious climate, the wide ocean prospect from its cliffs, and its extensive bathing beaches. Then, too, there was about it a delightful historic afterglow. Nobody there was very busy now. The shipping — huge East Indiaman and small trim slaver — had disappeared. The wharves and slave-pens were falling to decay. No Red Rover lay mysterious in the outer harbor. But local circles were charged with anecdotes of many a slaver and many a rover ; and the local spinster, proud of the claims of long descent, was proud also to produce for the benefit of those sufficiently accredited the heirloom London gown, the heirloom invitation to the Washington-Rochambeau ball, or the heirloom set of priceless " china " from Canton.

Nor yet in other ways did latter-day Newport fail in suggestiveness. The gentle and flower-like genius of Edward G. Malbone — a natural son of John Malbone the merchant magnate — served to re-create a Berkeleyan atmosphere in art. Born in 1777, Malbone painted miniature portraits unmatched for loveliness, and died at the age of thirty. But in no son of Newport, perhaps — whether of a latter day or a former — was the Berkeleyan or idealistic element fundamental in Rhode Island character brought to such perfection as in William Ellery Channing. On the 9th of May, 1773, Dr. Ezra Stiles made entry in his diary : " In the eveng I married Mr. William Channing and Miss Lucy Ellery." William Ellery Channing was a fruit of this union. He opposed slavery and forecast Transcendentalism. His death occurred in 1842. After 1840 — the era of railroads — Newport, and with it Rhode Island at large in so far as the latter depended upon the sea, became an American Venice. It could only look forth helpless upon that element which erstwhile it had been its mission to subdue.

It has been said that Providence at the close of the Revolution glanced forward as well as backward. Its first vigorous glance was unmistakably forward. On December 2, 1789, nearly six months before

Rhode Island ratified the Federal Constitution, Samuel Slater, a young Englishman of Derbyshire who had been attracted to America by a prospect of advancement in connection with the manufacture of cotton yarn, wrote thus to Moses Brown: " A few days ago I was informed that you wanted a manager of cotton spinning, &c., in which business I flatter myself that I can give the greatest satisfaction, in making machinery, making good yarn, either for stockings or twist, as any that is made in England; as I have had opportunity and an oversight, of Sir Richard Arkwright's works and in Mr. Strutt's mill upwards of eight years." When this letter was received, Brown (the financial stay of the firm of Almy & Brown) had for some time been struggling at Pawtucket with imperfect imitations of the Arkwright patents. " If thou thought," he at once replied to Slater, " thou couldst perfect the machines and conduct them to profit, if thou wilt come and do it, thou shalt have all the profits made of them over and above the interest of the money they cost and the wear and tear of them." Slater came, and his triumph will ere long engage our attention. Meanwhile a word regarding that upon which Providence in common with Newport was casting backward glance — commerce.

In this domain it is our acquaintance John Brown — the brother of Moses — that bespeaks attention. No whit less restive now was John than when we beheld him upbraiding Sullivan (through Greene) for the failure of the Franco-American movement against the British under Pigot. One of the few Providence merchants to reënter the slave trade, he was a member of the General Assembly in March, 1784, when the emancipation bill was passed ; and although instructed by the Providence town meeting to support the measure, he made over it a very wry face indeed. A "shaller policy," he stigmatized it, to prohibit slave holding or to interfere with the lucrative business of slave trading. His course on slavery, like his course in relation to the Continental frigates and in denunciation of Sullivan, was but a variation at considerable moral cost upon the precept, " Put money in thy purse." It is true that in 1787 we find him (under the spur of a desire to enlist in a commercial venture the capital of his brother Moses) actually proposing to quit the " Giney " trade, and urging Moses to enter the General Assembly, where he could work for the suppression of slavery. But in 1797 he became the object of a legal prosecution at the hands of Caleb Greene of Newport for participation in this very trade to Guinea. The same year he wrote to Greene begging him to desist from the suit for the reason that " he had done with the trade now ; " yet in 1799, as a member of the lower house of Congress, he did not scruple to proclaim from his seat that all the existing legislation against slavery should be repealed ; " for why," he asked, " should we see Great Britain getting all the slave trade to themselves ? "

The commercial venture of 1787 in which John Brown endeavored to enlist the support of Moses Brown was a voyage to the East Indies. The idea was a bold one. It was only since 1783 that the mariners of Salem, Massachusetts, following a lure which had enthralled Marco Polo, Columbus, and Da Gama, had adventured to the Orient; but Brown, as the affair of the Gaspee had shown, was nothing if not bold. Besides (and this perhaps was the main consideration) the slave trade was now so obstructed by local penal legislation, and the West India trade by British restrictions, that a departure in commerce had become almost a necessity.

As far back as 1782 the historic house of Nicholas Brown & Company had been dissolved, and in its stead there had arisen under Nicholas Brown the house of Brown & Benson, and under John Brown the house of Brown & Francis. Between 1787 and 1807 the latter house, which owned its own docks and yards and built its own ships, employed in the East India trade four vessels, — the General Washington, the Warren, the President Washington, and the George Washington. Of these the largest was the President Washington (950 tons), and all were uniformly successful in their voyages. Outward bound, they made the ports of Madeira, Calcutta, Madras, Batavia, Pondicherry, and Canton. Returning, they touched

at St. Helena, St. Ascension, and St. Eustatia.
Their cargoes of anchors, cordage, cannon and
shot, bar iron, Narragansett cheese, spermaceti
candles, wine, brandy, spirits, and rum were exchanged for tea, silks, "china," cotton goods,
lacquered ware, cloves, and flannels, and the profits earned cast those even of slave-trading into
the background.

In 1794 Brown & Benson (now Brown, Benson
& Ives), stimulated by the success of Brown &
Francis, determined likewise to adventure in the
East. They sent out (respectively in 1794 and
1798) two notable ships, the John Jay and the
Ann and Hope. Both made successful voyages,
but both alike (in strong contrast to the vessels
of Brown & Francis) led checkered careers ending in disaster. The John Jay on her first voyage
(to Bombay and Canton) was caught in a mon-
soon and lost nearly all her masts and all her
sails and spars. She furthermore was scourged by
small-pox and narrowly escaped seizure by pirates
in the China seas. When finally, in 1796, she got
home she brought with her, besides 560,000 pounds
of tea, such articles of interest as silks (13 boxes
and 14 pieces), umbrellas (2 boxes and 64 single
umbrellas), china-ware (138 boxes), fans (3 boxes),
quicksilver (2 tubs), sugar candy (2 tubs), preserved fruits (4 tubs), ostrich feathers (610), rat-
tans and canes (1800), one bundle of window
screens, one backgammon board, and what not.

The John Jay in 1806 was captured by a British sloop-of-war, and in order to effect her release it became necessary to appeal to the High Court of Admiralty. In 1807 she struck a reef off Pigeon Island (near Java) and went to pieces.

As for the Ann and Hope, her career was varied in the extreme. She was a fast ship, and carried a good armament. In 1798 she sailed for Canton. She stopped at Sydney, Australia, and afterwards át the uninhabited island of Tinian. Here there was discovered, wildly pacing the sands, a Lascar (East India sailor) who had been cast away in a brig manned by whites and East Indians. The whites had been rescued by a passing vessel, but the Lascars had been left to their fate. At length a Spanish slave ship had touched at the island. By this craft the Lascars (all save the narrator) had been carried away in irons. The narrator had escaped by concealing himself in the woods. Subsisting on oranges, cherries, plums, and cocoanuts, — products of the spot, — he had passed his time in solitude and tears, watching for a sail. A man not without parts was this Robinson Crusoe of the Orient, for he spoke English, French, Spanish, Portuguese, and Malay. He was taken to Macao, whence he could ship readily for Bengal. On the same voyage the Ann and Hope fell in with a French privateer, which gave her chase and fired three shots at her. These were returned with emphasis, and the privateer drew off. In 1806, on a return voyage from the East, the vessel, together with her cargo, was lost on Block Island.

Commodities imported from the East Indies into Providence in 1795 were valued at $311,910; in 1800 at $726,924; in 1804 at $887,000; in 1806 (the year of the loss of the Ann and Hope) at $662,200. The trade lasted until 1841, but its heyday was over by 1807.[1]

The trade of Rhode Island with the East was free from the peculiar embarrassments that beset the slave trade and the West India trade, but it suffered from others common at the time to American trade everywhere. John Brown died in 1803, and before his death the embarrassments spoken of had become serious. Among them after

---

[1] The registered tonnage of the United States calculated on an average of ten years, 1800–1809, was held in the following ratio compared to population : —

New Hampshire	0.09	tons to the inhabitant.
Vermont	.001	tons to the inhabitant.
Massachusetts	.37	tons to the inhabitant.
Rhode Island	.19	tons to the inhabitant.
Connecticut	.10	tons to the inhabitant.
New York	.13	tons to the inhabitant.
New Jersey	.01	tons to the inhabitant.
Pennsylvania	.10	tons to the inhabitant.
Delaware	.02	tons to the inhabitant.
Maryland	.17	tons to the inhabitant.
Virginia	.03	tons to the inhabitant.
North Carolina	.03	tons to the inhabitant.
South Carolina	.09	tons to the inhabitant.
Georgia	.03	tons to the inhabitant.

Seybert, p. 308.

Quoted by Dr. William Jones in his *Transition of Providence from a Commercial to a Manufacturing Community*.

1793 was (as has been said) interference by foreign powers. Interference was of two kinds — depredations by Barbary pirates and seizures by the British and French (then at war) under the orders and decrees of their respective governments with regard to neutrals.

The Barbary pirates were the same marauding race that in 1680 had taken captive William Harris, the antagonist of Roger Williams. European States had long been paying them tribute, and since 1785 tribute had been accumulating against the United States. It had not sooner been collected, because hitherto the Algerians and Tunisians had been confined by Portugal within the Straits of Gibraltar and so had been unable to lay hands upon American ships. In 1793, through British contrivance, the Portuguese blockade was suspended for a twelvemonth and the pirates flocked out into the Atlantic. In one cruise they captured ten American merchantmen and enslaved one hundred and five citizens.

The news when received at Providence caused the greatest concern. Theodore Foster, one of the United States senators from Rhode Island, was beset with requests to make known what Congress would do. " We can't send out a ship," wrote Welcome Arnold in January, 1794, " without stipulating to redeem the seamen from the Algerines. Will Congress set about building a navy immediately? . . . If Congress must buy peace it can

do it cheaper with a navy building." On the 4th
of February the town of Warren, with commend-
able forethought, wrote asking to be given a chance
to build some of the ships for the projected navy.
On February 13 George Benson, of the house of
Brown & Benson, inquired anxiously : " Why is
there no decision on the proposal to equip a small
fleet ? The season for cutting ship-timber is fast
closing, and we learn 'by an arrival from South
Carolina that a vessel from Gibraltar brings authoritative information that the Algerine fleet is
refitting and actually means to cruise on our coast
next summer." Letters like the foregoing were
productive of results. On March 27, 1794, Congress ordered six frigates to be built — among
them the ever famous Constitution. Despite the
plea of the town of Warren, none was ordered
to be built in Rhode Island, yet the State was not
permitted to go unrecognized. In June, 1794,
Silas Talbot, the hero of the capture of the Pigot
galley, was appointed one of six new naval captains.

Rhode Island built neither the Constitution, the
President, the United States, the Chesapeake,
the Congress, nor the Constellation ; in 1798,
however, the Federal government purchased from
John Brown the Indiaman George Washington.
In 1800 (fact humiliating and strange) this vessel
under Captain Bainbridge was sent to Algiers
as bearer of tribute to the Dey. The story how

the George Washington, as the ship of a tributary nation, was compelled to carry a party of two hundred Algerine envoys to Constantinople that they in turn might render tribute to the Sublime Porte, is interesting, but cannot here be repeated. Suffice it to say, that soon after the return of the ship to the United States, there came an end to tribute — an end which Stephen Decatur, son and grandson of a Decatur of Newport, did not a little to bring about.

Toward the War of 1812 — a contest for commercial rights forced upon America by the Anglo-French wars which had begun in 1793 — the attitude of Rhode Island was peculiar. Its seamen ever and anon were impressed,[1] and between 1804 and 1807 its ships suffered from the British orders-in-council. But the Jeffersonian embargo, imposed in 1807, proved more destructive to its interests than impressment and orders-in-council combined. The measure gave a foretaste of absolute cessation

---

[1] In May, 1794, the British man-of-war Nautilus put into Newport Harbor for supplies. It became known that there were on board the vessel a number of impressed American seamen. The General Assembly thereupon detained the captain (Boynton) and his first lieutenant until a search could be made. As a result of the search, six men were found who claimed to be American citizens : one from Martha's Vineyard ; one from Charleston ; one from Boston ; one from Georgetown, S. C. ; one from Portsmouth, Va. ; and one from New York. All were liberated. This probably is the earliest case of resistance by an American government to the British claim of right of impressment. S. S. Rider, *Book Notes*, vol. i.

of trade with Great Britain. When, therefore, in 1812 war with Great Britain was declared, Rhode Island was emphatic in protest. The General Assembly denounced a resort to arms; the town of Providence tolled its bells and lowered its flags to half-mast; Napoleon Bonaparte was denominated an "atrocious murderer and incendiary," and Great Britain was lauded as an " oppressed nation gloriously struggling for the preservation of its liberties." These utterances were supplemented by others more specific. In 1813 Governor William Jones denied the right of the president to summon the militia out of the State, and in 1814 the same official gave warning that " notwithstanding our respect for the law and our strong attachment to the union of the States, there may be evils greater than can be apprehended from a refusal to submit to unconstitutional laws." After such an assertion of particularism as this the State was ready for the Hartford Convention, the initial step toward which it took, and the sessions of which it honored with four delegates.

Rhode Island, although refusing to sanction the War of 1812, furnished in the person of Oliver Hazard Perry of South Kingstown the most picturesque naval hero of the conflict. In 1775 James Wallace, captain of the British frigate Rose, had written to Abraham Whipple: "You, Abraham Whipple, on the 10th June, 1772, burned his Majesty's vessel, the Gaspee, and I will hang you at the

yard-arm," whereupon Whipple had replied : " Sir,
always catch a man before you hang him." Perry
thus had before him a model of the epigrammatic
in a naval dispatch, when, on September 10, 1813,
he wrote : " We have met the enemy and they are
ours." Another Rhode Island figure of interest in
connection with the War of 1812 was James De
Wolf the slave trader of Bristol. In 1812 De
Wolf put in commission the privateer Yankee.
The vessel in three and one half years made six
cruises, captured in all forty prizes, destroyed
British property to the value of five millions of dollars, and sent into Bristol a million dollars' worth
of goods. On the fifth cruise alone the profits were
so great that the two negro cabin waiters, Cuffee
Cockroach and Jack Jibsheet, received respectively
eleven hundred and twenty-one dollars and eighty-
eight cents, and seven hundred and thirty-eight
dollars and nineteen cents.

It remains for us to follow the fortunes of Samuel Slater. On reaching Pawtucket Slater did three
things : he secured lodgings at the house of the
Quaker machinist, Oziel Wilkinson ; he fell deeply
in love with Wilkinson's daughter, the laughing-
eyed Hannah ; and he inspected carefully the spinning appliances of the factory operated by Almy
& Brown. The appliances he pronounced worth-
less, and he at once set to work to replace them by
a full set of machines constructed after the Ark-

wright designs. Models he had none, nor even drawings, for the exportation of these things from England was forbidden under heavy penalties. But he was able to make drawings from memory, and by the aid of them models were constructed. On December 20, 1790, the Almy & Brown factory was newly equipped and ready to start.

By reason of improved machinery, masterly superintendence, and ample capital, the firm of Almy & Brown was successful in producing cotton yarn. As late, however, as 1803 it was the only successful cotton firm in New England. In all the country besides there was but one other cotton firm and that soon failed. What was needed to establish the industry of cotton manufacturing in America was protection against English goods, and this came unbidden and unwelcome with the embargo of 1807 and the War of 1812. The disturbances which were wrecking commerce — carrying Newport down to commercial death and sadly injuring commercial Providence — disturbances which a Providence town meeting on January 28, 1809, denounced as subversive of the natural right of navigating the ocean — these disturbances, unknown to Rhode Island, were preparing the way for its greatest prosperity.

Within thirty miles of Providence in 1805 there were five small cotton factories operating 4000 spindles. In 1815, within the same radius, there were 171 factories employing 26,000 workmen,

operating 134,588 spindles, and consuming annually 29,000 bales of cotton in the production of
27,840,000 yards of cloth. The cessation of the
war brought with it the removal of barriers to
foreign trade and an influx of English and India
cotton goods with a lowering of prices. Thereupon Rhode Island cast in its lot definitely with
those demanding a national protective system and
supported the tariff of 1816.

To provide the capital for the operating of factories, banks early became indispensable. Between
1817 and 1819 such institutions increased from
seventeen to thirty. To connect the numerous
small mill villages with Providence — their *en-
trepôt* and their *dépôt* — good roads early were
required. Between 1803 and 1842 thirty-six turn-
pike companies were incorporated. Mill employees
were growing in number, and the problem of
education arose. It was met in part in 1796 by
Samuel Slater. He established at Pawtucket a
Sunday-school at which there were taught the
rudiments of knowledge. His efforts were supplemented by those of John Howland at Providence,
who as a barber was a member of the Association
of Mechanics and Manufactures, a society organized in 1789. By the energy of Howland the General Assembly in 1800 was led to pass an act
creating free schools. The act was repealed in
1803, and no other was passed until 1828.

In illustration of the transition in Rhode Island

from commerce to manufactures there may be cited the case of the great commercial house of Brown & Ives, formerly Brown, Benson & Ives. As late as 1828 this house was commercial, although manufactures largely concerned it. To guard its commercial interests it joined in a petition to Congress against the tariff of 1828, a measure which bore heavily on hemp, sail-cloth, iron, and molasses. But in 1834 Edward Carrington, Wilbur Kelley, Nicholas Brown, Thomas P. Ives, Moses Brown Ives, John Carter Brown, and Robert H. Ives formed the Lonsdale Cotton Company, and soon afterwards the house which had sent forth the John Jay and the Ann and Hope sold its last ship and ceased to tempt fortune on the sea.

Commerce in Rhode Island having been supplanted, the fact was not long in pointedly disclosing itself. The magnate now was no Wanton (William or John) or Godfrey Malbone eking out privateering with mercantile adventuring. The magnate of this order had been swept as ruthlessly into the realm of anecdote as earlier had been swept into the same realm the William Harrises, the William Coddingtons, and the William Brentons of the order of agriculture. Now the magnate was a less picturesque but more ample and utilitarian figure — the cotton-mill owner. Such was William Sprague the son of the founder of the family of Sprague, and such was William Sprague the grandson. Under the firm name of " A. & W. Sprague,"

the Spragues junior owned and administered pos-
sessions princely in extent and magnitude in the
valley of the Pawtuxet. William, the son of the
founder, became governor of Rhode Island in 1838
and United States senator in 1842. William,
nephew to the latter, became governor in 1860 and
United States senator in 1863.

The period of fifty years dealt with in the present chapter is noteworthy in Rhode Island history
for the gubernatorial administrations of Arthur
and James Fenner, father and son.[*] Arthur held
office continuously from 1790 to 1805, and James
continuously from 1807 to 1811; an interval as a
whole comparable with that during which Samuel
Cranston held the same office a century earlier,
or with that during which the office was held by
various members of the Wanton family. The Fenner administrations were coincident largely with
the administrations of Washington,[1] Adams, Jef-

[1] The topics of national politics which were of special interest
to Rhode Islanders at this time were the location of the national
capital and the assumption of the State debts. Of almost equal
interest was the matter of appointments to Federal office. Washington, who in the other States ignored party considerations, in
Rhode Island (because of the obstinacy of that commonwealth in
withstanding the Union) paid attention to them. Arthur Fenner,
Jabez Bowen, Henry Marchant, William Ellery, John Collins,
William Channing, John Carter, and many others were appli-
cants for favors. — J. F. Jameson, " The Adjustment of Rhode
Island into the Union in 1790," *Pub. R. I. Hist. Soc.* vol. viii ;
Gaillard Hunt, " Office Seeking during Washington's Adminis-
tration," *Am. Hist. Rev.* vol. i.

ferson, and Madison. Under Washington and
Adams Rhode Island was Federalist. The treaty
of Jay with England and the resistance to French
spoliations were favorable to the interests of the
State as a commercial community. Under Jefferson the Republicans gained control, but under
Madison they lost it because of their advocacy of
the War of 1812. After the rise and development
of the protective tariff issue the State became
Whig.

But not thus alone is our period one of note. In
1790 the Providence Society for Promoting the
Abolition of Slavery was chartered. In 1799 resolutions were passed by the General Assembly condemning the Virginia and Kentucky Nullification
Resolutions. In 1822 the Rhode Island Historical
Society was founded. Between 1831 and 1837
there took place an anti-Masonic agitation, and
in 1835 the Boston and Providence Railroad was
opened.

The Abolition Society of 1790 owed its existence
to Moses Brown and "College Tom" Hazard of
South Kingstown; but associated with these leaders were David Howell, Arthur Fenner, and
Samuel Hopkins; and Jonathan Edwards was
associated by correspondence. Over the anti-Nul-
lification resolutions of 1799 one pauses amazed at
the irony of Time in his revenges. In 1798 Virginia had declared: "In case of a deliberate, palpable
and dangerous exercise of . . . powers not granted

[to the Federal government], the States . . . have the right and are in duty bound to interpose for arresting the progress of the evil." In 1815 Rhode Island, through its governor (William Jones), indorsed the report of the Hartford Convention, a report which said : " In cases of deliberate, dangerous, and palpable infractions of the Constitution, affecting the sovereignty of a State and the liberties of the people, it is not only the right but the duty of such State to interpose its authority. . . . When emergencies occur which are either beyond the reach of the judicial tribunals, or too pressing to admit of the delay incident to their forms, States which have no common umpire must be their own judges and execute their own decisions."

With the mention of some interesting names the present chapter may be dismissed. Between 1787 and 1824 Rhode Island was visited by the travelers J. Hector St. John de Crèvecoeur, J. P. Brissot de Warville, and the Duc de La Rochefoucauld-Liancourt; and by the statesmen Talleyrand and the Marquis de Lafayette. Talleyrand came in 1794, and he alighted at Newport. He tarried several weeks, received no letters, asked no questions, paid his reckoning and went his way. Why had he come ? Mr. George Champlin Mason, writing in 1884, conjectured that Talleyrand's " Memoirs " when printed might solve the little mystery. The " Memoirs " at length have been printed. Is the mystery solved ? As for the Marquis de Lafayette, his coming, which made memorable the year 1824, was to renew associations of the time of D'Estaing. Nor are the names here to be mentioned exclusively foreign. They include Elisha Potter and Benjamin Hazard, members of the General Assembly, and Tristam Burges, the " bald eagle " of the national House of Representatives. Pitted in many a contest against John Randolph of Roanoke, Burges proved himself a doughty defender of Rhode Island's bulwark, the protective tariff system.

Yet of all the names of our period those which chiefly are of interest are John and Moses Brown. John established trade with the Orient. Moses established the spinning of cotton yarn.

CHAPTER XIV

THE DORR REBELLION

Suffrage and Representation — Thomas W. Dorr — Rival Conventions and Governments — Dorr the Fanatic — *Luther vs. Borden* — National Party Politics.

ORIGINALLY in the four Rhode Island towns the suffrage was coupled with the freehold. The adjustment was agricultural, and so long as the towns remained agricultural it was natural. When, however, Rhode Island life expanded, when to agriculture there was added commerce, and when to commerce there were added manufactures, a readjustment was required; one that would admit to a share of power the newer element in the body politic — the artisan class as distinguished from the class that was land-owning. Readjustment the freeholders (powerholders) for over fifty years refused to grant. Their close corporation based upon property they guarded from profanation as jealously as had the Puritans their close corporation based upon religion. In Massachusetts it took a revocation of charter to get rid of religious exclusiveness. In Rhode Island it took a rebellion — a rebellion of the unifying present against the separatist past — the rebellion headed by Thomas

W. Dorr — to get rid of the exclusiveness of proprietaryism.

The movement which culminated in the Dorr revolt was directed principally against the restriction on the suffrage, but it also was directed against inequality of town representation in the General Assembly. Both grievances were grounded in the actual constitution of the State: the suffrage grievance in the rule of freehold qualification expressed in the statute of 1724, and the grievance as to representation in the apportionment provision of the Charter of 1663.

Of the two grievances that in respect to representation was the earlier felt. Providence by the close of the Revolution had so gained in population as to be entitled to the same representation as Newport. As a matter of fact, it was represented by four assemblymen or deputies, and Newport by six. In 1791 a commencement orator of Brown University alluded to Rhode Island as possessing no constitution or political compact entered into by the people, and described the charter as an old musty document from Charles Stuart. The antiquity of the charter would have weighed little at this time had not the feature of inequality of representation been joined to the feature of age. It was in relation to State taxation that the inequality feature was most complained of. In 1796, therefore, Providence issued a summons for a convention of towns to take into consideration

the question of forming a "written" State constitution. Eight northern towns responded, and in
October the General Assembly appealed to the
towns as a body for instructions regarding a constitutional convention; further than this no result
was attained.

Providence, nevertheless, was in earnest. In
1797, one of its citizens, Colonel George R. Burrill, delivered a Fourth of July oration. In it the
declaration was made that "equal representation
is involved in the very idea of free government."
But how was such representation to be obtained
in Rhode Island? To petition the legislature for
it would, the speaker said, be to "require the
powerholders to surrender their power, — a requisition which it is not in human nature to
grant."

The only course left was to ignore the legislature and to form a constitution without its aid.
Thomas W. Dorr had not been born when the
Burrill oration was delivered, but what forty-four
years afterwards he did was in full consonance
with it. The legislature was ignored and the people in their primary capacity were invoked to
act.

Between 1797 and 1829 at least one attempt
(1811) was made to secure through the legislature an enlarged suffrage, and at least five
attempts were made (1799, 1817, 1821, 1822, and
1824) to secure through a new constitution a

more just legislative apportionment. None of the
attempts were crowned with success. The General Assembly indefinitely postponed the measures of 1811 and 1817, and those of 1821 and
1822 (which, together with the measure of 1817,
were resolutions that a constitutional convention
be called) were defeated at the polls. The attempt
of 1824 brought about the submission of a constitution for acceptance or rejection, but rejection
was the fate encountered. Under the instrument rejected Newport would have lost one assemblyman
and Providence (now far larger than Newport)
and other northern towns would have gained one.
The scheme had been devised to please all the
towns; it pleased none.

With 1829 the movement for constitutional reform in Rhode Island became distinctly a movement for enlarged suffrage. Providence had risen
in population from 11,745 souls in 1820 to 15,941
in 1825, and of these a large fraction were mechanics and cotton-mill operatives, — men who
were not owners of land and who could not vote,
yet who regarded exclusion from the franchise as
more or less of an injustice. Petitions in relation
to the suffrage were presented in the lower house
of the General Assembly on behalf of the unen-
franchised in the towns of Providence, North
Providence, Bristol, and Warren. The petitions
were referred to a committee of which Benjamin
Hazard was chairman, and by that committee were

somewhat contemptuously dismissed.[1] At this time
Thomas W. Dorr was twenty-four years old. He
was the son of Sullivan Dorr, a successful Providence manufacturer, and as such had received a
careful education. From Phillips Exeter Academy
he had gone to Harvard College. There he had been
graduated in 1823. Afterwards he had studied
law with Chancellor Kent of New York, and now
was a respected and rising man practicing his profession in his native town. Just how much of a
Tiberius Gracchus, revolving in his ardent mind
the lot of the downtrodden in Rhode Island, Dorr
may have been prior to 1833 (the year of his election
to the General Assembly), we do not know. That
by nature he was a reformer, an idealist, we are led
to surmise. Among his early legislative acts were
a bill (which became law) in favor of poor debtors, and a protest against interference with the
Abolitionists. His first unequivocal revelation of
himself, however, was in an address to the people
of Rhode Island issued in 1834. In that year a
convention of northern towns was held at Provi-

1 " The committee have not thought it necessary to inquire
particularly how many of the signers are native citizens of the
State, but they are sufficiently informed to be satisfied that a
very great proportion are not so, and it is ill calculated to produce a favorable opinion of their qualification . . . that persons
who have adventured, and are every day adventuring among us
from other States or countries, to better their condition; who
enjoy, in common with ourselves, all the protection and benefits
of our equal laws, *and upon whose departure there is no restraint;*
should still be restless and dissatisfied," etc.

dence " to promote the establishment of a state
constitution," and Dorr was selected to voice to
the world the convention's purpose.

What constitutionally was the condition of
Rhode Island in 1834? The suffrage was restricted to such as were owners of land, or were
the eldest sons of owners of land, of the value of
one hundred and thirty-four dollars : that we know.
Representation in the General Assembly was altogether unequal: that also we know. But there
was a further anachronism. The General Assembly persisted in arrogating to itself judicial functions — a proceeding rendered easier by the usage
under the charter of an annual election of judicial officers.

In point of ability Dorr's address was worthy
of his Harvard training. It was perspicuous and
temperate and it dealt with each of the several elements of injustice in the Rhode Island system:
with the narrow suffrage, the unequal apportionment, and the dependent judiciary. The author's
conclusion — in the light of the provision of the
Federal Constitution guaranteeing to each State
a republican form of government — was that in
Rhode Island the form of government was not
republican and should be changed. But in reaching his conclusion he, as an idealist, advanced one
radical, one revolutionary, doctrine : namely, that
the suffrage was in no sense a political privilege
but a native and natural right. It is important

that Dorr's advocacy of this doctrine be borne
in mind, for upon it in a short time his personal
fortunes and those of his supporters were wrecked.

The plea of Dorr for a constitution was productive of no considerable effect. Time sped and there
was reached the year 1840. By that year Providence had increased in population until it numbered 23,172 souls. Warwick, Smithfield, Cumberland, North Providence, and Bristol had also
increased heavily in population. The newcomers,
both American and foreign, sympathized with the
ideas of the Dorrites or Constitutionalists in favor
of an enlarged suffrage, and through their interest
and support agitation was renewed. In January,
1840, an " Address to the Citizens of Rhode Island," printed in New York, was widely distributed;
in March " The Rhode Island Suffrage Association " was formed; and in November there appeared in Providence a suffrage newspaper, the
" New Age."

" Our first appeal," the Suffrage Association declared, " is to heaven for the justice of our cause.
Next to the whole people of Rhode Island . . .
through the medium of the ballot-box. Next to
the General Assembly of the State. These failing,
our final resort shall be to the Congress of the
United States . . . and if need be to the Supreme
Judicial Power to test the force and meaning of
that provision in the Constitution, which guaran-
tees to every State in the Union a republican form

of government." Neither by Dorr nor any other
suffragist in 1840 would it seem seriously to have
been contemplated that, in seeking to set up a government opposed to that of the charter, force might
have to be employed, and that in a conflict between
a government *de jure* and the government *de facto*,
the *de facto* government would have on its side
the immense advantage of organization, regularity,
and law, to the ultimate sanctions of imprisonment
and death.

In January, 1841, the General Assembly again
was appealed to by the suffragists to call a convention to adopt a constitution. The Assembly merely
repeated its time-worn tactics. The suffrage question it passed over, and the question of apportionment it resolved to submit for consideration to a
constitutional convention to be composed of delegates in the number of members of the General
Assembly, and, like them, chosen by the freemen
under the existing law. Disgusted with the Assembly's disingenuousness, the suffragists called a
mass meeting to be held at Providence on April
17. The meeting was a success. Three thousand
men formed themselves in civic procession to
march to the State House. Each participant wore
a badge stamped with the words, " I am an American Citizen ; " and banners were carried displaying
the mottoes : " Worth makes the Man, but Sand
and Gravel make the Voter ; " " Virtue, Patriotism and Intelligence versus $134 worth of Dirt."

At the State House a collation was served and speeches were made by ex-Congressman Dutee J. Pierce and Samuel Y. Atwell — men who as suffragist leaders stood next in prominence to Dorr himself.

On May 5 a mass meeting was held at Newport, and on July 5 such a meeting for a second time was held at Providence. At the Providence meeting resolutions were passed demanding a constitutional convention and affirming: "We will sustain and carry into effect [the proposed] constitution by all necessary means." On July 20 it was announced that a convention would be held at Providence on October 4. To this convention delegates were to be chosen by the votes (delivered on August 28) of "every American male citizen, of twenty-one years of age and upwards, who has resided in this State one year preceding the election of delegates."

Promptly on the day appointed the suffragist, or, as it now had come to be called, the People's Convention, met. On November 15, after an adjournment, it met again; and by the 18th its work was completed. The constitution which it framed sought to correct the three evils emphasized by Dorr in his address. It extended the suffrage to each white male citizen of the United States, of the age of twenty-one years, who should have resided one year in the State and six months in the town or ward where his vote should be offered. It remedied the inequitable apportionment, and it removed from the General Assembly the judicial power and the power of pardon. The instrument provided that the vote upon adoption should be taken on December 27, 28, and 29. On these days, accordingly, the vote was taken, and it was large. Thirteen thousand nine hundred and forty-four ballots were cast. Each voter had been instructed to indorse his ballot with the statement that he was a freeman or a non-freeman, as the case might be, and the indorsements disclosed a vote of 4960 freemen and of 8984 non-freemen. On January 12, 1842, the People's Convention reconvened and the returns were canvassed by a duly authorized committee. Estimating the adult males of the State qualified to vote under the People's Constitution at 23,142 (an estimate not gainsaid), the instrument had been adopted by a decisive popular majority. The claim was made that it also had been adopted by a majority of the actual freemen of the State. The final act of the convention was to proclaim the constitution in force and to send a copy of it to the governor to be communicated to the General Assembly.

Meanwhile, what concerning the convention which in January, 1841, had been decided upon by the General Assembly itself? It met on November 1, remained in session two weeks, and adjourned until February, 1842. The truth is that the convention was in sore distress. It did not know what to do regarding the suffrage. When it reconvened it found the situation to be this: The General Assembly had refused to recognize the People's Constitution, but it had resolved that those whom the Freemen's Constitution might by its terms enfranchise should be permitted to vote upon the question of adoption. Grateful for the cue, the convention on February 19 submitted a constitution abolishing the freehold qualification in the case of citizens of Rhode Island who were native Americans, and rectifying in some degree the unequal representative apportionment. Upon this constitution a vote was taken on March 21, 22, and 23, with the result that it was defeated by the narrow majority of 676.

Driven step by step by the agitation and acts of the suffragists from an attitude of uncompromising opposition to an extension of the suffrage, the General Assembly and its constitutional convention had at length granted substantially what the suffragists demanded. Why, then, was the Freemen's Constitution not adopted? Because, under the advice of Dorr, the suffragists voted against it. Feeling toward the anti-suffragists was bitter, and, moreover, the belief was still cherished that the People's Constitution itself could be put legally, and hence peaceably, into effect.

From a legal standpoint the outlook for the suffragists was not reassuring. Early in March the State Supreme Court unofficially, but none the less emphatically, let it be known that in their judgment the People's Constitution was wholly illegal, and that any attempt to proceed under it would be treason against the State. A little later (March 25) the chief justice (Job Durfee), instructing the grand jury at Bristol, asserted that the only sovereign people anywhere were the corporate people, that no change of government could anywhere legally be effected save through and by the act of the corporate people, and that if the existence of a new constitution in Rhode Island were affirmed to the Supreme Court of the United States, the question to be answered would not be who voted for it, nor how many, but what right anybody had to vote for it at all. Then, late in March, the General Assembly enacted a law (called because of its ruthlessness the " Algerine Law ") which declared all meetings for the election of State officers, other than in accordance with existing statutes, illegal and void. Penalties of fine and imprisonment were prescribed against any and all persons who should assist at such meetings or should accept from them nominations to office. Finally, about the middle of April, a letter from President John Tyler to Governor Samuel W. King of Rhode Island was published, which stated that in case of violence it would be the duty of the president " to respect the requisitions of that government which had been recognized as the existing government of the State through all time past, until he was advised in regular manner that it had been altered and abolished and another substituted in its place by legal and peaceable proceedings adopted and pursued by the authorities and people of the State."

So far as the views of the State Supreme Court were concerned, Dorr had sought to neutralize the effect of them by circulating in reply a legal opinion signed by nine lawyers of Providence (of whom he was one), asserting "that the People's Constitution is a republican form of government as required by the Constitution of the United States, and that the people of this State, in forming and in voting for the same, proceeded without any defect of law, and without violation of any law."

Under the People's Constitution there was held, on April 18, an election of State officers and of both branches of the General Assembly. Dorr himself was chosen governor, and on May 3 he was inducted into office by a great concourse, civic and military. On the same day the legislature-elect convened in a foundry building and Dutee J. Pierce was chosen temporary speaker of the house. In the presence of the house and senate Dorr delivered his inaugural address. The legislature remained in session two days. It requested the governor to make known to the president of the United States, to Congress, and to the various State governors, the fact of the adoption of a re-

publican constitution in Rhode Island, and passed
an act repealing the Algerine Law. Two things of
obvious importance the legislature failed to do.
One was to take possession of the State House
with its records, and the other was to install a new
judiciary.

•On May 4 the regular General Assembly under
the charter met at Newport and Samuel W. King,
who had been reëlected governor, was inaugurated.
The Assembly then dispatched an appeal for help
to President Tyler. A letter to the president was
dispatched also by the Dorr government; but not
content with a mere letter, Dorr personally set
forth for Washington to see the president. On the
theory of the People's governor respecting a Federal guaranty of republicanism to the States, the
Federal government of course could not do otherwise than recognize the validity of the People's
Constitution. Still the president, and likewise
the Senate, beset as they were by communications
from the charter government, might be misled ;
hence the journey of Dorr. In Washington nothing was accomplished. The president adhered
to the position assumed in his letter to Governor
King, and the Senate laid the Dorr papers upon
the table. On May 12 Dorr, on his way back
from his fruitless mission, was in New York. His
view of the suffrage as a natural right, a right so
obvious and of such magnitude as to be guaranteed
to every American State by the Constitution of the

United States, had in practice utterly collapsed. The People's governor was discouraged, and so frankly avowed himself. He could, he said, do no more ; he must hope for an act of amnesty.

Thomas W. Dorr went to Washington a pronounced reformer — a reformer dominated by an idea (as reformers are wont to be) — but not an unrecking fanatic. He returned to Providence a fanatic, not only unrecking but vehement. After May 16 there was manifest in him the rigor and relentlessness of those whose souls, disdainful of prudence, go fiercely marching on.

From his fit of depression in New York the People's governor had been roused by an unexpected and timely proffer of help. Tammany Hall had rallied to his support. Under Tammany guidance he had attended the Bowery Theatre. Under Tammany auspices he had been given a public reception. By Tammany braves and henchmen he had been escorted to the New York pier, whence he was to embark for Stonington. The demonstration last named may be found described in the New York " New Era " as " a vast civic procession which numbered thousands of our most worthy, industrious, and respectable citizens." In the New York " American " the description to be found runs thus : " We never in our lives saw a worse looking set than the governor's escort — the Five Points could not have beaten it at election. The governor sat bareheaded, looking as grave as an owl. He is a man of nerve and no mistake — any but such a person would have broken down in a fit of laughter at the absurdity of the thing."

On the whole, something more substantial than the memory of a theatre party, a reception, and a procession was carried back by Governor Dorr from New York to Rhode Island. He bore with him a written request from the colonel of the Thirteenth Regiment of New York Artillery and the lieutenant-colonel of the Two Hundred and Thirty-Sixth Regiment of New York Infantry to be permitted to attend him with their respective commands. In Providence three thousand people gathered to welcome him home, and from a carriage he delivered to them an impassioned speech. He declared that in New York he had been promised five thousand men for use against any troops that the government of the United States might send into the State, and by way of emphasizing the point he drew a sword and flourished it. During the absence of Dorr a number of participants in the People's government (Dutee J. Pierce among them) had been arrested by the charter authorities. A warrant had been issued for the arrest of Dorr, but as yet there had arisen no moment favorable for serving it.

Such was the situation when, on the afternoon of May 17, Dorr's followers by command of their leader seized some pieces of artillery. On the 17th, about midnight, these same followers — a force of perhaps two hundred and thirty-four men with two cannon — set forth under the governor to take possession of the town arsenal on Cranston Street. The structure, a stone building, was held by a guard which refused a summons to surrender, and Dorr at once unflinchingly gave orders to discharge the cannon. They had been tampered with and merely flashed twice without result. It was a foggy night; there was great confusion; alarm bells were ringing; all over the city the militia and citizens were turning out; nobody knew what to expect; nobody knew who was friend or who was foe. Suffice it to say that when day broke Dorr (who in any event was possessed of no military capacity) stood revealed a revolutionary leader abandoned by all save a handful of friends. At eight o'clock a letter was handed to him announcing the resignation of substantially his entire government, and before nine o'clock the People's governor was in flight for Connecticut.

The remainder of May and the greater part of June passed without incident. By June 25 a small force of suffragists had assembled at the village of Chepachet in the Rhode Island town of Glocester, which borders upon the Connecticut line. The spot had been chosen as a safe rendezvous for such sympathizers with the fugitive leader as were willing to fight for him, but only a few had come. Dorr himself, after an inspection of the men, their poor munitions, scant subsistence, and haphazard fortifications on Acote's Hill, disbanded them and sought again his Connecticut refuge.

Martial law in Rhode Island was proclaimed by Governor King on June 26. Arrests were freely, even indiscriminately, made. The prisons were filled. For the People's governor a reward of five thousand dollars was offered. Nobody came forward to claim it, and requisitions for the fugitive upon the governors of Connecticut and New Hampshire were not complied with. In Providence the occasion was not permitted to go unimproved by the pulpit. On May 22, the Sunday after the attack on the arsenal, Dr. Francis Wayland, president of Brown University, preached an impressive sermon; and on July 21 the Rev. Mark Tucker (Congregationalist) followed Wayland's example. A parallel has been suggested between Dorr with his youth, good birth, unusual education, and superior social position, and Tiberius Gracchus. No such parallel was sanctioned by the Rev. Mark Tucker. In his eyes young Dorr was a young Catiline, talented and mad; or, to make use of the clergyman's own illustration, "a William Lloyd Garrison propagating errors of the worst character, assailing all government, the Holy Sabbath, and the Christian Ministry."

For more than a year Dorr kept aloof from Rhode Island. At length, on October 31, 1843, he came to Providence. He was immediately ar-

rested under an indictment for high treason, and
on April 26, 1844, was brought to trial before the
State Supreme Court with Chief Justice Durfee
presiding. The trial was held at Newport — a place
other than that where the crime was alleged to
have been committed — before a jury who to a man
were, as has well been said, "Algerines and Whigs."
Samuel Y. Atwell was the principal attorney for
the prisoner, but at the time of the trial he was ill,
and Dorr, although assisted by other counsel, conducted in the main his own case. His chief reliance was upon the contention that treason could not
be committed against an individual State of the
Union. The point in 1844 was more novel than it
is to-day. It had not been illustrated by the acts
of John Brown in Virginia. The ruling of the
Rhode Island court, nevertheless, was that treason
against a State was an offense altogether possible,
and, under instructions which left nothing to the
discretion of the jury, Dorr was convicted. Sum-
ming up — with allusion to the capital failure of
the suffragist legislature to seize the opportunity
open to it in May, 1842 — his own unfortunate
career, the prisoner recited the familiar lines : —

> "There is a tide in the affairs of men,
>   Which, taken at the flood, leads on to fortune;
>   Omitted, all the voyage of their life
>   Is bound in shallows and in miseries."

Governor Dorr was sentenced by the court to

imprisonment for the term of his natural life, at hard labor, and in separate confinement. A reaction of sentiment soon set in, and in January, 1845, he was offered his freedom on condition of subscribing to an oath of allegiance to the state of Rhode Island. This offer he proudly declined to accept. In June, 1845, he was unconditionally liberated by act of the General Assembly, and in May, 1851, his civil and political rights were restored to him. On December 27, 1854, he died at the age of forty-nine years.

To the cause of enlarged suffrage, and hence to the cause of human freedom, Dorr made sacrifice of professional and political advancement, of family and social sympathy, and ultimately of life itself. The conclusion is hard to escape that much of this sacrifice was unnecessary. Success he achieved twice, — once when unable to realize that he had done so. The Freemen's Constitution was his work and his triumph. Wrung piecemeal from a reluctant legislature and equally reluctant convention, it was granted at all because of the agitation which he had instigated. In November, 1842, during his absence from the State, practically the same constitution (the one to-day in force) was resubmitted to the people and adopted. Resubmission should not have been required. Had Dorr not been primarily an idealist and doctrinaire, and secondarily a lawyer and statesman, it would not have been required. The reformer in him was his paradox, his irony. It led him to victory, but so blinded him in the moment of it as to rob his career of symmetry and spoil it by anti-climax.

Divers are the queries to which the Dorr Rebellion gives rise. What, for example, was its relation to Federal law? What was its relation to national party politics?

The first query was propounded in the judicial action, *Luther vs. Borden*, a cause which grew out of the assertion and exercise of martial law by Governor King. Martin Luther, a shoemaker of the town of Warren, had acted as moderator of a town meeting held under the People's Constitution. For this crime (by the Algerine Law it was a crime) the charter government sought to arrest him. The government failed, owing to the fact that Luther had fled to Fall River, Massachusetts, but in searching for him a squad of militia broke open his house and maltreated his family. As a citizen of Massachusetts (which he now claimed to be) Luther, in November, 1842, brought suit in the Federal court against the trespassers, and in January, 1848, the case was heard on appeal before the United States Supreme Court. Whether, as so pertinaciously maintained by Dorr, political power under the Constitution of the United States be vested in the people as a congeries of adult males, or whether it be vested in such of the people only as hold it by preëxisting law, is a point which

in this case was ably dealt with by Daniel Webster,
who, with John Whipple, was counsel for the ap-
pellees.

"Is it not obvious enough," asked Webster,
"that men cannot get together and count themselves, and say they are so many hundreds and so
many thousands, and judge of their own qualifications, and call themselves the people and set up a
government? Why, another set of men forty miles
off, on the same day, with the same propriety, with
as good qualifications, and in as large numbers,
may meet and set up another government; one
may meet at Newport and another at Chepachet,
and both may call themselves the people. What is
this but anarchy? What liberty is there here but
a tumultuary, tempestuous, violent, stormy liberty
— a sort of South American liberty, without power
except in spasms — a liberty supported by arms
to-day, crushed by arms to-morrow. Is that our
liberty?"

As for the Dorr Rebellion and national party
politics, there is a sense in which at first there was
no connection between them. The suffragists were
composed of Whigs and Democrats alike. Outside
of Rhode Island the movement was given a political bearing through the action of Tammany Hall;
action which enlisted for Dorr the lively sympathy
of Democrats such as William Cullen Bryant and
Samuel J. Tilden. Within the State, Dorrites and
Democrats, Algerines and Whigs, became respec-

tively identified after the adoption of the Constitution of 1842. It was by Whigs (chiefly) that
Dorr was brought to trial and prison ; and it was
by Democrats (after a hotly contested gubernatorial campaign) that the People's governor was
liberated. Moreover, it was by the Rhode Island
Democracy that, in 1844, the national House of
Representatives (then Democratic) was led to
make an investigation of the "rebellion" in an
attempt to discredit the course of President Tyler.

But in a deeper sense the suffrage agitation in
Rhode Island owed its inception to national party
politics. At this period the Whigs — Daniel
Webster, Joseph Story, Chancellor Kent — stood
for property as the basis of the suffrage and of the
State. The Democrats, on the other hand, — the
followers of Andrew Jackson, the man of the frontier, — stood for manhood as the basis. A struggle
between these ideas took place in most of the older
commonwealths. In Rhode Island the abrogation
of the Charter of 1663 and of the Freehold Act
of 1724 was a triumph fundamentally of the Jack-
sonian Democracy. The triumph here, though, was
marked by a feature peculiarly its own. In 1854
the General Assembly (still omnipotent) passed
an act reversing and annulling the judgment of
the Supreme Court rendered against Thomas W.
Dorr.

CHAPTER XV

THE CIVIL WAR AND AFTER

From Charter to Constitution — Survivals — Manufactures and Slavery — A Fighting Commonwealth — The Franchise — Corrupt Politics — Reform — Providence and Newport.

THE transfer of government in Rhode Island from officers elected under the Charter of 1663 to officers elected under the Constitution of 1842 was a work of extreme simplicity. On May 1, 1843, the last charter Assembly convened at the State House in Newport. On the following day the first constitutional Assembly convened in the same place, effected an organization, and adjourned. Straightway the charter Assembly reconvened, received a report of the organization of the constitutional Assembly, and adjourned *sine die*.

On May 3 installation of government under the constitution was made the occasion of a celebration by the citizens of Newport. A procession, composed of the incoming and outgoing State officers and assemblymen, the president and members of the State Historical Society, the president and officers of Brown University, and other dignitaries, formed in front of the State House and marched to the North Baptist Church. Here Cap-

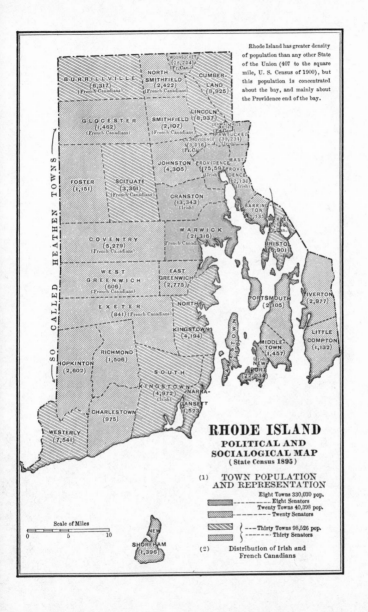

Rhode Island has greater density of population than any other State of the Union (407 to the square mile, U. S. Census of 1900), but this population is concentrated about the bay, and mainly about the Providence end of the bay.

SO CALLED HEATHEN TOWNS

BURRILLVILLE
(6,317)
(French Canadians)

WOONSOCKET
(28,204)
(Fr. Can.)

NORTH
SMITHFIELD
(2,422)
(French Canadians)

CUMBER-
LAND
(8,925)

GLOCESTER
(1,462)
(French Canadians)

SMITHFIELD
(2,107)
(French Canadians)

LINCOLN
(8,037)

PAWTUCKET
(39,231)
(Irish)

N. PROVIDENCE
(3,016)
(Fr. Can.)

FOSTER
(1,151)

SCITUATE
(3,361)
(French Canadians)

JOHNSTON
(4,305)

PROVIDENCE
(75,597)
(Irish)

EAST
PROVI-
DENCE
(2,130)

CRANSTON
(13,343)
(Irish)

WARWICK
(21,316)
(French Canadians)

BARRING-
TON
(1,135)

WARREN
(5,128)
(Fr. Can.)

BRISTOL
(6,901)
(Irish)

COVENTRY
(5,279)
(French Canadians)

WEST
GREENWICH
(606)
(French Canadians)

EAST
GREENWICH
(2,775)

NORTH

PORTSMOUTH
(2,105)

TIVERTON
(2,977)

EXETER
(841) (French Canadians)

KINGSTOWN
(4,194)

PRUDENCE ISLAND

MIDDLE-
TOWN
(1,457)
(Irish)

LITTLE
COMPTON
(1,132)

HOPKINTON
(2,602)

RICHMOND
(1,506)

SOUTH

NEW-
PORT
(22,034)

KINGSTOWN
(4,972)
(Irish)

NARRA-
GANSETT
(1,523)

CHARLESTOWN
(975)

WESTERLY
(7,541)

Scale of Miles

0   5   10

NEW
SHOREHAM
(1,396)

RHODE ISLAND
POLITICAL AND
SOCIALOGICAL MAP
(State Census 1895)

(1)   TOWN POPULATION
AND REPRESENTATION

Eight Towns 330,030 pop.
———— Eight Senators
Twenty Towns 40,398 pop.
———— Twenty Senators

} ——— Thirty Towns 98,526 pop.
———— Thirty Senators

(2)   Distribution of Irish and
French Canadians

tain David M. Coggeshall of Newport (a descendant of John Coggeshall, the first president of Providence Plantations) brought forth the identical box
in which the Charter of 1663 had been conveyed
across the Atlantic by "Captyne George Baxter,"
and for the last time the venerated instrument was
"held up on hygh and presented to the perfect
view of the people." The principal feature of the
exercises at the church was an oration by William
G. Goddard. The orator — something of a reactionary — extolled the days of charter rule. "Then,"
proudly declared he, "the men who governed the
State owned the State." "Can we pass, my fellow
citizens," he asked, "without emotions allied to
filial sorrow, from under the beneficent dominion
of the old charter — the oldest constitutional
charter in the world? — the charter under which
"Hopkins and Ellery affixed their signatures to
the immortal Declaration of American Independence;" under which "the Rhode Island line
stood foremost in fighting the battles of liberty;"
under which "this State joined the Confederacy
established by the glorious old thirteen;" under
which "Rhode Island by the adoption of the
American Constitution added the last link to that
chain of more perfect union which binds these
States together?"

In getting rid (even by help of a Dorr) of a frame
of polity sanctioned by observance during one hun-

dred and eighty years, it was well-nigh inevitable
that some of the separatism of the age of Roger
Williams (when the charter originated) should be
carried into the era of the new régime — the era
of unification and manufactures. In part what
was carried was separatism modified ; in part it
was separatism intensified. In the continued itin-
erancy of the General Assembly, in the yet narrow
suffrage, in the yet unequal representation, and in
the yet anomalous position of the judiciary, there
was separatism ; but it was separatism of an ameliorated kind. Not for many years had the Assembly been wont to meet at Portsmouth and Warwick, but down to 1843 it had met regularly at
some point in each of the five counties of Newport,
Providence, Washington, Bristol, and Kent. Now
(1854) its meeting places were restricted to Newport and Providence. Hitherto the suffrage had
been perquisite to the ownership of a freehold or
to the relationship of first born son to one distinguished by such ownership. Now it was open to
adult males who were native Americans, with the
saving limitation that only the possessors of one
hundred and thirty-four dollars' worth of land
might vote on questions of taxation. Hitherto
representation in the lower house had been the arbitrary device, — six from Newport ; four from
Providence, Portsmouth, and Warwick ; and two
from each of the other towns. Now representation
was based on population ; but membership of the

house might never exceed a total of seventy-two, and to no single town was there to be accorded membership in excess of one sixth of the total. The judiciary hitherto had been slavishly dependent upon the legislature. Now the members at least held office during good behavior and at a fixed minimum remuneration.

Where, under the new régime, an intensification of separatism was to be remarked was in the form of the senate and in the rule for amending the constitution. Under the charter, the upper house had been composed of ten members chosen by general ticket — ten members at large. Under the constitution, senators — after the precedent set in the case of the Federal system — were alloted one to each political unit [town].[1] Under the charter (subsequent to the Revolution) amendment had been obtainable by vote of a simple majority of the qualified people. Under the constitution (in view of

[1] The organization of the Rhode Island senate has found its strongest justification in the argument that in Rhode Island (a diminutive State) it is essential to keep political power in the hands of the rural districts as an offset to the economic power of the growing municipality of Providence (W. P. Sheffield, *The Mode of Altering the Constitution of Rhode Island*, pp. 40–41). One thing, however, this argument overlooks, and that is that in human affairs power of whatever kind should be conceded a due share of political responsibility. The principle, it is true, is not recognized in the organization of the senate of the United States, but the question arises whether a senate for a continental area is a fit archetype for one for an area strictly limited and local. It is not without suggestiveness that even a continental area has its corrupt burroughs — its Nevadas and Delawares.

the results wrought by simple majorities through
Thomas W. Dorr) amendment was only to be obtained by vote of the qualified people in a majority
of three fifths.

Survivals — the survivals recounted above — constitute the most significant fact in the later history
of Rhode Island. It is in the light of them that the
politics of the State, both legitimate and debased,
are to be understood. One after another they have
yielded to the power of the uncongenial age into
which they have been brought; but they have
yielded slowly and in no case without a struggle.
The first to yield was legislative surveillance of the
judiciary.

Athwart the face of the judgment recorded
against Thomas W. Dorr the General Assembly
in 1854 ordered to be written, "Reversed and annulled." The succeeding Assembly asked of the
Supreme Court its opinion of the constitutionality
of this act, and received in reply, through Chief
Justice Richard W. Greene, the statement that the
particular act was unconstitutional, but that the
long-continued exercise by the Assembly of judicial functions derived a kind of sanction through
acquiescence. Once again had the Rhode Island
judiciary receded from before the legislature. It,
however, was for the last time. In 1856 there came
up for determination the case of *Taylor vs. Place*,
a case in which an appeal to the General Assembly

had been entertained. The chief justice now was
Samuel Ames, a man of wide legal learning, of
marked judicial talent, and of a personal presence
not unlike that of Salmon P. Chase. In the opinion
which he proceeded to render he set forth fully the
nature of judicial power, pointed out that the Constitution of 1842 vested such power in "one"
Supreme Court with appropriate inferior courts,
and voiced the irresistible conclusion that it was the
whole and not a part of judicial power which thus
had been conferred. It remained for the legislature to confess the correctness of Ames's position.
The confession was not made at once. Not until
1860, in the case of *Hazard vs. Ives*, did the legislature after an elaborate debate tacitly and, as it
were, sullenly lay down a power which it had exercised from the earliest days, and in defense of
which it had ventured to antagonize both the Earl
of Bellomont and Queen Anne.

Two other matters of importance claimed the attention of Rhode Islanders at this period: manufactures and the question of African slavery. By
1840 (owing to a tariff, to steam, and to the power
loom) the cotton manufacture had become thoroughly established. After that year cotton was confronted by a rival industry in woolens — a manufacture identified in origin with the energetic Hazards
of Peacedale, and with the ingenious and versatile
Zachariah Allen. Implements and machinery, now,

too, were notable local industries. In the time of
the Revolution, Pawtucket, Providence, and other
towns had been centres for the production of cannon and small arms. By 1794 Elijah Ormsbee
and David Wilkinson, the latter a brother of the
wife of Samuel Slater (she of the laughing eyes),
had invented a steamboat which would run, and by
1849 George H. Corliss of Providence had invented
the Corliss engine. The cotton and woolen industries, the manufacture of tools and implements, and
the fabrication of jewelry (an industry which from
1810 to 1857 had steadily augmented in importance)
made Rhode Island, and especially Providence with
its 50,000 souls, a point of exceeding interest by
1860.

Toward the question of slavery in the South, the
attitude of Rhode Island was neither more nor less
advanced than that of New England in general.
After 1820, when the slave trade was declared
piracy, Newport and Bristol by degrees declined its
fascinations, and the sentiment of the State — dictated by the industrialism of Providence — became
a sentiment increasingly for freedom. The Mexican
War was not liked, but the temptation to rejoice
over the victories of General Zachary Taylor at
Palo Alto and Resaca de la Palma proved too great
to be resisted. Atonement was sought to be made
by legislative resolutions condemnatory of the war
and of President Polk for inaugurating it. The
electoral vote of the State, which in 1852 had been

cast for Franklin Pierce, was given in 1856 to John C. Fremont. In 1854 State officers were forbidden to lend aid in the rendition of fugitive slaves, and in 1859 the people were profoundly stirred by the raid of John Brown.

Not long after the raid in question, Abraham Lincoln (February 28, 1860) delivered a political speech in Providence; and not long after the Lincoln speech Stephen A. Douglas (August 2, 1860) was given an ovation and a "clam bake" at Rocky Point. Lincoln's thesis was the memorable one, "This government cannot permanently endure half slave and half free." "He abounds in good humor and pleasant satire," was the comment of the Providence "Journal," "and often gives a witty thrust that cuts like a Damascus blade." At the Douglas ovation, the little giant took occasion to observe that one of his ancestors on the maternal side [an Arnold] had been an associate of Roger Williams, and that the latter was really the first American "squatter sovereign."

In spite of its Quakers, Rhode Island may accurately be described as a fighting commonwealth. It preferred at first to fight upon the sea, but as far back as the Canadian and Cuban expeditions of the early eighteenth century it fought with conspicuous bravery on land. In the war of the Revolution the doughtiness of the Rhode Island line at Monmouth, Long Island, Red Bank, Princeton, and Trenton, under leaders such as Christopher Lippitt, Israel Angell, and Christopher C. Greene, was proverbial, and the war for the Union showed that in martial spirit there had been no decline. William Sprague was elected governor in 1860, and before the inauguration of Abraham Lincoln he offered to President Buchanan the use of the Rhode Island militia for the defense of the national capital and for the maintenance of the Constitution and laws. After Lincoln's inauguration and the outbreak of actual war, the military efforts of the State were unceasing until the restoration of peace in 1865. During this interval there were sent into the field 23,457 men, — a force comprising eight regiments of infantry,[1] three of cavalry, three of heavy artillery, and one regiment of light artillery. The force was in excess of the quota of the State; it was greater in proportion to population than that sent into the field by any other State save perhaps one, and its cost was $6,500,772. No part of it was raised by conscription. To conscription the individualism of the people was unalterably opposed.

[1] As in the Revolution, so in the war for the Union Rhode Island raised a regiment of colored troops. An attempt to form such a regiment was made in 1861, but only a few enlistments were secured. In 1863 a second attempt was made which resulted in the formation of the Fourteenth Rhode Island, a regiment of heavy artillery. The regiment cost nearly a million of dollars in bounties, showed little physical endurance, and was made the object of systematic frauds.

Unlike the war of the Revolution, the Civil War was fought at points wholly beyond the jurisdiction of the Narragansett Bay commonwealth. None of the operations, therefore, call for detailed consideration. Rhode Island troops were with Grant before Vicksburg, and helped contest the bloody actions of Antietam, Fredericksburg, Gettysburg, and those of the Wilderness Campaign. The most prominent officer whom the State gave to the conflict was General Ambrose E. Burnside. He fought as a colonel at Bull Run; led in 1862 the "Burnside Expedition" against North Carolina; commanded, the same year, the Ninth Army Corps, and the Army of the Potomac before Fredericksburg; and in 1863, in Ohio, promulgated the orders which resulted in the arrest of Clement L. Vallandigham. His subsequent service was with the Ninth Corps under Generals Meade and Grant. Burnside was a native of Indiana, but his wife was from Providence, and to Rhode Island, his adopted State, he devoted his life and talents as warrior, governor, and United States senator. Rhode Island, it has been said, preferred originally to fight upon the sea. It so preferred until after the War of 1812. With the decline, first, of privateering, then of the slave trade, and finally of legitimate commerce itself, there supervened (along with the rise of manufactures) a comparative indifference to the sea. Owing to this indifference it perchance was that the commonwealth

which in the Old French War had kept a large
quota in the royal navy, and fifteen hundred men
on board of privateers, contributed to the navy in
the war for the Union 480 men.

Distrust of delegated power had made it hard
for Rhode Island to ratify the Federal Constitution. A like distrust made it hard for the State to
put aside the Charter of King Charles II in favor
of the Constitution of 1842, and in the case of
the Constitution of 1842 made it hard to secure
amendments. The amendment chiefly desired was
one eliminating the separatist survival which withheld from naturalized citizens, not possessed of a
freehold, the privilege of voting. Already the survival which kept the judiciary under surveillance
had been gotten rid of; but it had not been gotten
rid of by amendment to the constitution. In fact,
down to the time of the Civil War, the only amendments adopted had been three: one taking the
registration of voters out of the hands of the towns;
one investing the governor with the pardoning
power; and one shortening the itinerary of the
General Assembly.[1]

After 1842 it had been the Democrats that had

[1] On April 7, 1886, there was adopted an amendment (the Fifth)
prohibiting the manufacture and sale of intoxicating liquors to be
used as a beverage. By a further amendment (the Eighth) adopted
June 20, 1889, Amendment five was annulled. For the history of
liquor legislation in Rhode Island see J. H. Stiness, *Two Centuries
of Rhode Island Legislation against Strong Drink*, 1882.

advocated an extension of the suffrage to the foreign born. After 1842 it had been the Whigs that
had declared peril to lurk in a suffrage that was
undiscriminating. Force, now, was imparted to
the declaration of the Whigs by an arrival of
Irish immigrants — people poor, untutored, and
driven from home by famine. In 1854 the Whig
party began to disintegrate, but the fact proved
to be little to the advantage of the Democrats.
On the ruins of the Whig organization there arose
that of Know-Nothingism. The Know-Nothings
were the "A. P. A." of their day. They were
for America for the Americans. In Rhode Island,
therefore, they were against Irishmen and Catholics, and by a sweeping victory at the polls in 1855
put a temporary check to agitation in favor of
widening the suffrage. In 1862 and 1863, however, when the Republican party was in control of
the legislature, serious effort was made to secure
for soldiers and sailors who had been naturalized
in Rhode Island the privilege of voting. The effort
met with failure, and was not renewed with success
until 1886.

Yet even in Rhode Island the trend of the age
toward manhood suffrage was not permanently to
be stayed. In 1871, and again in 1876, the question of enfranchising foreign-born citizens was
submitted to the people, and in 1878 a systematic
and determined scheme of agitation was put in
operation. The difficulty was not to obtain a ma-

jority vote in behalf of the naturalized foreigner.
It was to obtain a majority vote of three fifths.
The situation was not unlike what it had been in
1840, when Dorr began his memorable crusade.
The powerholders — the legally qualified electors
— would not yield the boon desired. A three fifths
majority, it was averred, never could be secured.
What recourse was left? The same that in 1840
was left to the Dorrites, — either a new State
constitution or interposition by the Federal government.

At first interposition by the Federal government was sought. In 1878 Charles E. Gorman
(a naturalized citizen of the United States for
nearly forty years, and since 1848 a citizen of
Rhode Island) presented a memorial to the Senate and House of Representatives claiming for the
subscribers the privilege of the suffrage in Rhode
Island under the Fourteenth and Fifteenth Amendments to the Constitution of the United States.
Said the memorial: "The naturalization laws of
the United States are, within the State of Rhode
Island, nullified. . . . The naturalized citizens,
who have renounced claim to the protection of the
country of their origin, and either are, or are entitled to be, citizens of the United States, are rendered, unless in exceptional cases, utterly alien to
the institutions of their adopted country." In the
Senate the memorial was referred to the judiciary
committee, but the report upon it was unfavorable.

If, observed Senator Edmunds, chairman of the committee, voting were one of the privileges or immunities of citizens of the United States as such, it must be a privilege or immunity of all citizens, male and female, infants, lunatics, and criminals.

Having failed with the Federal government, the Gormanites devoted every energy to the task of securing a new constitution. And here the parallel between them and their predecessors the Dorrites is of special interest. Like the Dorrites, the Gormanites contended that the right and power of framing a constitution was, in every State, a right and power inherent in the people, and that it was not limited in the mode of its exercise by provisions of the existing constitution with regard to mere amendment. On one point, however, the Gormanites stopped short of their predecessors. They did not assert a right in the people of creating a new constitution regardless of the legislature. The General Assembly must take the initial step, must submit to the people the question, Shall a constitutional convention be called?

In 1880 there was formed an Equal Rights Association, prominent in which, besides Charles E. Gorman, were Abraham Payne and Dr. L. F. C. Garvin. The question of a new constitution was urged upon the attention of the legislature, and even in Congress agitation was renewed. By some members of the national House and Senate it was proposed in 1881 to reduce the congressional representation of Rhode Island under that clause of the Fourteenth Amendment which prescribes reduction for denying the right to vote to male citizens of the United States twenty-one years of age. But Rhode Island's senior senator, Henry B. Anthony, who had represented the State in the Federal upper house since 1859, was able to show in an elaborate speech that, counting against the State two thousand naturalized citizens disqualified as voters, the population was still sufficient to command the existing representation.

In the General Assembly, despite the defeat of successive proposals to submit the question of a constitutional convention, sentiment was disturbed. Accordingly in 1883 the senate asked of the Supreme Court its opinion regarding the power of the Assembly to submit such a question. The court unanimously replied that the power of the legislature, under the Constitution of 1842, was limited to proposing specific amendments, each of which required a three fifths majority of the electors for its ratification. By this opinion the purposes of the Gormanites — the neo-Dorrites — seemed to be definitely and finally set at naught. The situation found effective summary and burlesque in a squib : —

" Alas ! what a pity our fathers did n't mention,
   That we boys, if very good, could hold a convention.

They never said we should n't but did n't say we might,
' Ergo,' cry the sages, ' you have n't got the right.'
'T was very bad, indeed, their permission to deny,
But infinitely worse at once to up and die ;
For thus they turned the lock and flung away the key,
And Rhode Island's ' in a box ' for all eternitee."

But it is the unexpected that happens, and in 1888, on a further submission to the electors of the proposition to amend the State constitution by granting the suffrage to naturalized citizens, there was cast an affirmative vote in a majority of three fifths.

By the amendment of 1888 there was eliminated in Rhode Island the last but one (the dual capital) of those separatist survivals from the age of Roger Williams which were carried in ameliorated form into the Constitution of 1842. It was otherwise with the survivals which were of the nature of separatism intensified — town representation in the senate and the three fifths majority requirement for amending the constitution. The contest over these particular survivals (the corrupt politics contest) had in 1888 only just begun ; nor is it yet finished.

The history of corrupt politics in Rhode Island is curious, interesting, and suggestive. In the seventeenth century as early as 1649 it was found necessary by Providence Plantations to pass an act in restraint of fraudulent voting, and in 1666 (under the charter) a penalty of five pounds was prescribed against voting on the part of persons who were not freemen. In the eighteenth century — between 1710 and 1750, the paper money era — fraudulent voting and bribery were both practiced with extreme boldness. A law of 1715 required each freeman to indorse his ballot with his full name, and made illegal voting punishable by a fine of five pounds, by not to exceed twenty stripes, or by imprisonment for one month. After 1724 voters were required to be owners, each, of a freehold in the value of one hundred pounds, or to be the eldest sons of such owners ; but admission to freemanship was through the towns, and a landed neighbor was apt (for a consideration) to be willing to accommodate an unlanded one with the loan of a freehold until after election. In 1730, therefore, an act against fraudulent representations became necessary, one (in 1736 and 1738) supplemented by acts which prescribed for illegal voting the penalty of fine and suspension of electoral privileges for three years. Because of the depreciation of the currency, these various enactments were in 1742 followed by a law raising the nominal freehold qualification to two hundred pounds ; and by a law in 1746 raising it to four hundred pounds and decreeing that the election of a candidate should be invalidated by a single vote that was fraudulent. It was not until 1762 — twelve years after the interposition of Parliament — that it was deemed practicable to restore the original freehold qualification by lowering the nominal one to forty pounds. Nor even then did there come a cessation of fraud in elections. Throughout the period of the Hopkins-Ward controversy, which did not end until 1768, votes (especially in Narragansett) were bought quite systematically; and in 1790 ratification of the Federal Constitution is said to have been secured through purchased votes — those of delegates from " back towns." [1]

In the nineteenth century, after the town of Providence had attained a population of 23,000, it there became a practice on the part of dishonest freeholders to divide up tracts into house lots, and by conveying the lots for a limited time to accomplices — transactions evidenced by the notes-of-hand of the grantees — to multiply their electoral power many fold. With the rise to colossal wealth of divers individuals, just before the Civil War, the practice of influencing votes directly by money is again brought to notice. Since the war, in connection with the growth of the Republican political machine, the practice has become ingrained and widespread — a scandal of a magnitude that is portentous.

What, however, in the history of political degeneracy in Rhode Island is most noteworthy is the intimate connection maintained between that degeneracy and the rural districts. When, in the

---

[1] In this connection Rider's *Book Notes*, vol. xiii, p. 182, should be consulted.

eighteenth century, Rhode Island began to grow distinctly commercial and coöperative, the agriculturalists began as much as possible to withdraw themselves ; to erect between themselves and the urban centres barriers. These barriers were town lines. Between 1700 and 1800 twenty-one towns were created, many of them avowedly for the reason that (as stated in 1765 in the petition for the creation of North Providence) "the petitioners are near all farmers whose interest and business differ from the merchants." Thus barricaded, thus withdrawn and secluded, the country towns (not only in the eighteenth century but also in the nineteenth) became the stronghold of corruption.

The specific spots in rural Rhode Island where political corruption most prevails are the towns of Burrillville, Coventry, East Greenwich, Exeter, Foster, Glocester, Narragansett,[1] New Shoreham (Block Island), North Kingstown, North Providence, North Smithfield, Scituate, Smithfield, and West Greenwich. Of these towns six — Burrillville, Glocester, Foster, Coventry, West Greenwich, and Exeter — are on the Connecticut border, and are called significantly "heathen." Seven towns — Exeter, Foster, Glocester, North Smithfield, Scituate, Smithfield, and West Greenwich — are losing

---

[1] Narragansett, which comprises that portion of South Kingstown lying east of the Pettiquamscutt River, was created an administrative district on March, 22, 1888. The privilege of representation in the General Assembly was conferred upon it on March 28, 1901.

steadily in population, and are called "dying"
towns.[1] Indeed, Exeter, Foster, and West Greenwich have to-day each less population than they
had in 1790. Neither of them supports a resident
clergyman, and the three (along with Burrillville,
North Smithfield, and Smithfield) are handicapped
by superstition, ignorance, and certain forms of
immorality.

It would be an easy explanation were one at
liberty to ascribe the aforementioned conditions
primarily to the insidious influence of the State
machine, but to do this one is not at liberty. The
separatism of the Rhode Island agriculturalist —
due chiefly to an individualistic bent transmitted
from the age of Roger Williams — furnished to
the machine its opportunity. It furnished it, first,
with a senate so organized (upon separatist principles) as to be controllable through the control of a
few small electorates. It furnished it, second, with
electorates not only small but, through seclusion,
burdened with an ignorance and predisposition
to vice ancient enough to have been bewailed by
Roger Williams, Governor John Carver of Plymouth, and Governor John Winthrop, Jr., of Connecticut. It never is safe to indict a whole people,
nor, for that matter, the whole of any one class. It

[1] The Rhode Island State census of 1905 (now nearly completed) is expected to show little or no recovery on the part of the
dying towns. Providence (175,000 souls in 1900) should reach
190,000 in 1905.

therefore, perhaps, is rash to assert that the agriculturalists — the farmers — of Rhode Island are, as a class, corrupt in a political sense, or even corruptible; although the town of Coventry, which contains 5279 souls, and which in point of social morality stands well, has come to be thoroughly debauched politically. What reasonably may be asserted is, that in Rhode Island — a State cut up into small towns, each (regardless of population) possessed of a vote in the senate — there have been found with no great difficulty corruptible farmers in numbers sufficient to serve machine ends. Primarily it is to separatism — a survivalistic idea and habit wrought relentlessly into a system — that the political degradation of Rhode Island to-day is to be ascribed.

Since 1888 (the year of the adoption of the suffrage amendment) the task of the political reformer in Rhode Island has been that not of reforming decadent rural towns, or even of transforming them, but of destroying the system engrafted upon them. Under this system 330,030 (seventy-seven per cent) of the 428,556 inhabitants of the State constitute eight cities and towns, and are represented in the senate by eight members; while 98,526 (twenty-three per cent) constitute thirty towns, and are represented in the senate by thirty members. One section of population (a section 175,000 strong and with 29,030 qualified

voters — the section which constitutes the urban
division, Providence) is accorded one senator;
while another section (one 40,398 strong and with
5620 qualified voters — the section which constitutes twenty rural divisions) is accorded twenty
senators.

Prior to the adoption of the suffrage amendment, the hope of the Rhode Island reformer centred in the plan of a new constitution to be framed
and adopted by a convention of delegates chosen
upon a basis of population, and acting through a
simple majority. But the opinion of the Supreme
Court in 1883 denying the right of the General
Assembly to submit to the people so much even as
the question of a convention, coupled with the circumstance that in 1888 there was actually obtained
for an amendment so radical as that for an enlarged suffrage a three fifths majority, weakened
the convention plan. In 1897, therefore, when the
reformer again was urging his demand for constitutional betterment, he was forced to confine himself to asking from the Assembly the submission
to the people of an instrument in the form of an
amendment to the existing constitution, and, as
such, subject to defeat even though desired by a
majority.

During the year 1897 a new constitution was
draughted, but in the draughting the senate of
course took part, and although Dr. L. F. C. Garvin
earnestly pleaded for a section reorganizing the

senate on a basis of thirty-six members, to be
chosen from three senatorial districts on the principle of proportional representation, the old provision, " one senator from each town or city," was
left undisturbed. The proposed constitution nevertheless was an advance upon the Constitution of
1842. It vested the governor with a qualified
power of veto; it increased the membership of the
house of representatives from seventy-two to one
hundred, one fourth of which might be held by one
town (Providence); it provided for the adoption
of amendments by a majority vote of the electors;
and it provided for the submission to the people
every twentieth year, beginning with 1910, of the
question, " Shall there be a convention to revise
the constitution?" But when in 1898, and again in
1899, the instrument was tendered to the electors,
it was rejected; the rejection of 1899 being not only
by a majority but by a majority that was emphatic.

Thus far there has been little to show that
Rhode Island (including Block Island) has begun
to abandon venal politics and to dispense with
venal politicians, yet something has been accomplished. In 1902 Dr. Garvin — a Democrat — was
elected governor in protest against the Republican
State machine, and in 1903 he was reëlected.
Under the Constitution (that of 1842) and rules
adopted by the senate, a Democratic governor was
powerless. He could veto no bill; he could secure
the confirmation of no appointee. One thing, how-

ever, he could do: make in his official capacity a
revelation to the State and nation of the conditions politically which obtained about him. Accordingly, in March, 1903, Governor Garvin sent
to the General Assembly a special message on
bribery at elections. The document was treated
with scant respect by senators and representatives,
but it reached the ear of the nation and also to
some extent the ear of Rhode Island. Said the
Providence " Journal " on the day after the message
was submitted: " The blame for the present order
of things . . . belongs with the educated manu-
facturers and business men of the State who are
too busy making money to pay attention to political conditions." [1]

As has been observed, survivalistic separatism
is the fact in Rhode Island worthiest of note since
the Civil War. Other noteworthy facts are the
growth of foreign immigration and the economic,
educational, and social development of Providence
and Newport.

[1] In 1904 there was formed the Rhode Island Citizens Union,
an organization having for its object a convention to revise the
existing State constitution. In March, 1905, the Union secured a
hearing before the senate committee on special legislation, and on
May 4 it addressed to the committee a letter proposing a constitutional convention to be chosen on the basis of a hypothetical
membership of one hundred in the house of representatives. As
an alternative the Union offered to .support an amendment to the
constitution providing for a constitutional convention in 1906.
Nothing was done by the Assembly.

Since 1848 the Irish have been a strong invading element, and since 1880 the Canadian French. Indeed, within the last two decades the influx of the French has been phenomenal. As a result, over thirty per cent of the population of the State in 1900 (134,519 souls out of a total of 428,556) were foreign born. In the case of the Irish, immigration is a fact not especially significant. The people ally themselves readily with the native and other stocks, and they are not discouragingly illiterate. The towns in which they congregate — Bristol, Newport, Cranston, East Providence, Pawtucket, Providence, and South Kingstown — are among the thriftiest and most exemplary of all the towns. On the other hand, the Canadian French by their presence give rise to a problem. They do not amalgamate with other stocks; they are highly illiterate ; and the rural towns in which they preponderate among the foreigners — Warren, Coventry, Warwick, West Greenwich, Burrillville, Glocester, North Providence, North Smithfield, Scituate, Smithfield, and Exeter — are among the Rhode Island towns socially and politically most in disrepute.

Not that the Canadian French as such are degenerate. In Woonsocket, where they abound, morals and politics are excellent. The trouble with them is that wherever, as in the worst rural towns, they are brought as mill operatives into contact with a decadent American stock, they contribute to degeneracy by failing to withstand it. By temperament (save as to language and the domestic relation) they are a conformable race. They look to the Anglo-Saxon. Education, combined with an environment of wholesome politics, would beyond any reasonable doubt bring them effectually under the great Anglo-Saxon tradition.

Providence in 1860 was a city of 50,000 souls. In 1905 it is a city of 190,000 souls. Between these extremes of date and population much is comprehended. Industries have become greatly diversified. Woolen goods as an article of manufacture have taken precedence of cotton goods. Silverware, rubber commodities, and malt liquors have been added to the list of leading industrial products. In 1901, moreover, there was completed in Providence, at a cost of $3,000,000, a new State Capitol building. It is a structure of white marble, classic in design, and commanding in location. Just prior to its occupation there was adopted a constitutional amendment dispensing with sessions of the General Assembly at Newport. The long standing separatist survival of a dual capital has thus been eliminated.

In an educational respect Providence possesses features quite as remarkable as are its vast and varied manufactures. Brown University — exceptional in its traditions of a Francis Wayland, an Albert Harkness, a J. Lewis Diman, and an E. Benjamin Andrews ; of a Horace Mann, a Henry

Wheaton, a Richard Olney, and a John Hay — has grown steadily in equipment and importance. Its buildings now number more than a score, and its graduates are to be found in every State. Next to it in importance rank the Friends', or Moses Brown, School (an institution dating from 1819), the State School of Design (1877), and the State Normal School, admirably complete since 1898. Then there are the seven Providence libraries : the Athenæum (rich in the ownership of Malbone's "Hours"), the library of Brown University, the library of the Rhode Island Historical Society, the Providence Public Library, the John Carter Brown Library, the State Library, and the State Law Library. Of these the Athenæum is an outgrowth of the library established in 1750 by Stephen Hopkins, and the Brown University and John Carter Brown collections are memorials of the enlightened generosity of John Carter Brown, son and grandson, respectively, of the two Nicholas Browns, the principal benefactors of Brown University. The John Carter Brown collection is special in character, embracing Americana antedating the year 1800. In 1904 it was removed from the Brown residence on Benefit Street to a noble structure of the Greek order built especially for its use on the University campus.

To one limitation Providence finds it difficult to become habituated — that of inferiority as a seaport. Situated at the head of a charming and navigable bay, its ships between 1804 and 1806 brought home the spoil of the Indies ; and even as late as the period 1822–1825 its foreign commerce was almost equal to what it had been at the end of 1806. In the conversion of Providence from a mart to a producing centre three stages have been traversed : first (1787–1825) the stage in which the town, by reason of a position interior from the coast and by reason of the absence of competing canals and railways, was a natural distributing point westward to the Hudson ; second (1829–1840) the stage in which, by reason of embargoes and tariffs and of competing canals and waterways, the town was forced into production as a substitute for commerce ; and third (1840–1900) the stage in which, by reason of inferior railway communications with the great exporting regions of the West, it has been left behind by New York on the one hand, and by Boston on the other.

As early as 1796 it was realized by John Brown that Providence must hasten to avail itself of artificial waterways as a means of commercial stimulus, and the Blackstone Canal northward into Massachusetts was projected. But the work was deferred, and when in 1828 it at length was completed, the era of railways was at hand to render it useless. Yet to-day Providence possesses a coastwise trade in coal, lumber, and building materials that far exceeds in value and in the tonnage of the shipping employed the direct foreign trade of the period 1787–1825. Presumably with this not unsatisfactory showing local ambition will need long to be content.

Providence since the war has advanced industrially. Newport during the same period has continued its social advance.[1] But as a resort the Newport of the twentieth century is a place different far from the Newport of 1840 or 1860. The little harbor town, sustained by the patronage of the South and by that of its own sons, the little town dwelt upon so lovingly and oft by the pen of George William Curtis, has been replaced by a Newport sustained by patronage from a more opulent source.

The southerners of the eighteenth and early nineteenth centuries hired such Newport dwellings or lodgings as they could find. Between 1835 and 1840 gentlemen from Charleston and Savannah began building cottages on Bellevue Avenue, Narragansett Avenue, and the Old Beach Road. In 1844 the Ocean House was erected on Bellevue Avenue, and thenceforth, until 1861, the social life of Newport was both a cottage and hotel life, the latter hardly less fashionable than the former. The Ocean House was destroyed by fire in 1845, but it was at once rebuilt, and in 1846 it was in the hey-

---

[1] For a class comprehending both cottagers and hotel patrons Narragansett Pier in Narragansett and Watch Hill in Westerly have, since the Civil War, become prominent Rhode Island resorts.

day of its prominence. It possessed a wide veranda, was pierced by a corridor 252 feet long, and its chambers were spacious and high. On August 31, 1846, the hotel was the scene of a characteristic function — a magnificent ball. There were present three hundred guests at ten dollars a ticket. Dancing continued from half-past nine in the evening until four o'clock in the morning. It was described as "a medley of quadrilles, waltzes, polkas, and what is more delightful still, the redowa, an entirely new and perfectly bewitching dance." Bewitching, indeed (not to say excruciating), must have been life at the Ocean House in 1846 to be described as it was by the correspondent of the Providence "Gazette:" "We are well catered for by the musical world," he wrote. "Miss Northall — the plump Miss Northall — the charming throstle-throated Miss Northall — has delighted us with her vocal melody, while De Bignis — the big De Bignis — the prominent, aquiline-nosed De Bignis — has almost been the death of us with his Italian comicalities."

By 1852 the building of cottages at Newport had become an active pursuit. There now were twelve costly ones in existence, four owned by citizens of Boston, and eight by southerners. In the winter of 1853–54 more than sixty were erected. Among the owners were August Belmont, W. S. Wetmore, John Carter Brown, Alexander Van Rensselaer, Charlotte Cushman, Charles H. Rus-

sell, Peter Parker, Samuel Ward, Sara P. Cleve-
land, and H. Hunnewell. In 1852 Bellevue Avenue was extended to Bailey's Beach, and the same
year the sales of land by the principal agent of the
town reached $435,000. Between 1851 and 1879
the sales by this agent amounted to $13,746,000.
In 1860 the sales were $508,000; in 1863 $900,-
000; in 1864 $1,100,000; in 1871 $1,532,000; in
1872 $1,451,000; and in 1878 $791,000.

In an article printed in 1879 in the Providence
"Journal" it is stated that fifty thousand dollar
Newport cottages were then common, that a good
many cost over $100,000, and a select few $200,-
000. " Every known and unknown order of architecture was represented. The styles of old Germany
and of modern France, of Switzerland and Italy,
of England and the isles of the sea, were faithfully
reproduced." " Many of the cottages," to quote
again from the article mentioned, " are embowered
among trees, shrubs, and flowering plants. Borders
are cut so as to give the idea of deep vistas, and
hedges inclose beautiful lawns. Standing out in
bold relief are trees like the elm, the oak, and the
sugar maple. . . . Hidden among arbors and trel-
lises are spacious conservatories where flowers forever bloom; and graperies where delicious fruits
are ripened almost at will. Nectarines, apricots,
peaches, and figs grow in the graperies. Tiny
dwarf trees are set in pots, and when ripened fruit
hangs on the branches, the trees are placed upon

the dining-table that the guests may pluck the growing fruit themselves."

But the pastime of luxurious dining was but one Newport pastime of many. There were sports — polo and lacrosse ; there was bathing at Bailey's and Easton's beaches ; there was driving up the island, and, on "fort days," to Fort Adams. But more than anything else there was driving in full regalia in Bellevue Avenue. For what the Pincian was (and is) to the Roman, or the Park to the Londoner, or the *Bois* to the Parisian, that was (and is) Bellevue Avenue to the cottager at Newport.[1]

Between the Newport of 1879 and that of 1905

[1] " Newport is all shingle and clapboard, with a lot of pretentious wooden houses each on its little acre, or half-acre, of land, and subject each to the supervision of at least one neighbor. There is no such thing as privacy, and nobody seems to desire it. The great thing is to drive every day up and down the Avenue, as it is called, which is a loose line of wooden cottages with board ornamentation, or to bathe from the beach or to go on Saturday evening to the ' Ocean House ' to dance. The air is sirocco cooled off by the sea. Yesterday we went out on a yachting party — Commodore Stevens's yacht — The Maria — and had a charming sail in the bay. . . . There were two young girls, — one-inch-one in the waist and half-an-inch in the arms, and rather attractive notwithstanding ! In the evening, at the Ocean House, we were greatly amused. There was a great crowd, coming from everywhere, and among them some very pretty persons. The band played, and the great hall was crowded with dancers. People came in from the cottages — girls, old men, servants and shopkeepers mixed together, and yet there was nothing disagreeable in the manners of any of them — all were decorous and pleasant." — W. W. Story (after a long residence in Europe) to his daughter, summer of 1865.

the difference, though less than between the Newport of 1905 and that of 1860 or 1840, is yet a
difference to be remarked. The fifty thousand dollar cottages, and even the one and two hundred
thousand dollar ones, have been superseded by
structures costing nearly half a million. Hotel life,
which even after the war continued for some years
to be fashionable, has almost altogether ceased.
There consequently is less meeting and mingling
than of yore of representative people from different
parts of the Union. Society, which once was pan-
American, is now almost exclusively a reproduction
of New York.

Newport, the historic town, no longer commands
the unique position that it commanded in the days
of the Wantons and of Berkeley, or in those of the
Malbones and of Dr. Stiles — the days of its commercial and intellectual maturity; but it is not
therefore void of distinction. The stone windmill
of Governor Benedict Arnold is now more an
object of interest than it was in the eighteenth
century. Trinity Church and churchyard suggest loyalism under Queen Anne. The Redwood
Library perpetuates worthily a classic literary
tradition. The Jewish Cemetery blooms ever in
reminder of Spain, Portugal, and the East. The
State House enshrines the full length (replica)
portrait of Washington by Gilbert Stuart. Anti-
quarians are helped by the museum and collections
of the Newport Historical Society.

On Coaster's Island, withal, the United States Torpedo Station, Naval Training School, and Naval War College find congenial cohabitation; while in Newport Harbor there gracefully ride towering-masted miracles, creations of two descendants of John Brown of Providence, John Brown Herreshoff and Nathanael Greene Herreshoff, proprietors of the Herreshoff yacht works at Bristol. From the War College there has gone forth, in the lectures by Captain Alfred T. Mahan on "sea power," a characteristic Rhode Island influence. In the triumphs of the Defender, the Columbia, and the Reliance there are adumbrated the triumphs of the Prince Charles of Lorraine, the Defiance, and the Yankee.

In another way the southern section of Rhode Island has sustained the Rhode Island tradition. In South Kingstown, down nearly to the twentieth century, philosophical idealism (the soul of Rhode Islandism) was ministered to by Rowland G. Hazard, successor in spirit to Roger Williams, Samuel Gorton, and the individualists; to Anne Hutchinson and the Antinomians; to Mary Dyer, George Fox, and the Quietists; to Dean Berkeley and the Idealists; to Samuel Hopkins, Moses Brown, "College Tom," and the Abolitionists; to Stephen Hopkins and the Revolutionists; to David Howell and the political autonomists; to William Ellery Channing and the Transcendentalists; and to Thomas W. Dorr and the liberationists. Born near Tower

Hill in 1801, Mr. Hazard early became the friend
of Channing, and afterwards the antagonist,
friendly and admired, of John Stuart Mill. He
died at Peacedale on June 24, 1888. The depth
of his individualism, as Dr. Edward Everett Hale
has pointed out, may be gauged from his postulate
that man of himself is " a creative first cause."

The history of Rhode Island has been sketched
in three parts: the part Agriculture and Separatism embracing the period 1636 to 1689; the
part Commerce and Coöperation embracing the
period 1690 to 1763; and the part Unification and
Manufactures embracing the period 1764 to the
present day. The last two parts are important as
indicating the course of industrial development
and as revealing separatism in its deep power of
survival. But it is the first part that is most important. It comprehends the time when Rhode
Island alone among commonwealths exemplified
the two leading ideas of Christianity and the Reformation — the two leading ideas of modern life
and progress: the idea of Soul Liberty or Freedom of Conscience in religion; and the idea of the
Rights of Man in politics.

APPENDIX

APPENDIX

A

TOWNS AND COUNTIES OF RHODE ISLAND, WITH DATE OF SETTLEMENT OR OF INCORPORATION

TOWNS.

Providence, 1636.
Portsmouth, 1638.
Newport, 1639.
Warwick, 1643.
Westerly, 1669, May 14.
New Shoreham, 1672, Nov. 6.
North Kingstown, 1674, Oct. 28.
East Greenwich, 1677, Oct. 31.
Jamestown, 1678, Nov. 4.
South Kingstown, 1723, Feb. 26.
Glocester, 1731, Feb. 20.
Scituate, 1731, Feb. 20.
Smithfield, 1731, Feb. 20.
Charlestown, 1738, Aug. 22.
West Greenwich, 1741, April 6.
Coventry, 1741, Aug. 21.
Exeter, 1743, March 8.
Middletown, 1743, June 16.
Bristol, 1747, Jan. 27.
Warren, 1747, Jan. 27.
Little Compton, 1747, Jan. 27.
Tiverton, 1747, Jan. 27.
Cumberland, 1747, Jan. 27.

TOWNS.

Richmond, 1747, Aug. 18.
Cranston, 1754, June 14.
Hopkinton, 1757, March 19.
Johnston, 1759, March 6.
North Providence, 1765, June 13.
Barrington, 1770, June 16.
Foster, 1781, Aug. 24.
Burrillville, 1806, Oct. 29.
Fall River [now Mass.], 1856, Oct. 6.
Pawtucket, 1862, March 1.
East Providence, 1862, March 1.
Woonsocket, 1867, Jan. 31.
Lincoln, 1871, March 8.
North Smithfield, 1871, March 8.
Central Falls, 1895, Feb. 21.
Narragansett, 1901, March 28.

COUNTIES.

Providence, 1703, June 22.
Newport, 1703, June 22.
Washington, 1729, June 16.
Bristol. 1747, Feb. 17.
Kent, 1750, June 11.

B

CHIEF MAGISTRATES OF RHODE ISLAND, 1638–1905

PORTSMOUTH.

Judges.

William Coddington, March 7, 1638, to April 30, 1639.
William Hutchinson, April 30, 1639, to March 12, 1640.

NEWPORT.

Judge.

William Coddington, April 28, 1639, to March 12, 1640.

PORTSMOUTH AND NEWPORT.

Governor.

William Coddington, March 12, 1640, to May 19, 1647.

PRESIDENTS UNDER THE PATENT OF 1644.

John Coggeshall, of Newport, May, 1647, to May, 1648.
[1]Jeremy Clarke, of Newport, May, 1648, to May, 1649.
John Smith of Warwick, May, 1649, to May, 1650.
Nicholas Easton, of Newport, May, 1650, to Aug., 1651.

In 1651 a separation occurred between the towns of Providence and Warwick on the one side, and Portsmouth and Newport on the other.

PROVIDENCE AND WARWICK.

Presidents.

Samuel Gorton, of Warwick, Oct., 1651, to May, 1652.
John Smith, of Warwick, May, 1652, to May, 1653.
Gregory Dexter, of Providence, May, 1653, to May, 1654.

PORTSMOUTH AND NEWPORT.

President.

John Sanford, of Portsmouth, May, 1653, to May, 1654.

In 1654 the union of the four towns was reëstablished.

---

[1] William Coddington, of Newport, was elected, but the General Court would not engage him, for failing to clear himself of certain accusations.

Presidents.

Nicholas Easton, of Newport, May, 1654, to Sept. 12, 1654.
Roger Williams, of Providence, Sept., 1654, to May, 1657.
Benedict Arnold, of Newport, May, 1657, to May, 1660.
William Brenton, of Newport, May, 1660, to May, 1662.
Benedict Arnold, of Newport, May, 1662, to Nov. 25, 1663.

UNDER THE CHARTER OF 1663.

Governors.

Benedict Arnold, of Newport, Nov., 1663, to May, 1666.
William Brenton, of Newport, May, 1666, to May, 1669.
Benedict Arnold, of Newport, May, 1669, to May, 1672.
Nicholas Easton, of Newport, May, 1672, to May, 1674.
Wm. Coddington, of Newport, May, 1674, to May, 1676.
Walter Clarke, of Newport, May, 1676, to May, 1677.
[1]Benedict Arnold, of Newport, May, 1677, to June 20, 1678.
[1]William Coddington, Aug. 28, 1678, to Nov. 1, 1678.
[1]John Cranston, of Newport, Nov. 8, 1678, to March 12, 1680.
Peleg Sanford, of Newport, March 16, 1680, to May, 1683.
Wm. Coddington, Jr., of Newport, May, 1683, to May, 1685.
Henry Bull, of Newport, May, 1685, to May, 1686.
[2]Walter Clarke, of Newport, May, 1686, to June 29, 1686.
Henry Bull, of Newport, Feb. 27, to May 7, 1690.
John Easton, of Newport, May, 1690, to May, 1695.
[1]Caleb Carr, of Newport, May, 1695, to Dec. 17, 1695.
Walter Clarke, of Newport, Jan., 1696, to March, 1698.
[1]Samuel Cranston, of Newport, March, 1698, to April 26, 1727.
Joseph Jencks, of Providence, May, 1727, to May, 1732.
[1]William Wanton, of Newport, May, 1732, to Dec., 1733.
John Wanton, of Newport, May, 1734, to July 5, 1740.

---

[1] Died in office.
[2] The charter was suspended, by Sir Edmund Andros, till 1689.

Richard Ward, of Newport, July 15, 1740, to May, 1743.

William Greene, of Warwick, May, 1743, to May, 1745.

Gideon Wanton, of Newport, May, 1745, to May, 1746.

William Greene, of Warwick, May, 1746, to May, 1747.

Gideon Wanton, of Newport, May, 1747, to May, 1748.

William Greene, of Warwick, May, 1748, to May, 1755.

Stephen Hopkins, of Providence, May, 1755, to May, 1757.

[1]William Greene, of Warwick, May, 1757, to Feb. 22, 1758.

Stephen Hopkins, of Providence, March 14, 1758, to May, 1762.

Samuel Ward, of Westerly, May, 1762, to May, 1763.

Stephen Hopkins, of Providence, May, 1763, to May, 1765.

Samuel Ward, of Westerly, May, 1765, to May, 1767.

Stephen Hopkins of Providence, May, 1767, to May, 1768.

Josias Lyndon, of Newport, May, 1768, to May, 1769.

Joseph Wanton, of Newport, 1769 to Nov. 7, 1775. Deposed.

Nicholas Cooke, of Providence, Nov., 1775, to May, 1778.

William Greene, of Warwick, May, 1778, to 1786.

John Collins, of Newport, May, 1786, to 1790.

Arthur Fenner, of Providence, May, 1790, to Oct. 15, 1805.[2]

James Fenner, of Providence, May, 1807, to 1811.

William Jones, of Providence, May, 1811, to 1817.

[3]Nehemiah R. Knight, of Providence, May, 1817, to Jan. 9, 1821.

William C. Gibbs, of Newport, May, 1821, to 1824.

James Fenner, of Providence, May, 1824, to 1831.

[4]Lemuel H. Arnold, of Providence, 1831 to 1833.

[1] Died in office.

[2] Paul Mumford, deputy governor, died in office. Henry Smith, first senator, officiated as governor. In 1806, no election of governor; Isaac Wilbour, lieutenant-governor, officiated.

[3] Elected United States senator, Jan. 9, 1821, for unexpired term of James Burrill, Jr., deceased.

[4] In 1832, no election of governor, lieutenant-governor, or senators. Elections were successively ordered for May 16, July 18, Aug. 28, and Nov. 21, 1832, resulting without choice. At the January session, 1833, the officers who had not been reëlected in 1832 were continued in office until the next session.

John Brown Francis, of Warwick, 1833 to 1838.

[1]William Sprague, of Warwick, 1838 to 1839.

Samuel Ward King, of Johnston, 1840 to 1843.

UNDER THE CONSTITUTION OF 1842.

James Fenner, of Providence, 1843 to 1845.

Charles Jackson, of Providence, 1845 to 1846.

Byron Diman, of Bristol, 1846 to 1847.

Elisha Harris, of Coventry, 1847 to 1849.

Henry B. Anthony, of Providence, 1849 to 1851.

[2]Phillip Allen, of Providence, 1851 to 1853.

Francis M. Dimond, of Bristol, July 20, 1853, to 1854.

William Warner Hoppin, of Providence, 1854 to 1857.

Elisha Dyer, of Providence, 1857 to 1859.

Thomas G. Turner, of Warren, 1859 to 1860.

Wm. Sprague, of Providence, 1860, to March 3, 1863. Resigned.

[3]William C. Cozzens, of Newport, March 3, 1863, to May,
1863.

James Y. Smith, of Providence, 1863 to 1866.

Ambrose E. Burnside, of Providence, 1866 to 1869.

Seth Padelford, of Providence, 1869 to 1873.

Henry Howard, of Coventry, 1873 to 1875.

Henry Lippitt, of Providence, 1875 to 1877.

Charles C. Van Zandt, of Newport, 1877 to 1880.

Alfred H. Littlefield, of Lincoln, 1880 to 1883.

Augustus O. Bourn, of Bristol, 1883 to 1885.

George Peabody Wetmore, of Newport, 1885 to 1887.

[1] In 1839, no election of governor, or lieutenant-governor; Samuel Ward
King was first senator and acting-governor.

[2] Resigned July 20, 1853, having been elected United States senator, May 4,
1853. Francis M. Dimond, lieutenant-governor, officiated.

[3] Governor Sprague resigned March 3, 1863, to accept the office of United
States senator; and Lieutenant-Governor Arnold having been previously
elected to the senate of the United States to fill the vacancy caused by the
resignation of James F. Simmons, Mr. Cozzens became governor by virtue of
his office as president of the state senate.

John W. Davis, of Pawtucket, 1887 to 1888.

Royal C. Taft, of Providence, 1888 to 1889.

Herbert W. Ladd, of Providence, 1889 to 1890.

John W. Davis, of Pawtucket, 1890 to 1891.

Herbert W. Ladd, of Providence, 1891 to 1892.

D. Russell Brown, of Providence, 1892 to 1895.

Charles Warren Lippitt, of Providence, 1895 to 1897.

Elisha Dyer, of Providence, 1897 to 1900.

William Gregory, of North Kingstown, 1900 to Dec. 16, 1901.

Charles Dean Kimball, of Providence, Dec. 16, 1901 to 1903.

Lucius F. C. Garvin, of Cumberland, 1903 to 1905.

George H. Utter, of Westerly, 1905 to —.

BIBLIOGRAPHY

BIBLIOGRAPHY

PRINCIPAL CHAPTER SOURCES

THE most serviceable general bibliography of Rhode Island history is that prepared by the librarian of the Rhode Island Historical Society, Mr. Clarence S. Brigham, and printed as an appendix to volume iii of Mr. Edward Field's *Rhode Island at the End of the Century*. Other recent publications in Rhode Island history by Mr. Brigham are A List of Seventeenth Century Place-names in Providence Plantations (*R. I. Hist. Coll.* vol. x) and A Report on the Archives of Rhode Island (*Rep. Am. Hist. Assoc.* 1903, vol. i).

CHAPTER I. NARRAGANSETT BAY.

Anderson, R. B. America not discovered by Columbus, 1874.

Arnold, S. G. History of Rhode Island, 1636–1790, 2 vols. 1859, vol. i, chap. iii. (The Narragansett Indians.)

Brigham, C. S. Early voyages and the Indians. Field's *R. I. at End of the Century*, 1902, vol. i, chap. i, and notes.

Carpenter, E. B. South County Neighbors, 1887. (Character sketches.)

Channing, E. History of the U. S. 1905, vol. i, chap. i, note ii. (The Northmen and Vinland.)

De Costa, B. F. Pre-Columbian Discovery, 1868.

De Laet, J. Nieuwe Wereldt, 1625. *N. Y. Hist. Coll.* 2d ser. vol. i. (Block's voyage.)

Deming, C. In Wildest Rhode Island. *Outlook*, June 21, 1902.

Dorr, H. C. The Narragansetts, 1885. *R. I. Hist. Coll.* vol. vii.

Farnum, A. Visits of the Northmen to Rhode Island, 1877. Rider's *Hist. Tract No. 2.*

Gammell, W. Influence of Physiography upon R. I. History. *R. I. Hist. Soc. Proc.* 1885–86.

Hakluyt's Voyages. Hakluyt Soc. ed. 1850, p. 55. (Verrazano's letter.)

Haven, S. F. Archæology of the U. S. 1856. (R. I. as Vinland.)

Mason, G. C. The Old Stone Mill at Newport. *Mag. of Am. Hist.* 1879, vol. iii.

Miller, W. J. Notes concerning the Wampanoag Tribe of Indians, 1880.

Murphy, H. C. Voyage of Verrazzano, 1875.

Palfrey, J. G. Hist. of New England, 5 vols. 1858, vol. i. (The Old Stone Mill.)

Rafn, C. C. Antiquitates Americanæ, 1837.

Slafter, E. F. Voyages of the Northmen, 1877.

Williams, R. Key into the Indian Language, 1643. *R. I. Hist. Coll.* vol. i ; *Pub. Narr. Club*, vol. i.

Winsor, J. Narr. and Crit. Hist. of Am. 8 vols. 1889, vol. i, chap. ii. (The Northmen.)

CHAPTER II. THE AGE OF ROGER WILLIAMS.
1636–1689.

Adams, B. The Emancipation of Massachusetts, 1887. (Antinomians and Quakers.)

Adams, C. F. Three Episodes of Massachusetts History, 2 vols. 1892. (Antinomians.)

Adams, C. F. Antinomianism in the Colony of Masssachusetts Bay, 1894. Prince Soc. Pub. vol. 22.

Allen, Z. Memorial of Roger Williams, 1860. (Burial Place.)

Andrews, C. M. Colonial Self-Government, 1652–1689. A. B. Hart's *American Nation*, 1904, vol. v. (Navigation Acts, Lords of Trade, etc.)

Arnold, S. G. History of Rhode Island, 1636–1790, 2 vols. 1859. (A strictly chronological record.)

Ashley, W. J. Surveys Historic and Economic, 1900. ("England and America," and "American Smuggling," 1660–1690.)

Aspinwall, T. Remarks on the Narragansett Patent, 1863.

Baillie, R. Dissuasive from the Errors of the Time, 1647. (Roger Williams and the Independents.)

Barclay, R. Inner Life of the Religious Sects of the Commonwealth, 1877.

Benedict, D. History of the Baptists in America, 2 vols. 1813.

Bishope, G. New England Judged, 1661. (Persecutions of Quakers in Massachusetts.)

Bodge, G. M. Soldiers in King Philip's War, 1896.

Borgeaud, C. The Rise of Modern Democracy in Old and New England, 1894. (Relation of R. I. history to general history.)

Bowen, C. W. The Boundary Disputes of Connecticut, 1882.

Brayton, G. A. A Defence of S. Gorton, 1883. Rider's *Hist. Tract No. 17*.

Brennan, W. G. Roger Williams' Spring. *Pub. R. I. Hist. Soc.* vol. vii.

Brenton, E. C. History of Brenton's Neck, 1877. (Anecdotal and suggestive.)

Brigham, C. S. History of Rhode Island. Field's *R. I. at End of the Century*, 3 vols. 1902, vol. i, chaps. ii–x.

Brigham, C. S. ed. British State Papers relating to R. I. 1678–87. *Pub. R. I. Hist. Soc.* vols. vii and viii. (Contest for Narragansett.)

Brigham, C. S. Roger Williams' Wife. *Pub. R. I. Hist. Soc.* vol. viii.

Brigham, C. S. ed. Ten Letters of Roger Williams, 1654–78. *Pub. R. I. Hist. Soc.* vol. viii.

Brinley, F. Briefe Narrative of the Nanhiganset Country, 1696. *Pub. R. I. Hist. Soc.* vol. viii.

Brown Library, John Carter. Rhode Island Eastern Boundary, 1741. MS.

Bryce, J. Introduction to Richman's *Rhode Island*, vol. i.

Callender, J. Historical Discourse, 1739. *R. I. Hist. Coll.* vol. iv.

Campbell, D. The Puritan in Holland, England, and America, 1892, 2 vols. (Roger Williams and the Dutch.)

Channing, E. The Navigation Laws. *Proc. Am. Antiq. Soc.* Oct. 23, 1889.

Channing, E. History of the U. S. 1905, vol. i. Discovery of Am. to 1660. (Roger Williams, the Antinomians, etc.)

Clarke, J. Ill Newes from New England, 1652. *Mass. Hist. Coll.* 4th ser. vol. ii. (Persecutions by Massachusetts.)

Coddington, W. Letters to Governor John Winthrop. *Mass. Hist. Coll.* 4th ser. vols. vi and vii. (Dissensions in R. I.)

Connecticut Colonial Records, vols. i and ii. (Relations of R. I. and Conn.)

Deane, C. Some Notices of Samuel Gorton, 1850. *N. Eng. Hist. and Gen. Reg.* vol. iv.

Dexter, H. M. As to Roger Williams, 1876. (Strong statement of the case for Massachusetts.)

Diman, J. L. Address at the unveiling of the Roger Williams monument, 1877. (A moderate estimate of Williams.)

Dorr, H. C. The Planting and Growth of Providence, 1882. Rider's *Hist. Tract No. 15.*

Doyle, J. A. The English Colonies in America, 3 vols. 1882–89, vols. ii and iii. (Roger Williams to Sir E. Andros.)

Durfee, T. Gleanings from the Judicial History of Rhode Island, 1883. Rider's *Hist. Tract No. 18.*

Dyer, L. Review of Richman's R. I. *Eng. Hist. Rev.* Oct. 1903. (Origin of name " Rhode Island.")

Dyer, W. Letters to Massachusetts regarding Mary Dyer. N. Y. *Nation,* Nos. 1926, 1931.

Easton, J. Narrative of Causes of King Philip's War, 1858. F. B. Hough, ed.

Eggleston, E. Beginners of a Nation, 1896. (Roger Williams.)

Ellis, G. E. Life of Anne Hutchinson, 1847. Sparks's *Am. Biog.* 2d ser. vol. vi.

Foster, W. E. ed. Early Attempts at Rhode Island History. *R. I. Hist. Coll.* vol. vii.

Foster, W. E. The R. I. Charter of 1663. Prov. *Journal,* Nov. 14, 1888, and MS. of author.

Fox, G. ·New England Fire Brand Quenched, 1679. (Appendix contains statements by Richard Scott as to Roger Williams.)

Fuller, O. P. History of Warwick, 1875.

Gorton, S. Simplicitie's Defence, 1646. *R. I. Hist. Coll.* vol. ii.

Hallowell, R. P. The Quaker Invasion of Massachusetts, 1883.

Harris, W. William Harris Papers, 1902. *R. I. Hist. Coll.* vol. x.

Hazard, E. ed. Collection of State Papers, 2 vols. 1792, 1794.

Isham, N. M., and A. F. Brown. Early Rhode Island Houses, 1895.

Janes, L. G. Samuel Gorton, 1896. (His philosophical and religious views.)

Jellinek, G. Declaration of the Rights of Man and of Citizens, 1901. (Relation of R. I. history to general history.)

Kaye, P. L. English Colonial Administration under Lord Clarendon, 1660–67. *J. H. U. Studies,* 23d ser.

King, H. M. A Summer Visit of Three Rhode Islanders to

Massachusetts Bay, 1896. (Persecution of Holmes, Crandall, and Clarke.)

Knowles, J. D. Memoir of Roger Williams, 1834.

Kohl, J. G. How Rhode Island was named, 1883. *Mag. Am. Hist.* vol. ix.

Loundes, G. A. Letters of Roger Williams to Lady Barrington, 1889. *N. Eng. Hist. and Gen. Reg.* vol. xliii.

Mason, J. History of the Pequod War. *Mass. Hist. Coll.* 2d ser. vol. viii.

Masson, D. Life of John Milton, 6 vols. 1871–94, vols. ii, iii, iv. (Roger Williams in England.)

Matthews, A. R. Roger Williams and Sir Thomas Urquhart. *N. Y. Nation*, vol. lxx, p. 435.

McGovney, D. O. The Navigation Acts as applied to European Trade. *Am. Hist. Rev.* July, 1904.

Narragansett Club Publications, 6 vols. 1866–74. (The writings of Roger Williams.)

Old Indian Chronicle, 1867, Drake ed. (King Philip's War.)

Osgood, H. L. The American Colonies in the Seventeenth Century, 2 vols. 1904, vol. i, part ii, chaps. i–v ; viii ; xiv.

Paine, G. T. Denial of Charges of Forgery in Sachems' Deed, 1896.

Palfrey, J. G. History of New England, 5 vols. 1858–1890, vols. i–iii. (Roger Williams, the Antinomians, Navigation Acts, etc.)

Portsmouth Early Records, 1639–97, 1901. C. S. Brigham ed.

Potter, E. R. Early History of Narragansett. *R. I. Hist. Coll.* 1886, vol. iii.

Providence Records, 1892–1905, 17 vols.

R. I. Colonial Records (10 vols.), i and ii (1636–63).

R. I. Hist. Soc. Proceedings, 1874–75, 1876–77. (King Philip's War.)

R. I. Supreme Court, Opinion relative to the Narragansett Indians, 1898.

Richman, I. B. Rhode Island : Its Making and its Meaning, 1636–83, 2 vols. 1902. (Emphasizes relation of R. I. history to general history.)

Richman, I. B. The Land Controversies of William Harris. Introduction to William Harris Papers, 1902. *R. I. Hist. Coll.* vol. x.

Rider, S. S. The Origin of Rhode Island Institutions. *Book Notes*, vol. ix.

Rider, S. S. The Referendum in Colonial Rhode Island. *Book Notes*, vol. xi.

Rider, S. S. Soul Liberty, Rhode Island's Gift to the Nation, 1897. Rider's *Hist. Tract* (2d ser.) *No. 5*.

Rider, S. S. The King's Province. *Book Notes*, vol. xii.

Rider, S. S. The Forgeries connected with the Deed by the Sachems to Roger Williams, 1896. Rider's *Hist. Tract* (2d ser.) *No. 4*. See also *Book Notes*, vols. xiii, xiv. *Pub. R. I. Hist. Soc.* vol. iv.

Rider, S. S. ed. Unpublished Letters of Roger Williams, 1881. Rider's *Hist. Tract No. 14*.

Rider, S. S. Defence of the Founders of Warwick. *Book Notes*, vol. vii.

Rider, S. S. Petition of William Dyer for life of Mary Dyer. *Book Notes*, vol. v.

Rider, S. S. Origin of the name "Rhode Island." *Book Notes*, vols. vii and xx.

Rider, S. S. Concerning an alleged Portrait of Roger Williams. Rider's *Hist. Tract* (2d ser.) *No. 2*.

Rider, S. S. The Political Results of the Banishment of Roger Williams. *Book Notes*, vol. viii. (Pequod War.)

Rider, S. S. The Repeal of the Decree of Banishment of Roger Williams. *Book Notes*, vol. xi.

Rider, S. S. The Crimes of Roger Williams. *Book Notes*, vol. xi. (Causes of the banishment.)

Rogers, H. Mary Dyer of Rhode Island, 1896.

Rogers, H. The Importance of the Charter of 1663. " Providence Co. Court House," 1885.

Ross, A. A. Discourse on Civil and Religious History of Rhode Island, 1838.

Sheffield, W. P. Historical Address, Newport, 1876 (pamphlet).

Staples, W. R. Proceedings of the First General Assembly, 1647.

Staples, W. R. Annals of the Town of Providence, 1843. *R. I. Hist. Coll.* vol. v.

Stiness, J. H. The Return of Roger Williams with the Charter of 1644. " Providence Co. Court House," 1885.

Stokes, H. K. Finances and Administration of Providence. *J. H. U. Studies*, extra vol. xxv, 1903. (First four chapters constitute an admirable institutional and constitutional study of Rhode Island.

Straus, O. Roger Williams, 1894. See also *Book Notes*, vol. xi.

Trumbull Papers, *Mass. Hist. Coll.* 5th ser. vol. ix. (Narragansett country.)

Turner, H. E. Settlers of Aquidneck, 1880.

Turner, H. E. William Coddington in Rhode Island Colonial Affairs, 1878. Rider's *Hist. Tract No. 4.*

Tyler, M. C. History of American Literature, 1607–76, 1879. (Roger Williams.)

Warwick Records XV,II Century, Extracts. MS. vol. R. I. Hist. Soc.

Waters, H. F. Ancestry of Roger Williams, 1889. *N. Eng. Hist. and Gen. Reg.* vol. xliii. See also *Book Notes*, vol. vi.

Williams, R. Writings. *Pub. Narr. Club*, 6 vols. (Controversial works and letters.)

Winslow, E. Hypocrisie Unmasked, 1646. (Gorton.)

Winsor, J. Bibliographical Note on Roger Williams. (*Memorial History of Boston*, 4 vols. 1880–82, vol. i.

Winsor, J. Narrative and Critical History of America, 8 vols. 1889, vol. iii. (Early R. I. history.)

Winthrop, J. Journal, 1630–1649, 2 vols. 1853. (Anabaptists and Antinomians.)

CHAPTER III. PAPER MONEY. 1690–1786.

Arnold, S. G. History of Rhode Island, 1636–1790, 2 vols. 1859. (A strictly chronological record.)

Bates, F. G. Rhode Island and the Formation of the Union, 1898. *Columbia Univ. Studies*, vol. 10, chap. iv. (" The Paper Money Era.")

Brigham, C. S. History of Rhode Island. Field's *R. I. at End of the Century*, 3 vols. 1902, vol. i, chap. xii.

Bryce, J. The American Commonwealth, 2 vols. 1891, 2d ed. vol. i. (*Trevett vs. Weeden.*)

Comer, J. Diary, 1704–33. *R. I. Hist. Coll.* vol. viii. (Counterfeiting.)

Correspondence of the Colonial Governors of Rhode Island, 1723–75, 2 vols. 1902–03, G. S. Kimball, ed. (Attitude of English government toward colonial paper money.)

Davis, A. M. Currency and Banking in the Province of the Massachusetts Bay. *Am. Economic Assoc. Pub.* 3d ser.

Dewey, D. R. Financial History of the U. S. 1903, chap. i. (" Colonial Finance.")

Douglass, W. Summary of the British Settlements in North America, 2 vols. (1755), vol. ii, pp. 76–157.

Durfee, T. Gleanings from the Judicial History of R. I. 1883. Rider's *Hist. Tract No. 18.* (*Trevett vs. Weeden.*)

Durfee, T. The Judicial History of R. I. W. T. Davis's *New England States*, vol. iv. (*Trevett vs. Weeden.*)

Elliott, C. B. The Legislatures and the Courts. *Pol. Sci. Quart.* vol v, No. 2. (A highly instructive essay.)

Field, E. The Wars and the Militia. Field's *R. I. at End of the Century*, 1902, vol. i, chap. xiii. (Canadian expeditions.)

Parkman, F. Count Frontenac, 1893; A Half Century of Conflict, 2 vols. 1892 ; Montcalm and Wolfe, 2 vols. 1893. (Canadian expeditions.)

Potter, E. R., and S. S. Rider. Bills of Credit or Paper Money of R. I. 1710–86, 1880. Rider's *Hist. Tract No. 8.*

R. I. Colonial Records (10 vols.), iii, iv, v, and x, 1678–1792. (Canadian expeditions ; Paper money legislation.)

Rider, S. S. Remarks on *Trevett vs. Weeden. Book Notes*, vols. vi, 42, xi, 62, and xii, 24. (A criticism of James Bryce.)

Scott, A. *Holmes vs. Walton*. The New Jersey Precedent. *Am. Hist. Review*, vol. iv. (*Trevett vs. Weeden.*)

Stiness, E. C. The Struggle for Judicial Supremacy. Field's *R. I. at End of the Century*, 3 vols. 1902, vol. iii. (*Trevett vs. Weeden.*)

Stokes, H. K. Public and Private Finance. Field's *R. I. at End of the Century*, 3 vols. 1902, vol. iii, chap. iii.

Varnum, J. M. The Case of Trevett against Weeden, 1787 (pamphlet).

Weeden, W. B. Economic and Social History of New England, 2 vols. 1890, vol. i, chap. x (Currency problem); vol. ii, chap. xiii (Period of inflation).

White, H. Money and Banking Illustrated by American History, 1895, p. 120 *et seq.*

Winslow, J. The Trial of the R. I. Judges, 1887, pamphlet. (*Trevett vs. Weeden.*)

CHAPTER IV. RHODE ISLAND AND THE SEA. 1690–1764.

Arnold, S. G. History of Rhode Island, 1636–1790, 2 vols. 1859. (A strictly chronological record.)

Bartlett, J. R. History of the Wanton family, 1878. Rider's *Hist. Tract No. 3.*

Bartlett, J. R. Naval History of Rhode Island, 1869–70. *Hist. Mag.* vols. xvii and xviii.

Bellomont and the Lords of Trade, 1698–99. *N. Y. Col. Documents*, vol. iv. (Correspondence.)

British State Papers (MS. copies), John Carter Brown Lib. vols. covering period 1695–1700. (Deputy-Governor John Greene and the pirates Kidd, Paine, Bradish, and Gillam.)

Calendar of British State Papers, America and West Indies, 1696–97. (Piracy in Red Sea.)

Calendar of British State Papers, Colonial. *Pub. R. I. Hist. Soc.* vol. vii. (The privateer Thomas Paine.)

Correspondence of the Colonial Governors of Rhode Island, 1723–75, 2 vols. 1902–03, G. S. Kimball, ed. (Louisburg and the French.)

Fauque's Narrative of the Rhode Island Privateer Prince Charles of Lorraine. Kipp's *Historic Scenes from Old Jesuit Missions*, 1874.

Gardiner, A. B. The Havana Expedition of 1762 in the War with Spain. *Pub. R. I. Hist. Soc.* vol. vi.

Grieve, R. The Sea Trade and its Development. Field's *R. I. at End of the Century*, 3 vols. 1902, vol. ii, chap. iv. (Privateering as a source of profit.)

Johnson, C. History of the Pyrates, 2 vols. 1724. (Thomas Tew *et al.*)

Kimball, G. S. Introduction to Correspondence of the Colonial Governors of R. I. (The Wantons *et al.*)

Library of Congress. List of Vernon-Wager MSS. 1904. (Correspondence of Sir Charles Wager, 1707–43: piracy, slave trade, etc.)

Munro, W. H. History of the Town of Bristol, 1880. (Simeon Potter and the De Wolfs.)

Parkman, F. A Half Century of Conflict, 2 vols. 1892. (Louisburg and the French.)

Perry, C. B. Genealogy of the R. I. De Wolfs, 1902. (History of the De Wolf family.)

R. I. Colonial Records (10 vols.), iii and iv. (Bellomont and Dudley Papers.)

Sheffield, W. P. The City of Newport, 1876. (Sir Charles Wager.)

Sheffield, W. P. The Privateersmen of Newport, 1883. (Lists of men and ships.)

Smith, H. P. The Sea Force in War Time. Field's *R. I. at End of the Century*, 3 vols. 1902, vol. i, chap. xxiv.

Weeden, W. B. Economic and Social History of New England, 2 vols. 1890, vol. i, chap. ix. (Privateers, pirates, etc.); vol. ii, pp. 559 and 598 *et seq.* (Privateers.)

CHAPTER V. THE GOLDEN AGE OF NEWPORT — COMMERCE. 1730-1776.

Arnold, S. G. History of Rhode Island, 1636–1790, 2 vols. 1859. (A strictly chronological record.)

Bartlett, J. R. History of the Wanton Family, 1878. Rider's *Hist. Tract No. 3*.

Census of Rhode Island, 1885. (Summary of prior enumerations.)

Collins, E. D. Studies in the Colonial Policy of England. *Rep. Am. Hist. Assoc.* 1900, vol. i. (Royal African Co. and the Slave Trade.)

Correspondence of the Colonial Governors of Rhode Island, 1723–75, 2 vols. 1902–03, G. S. Kimball ed. (Sugar Act, 1733.)

Cranston, S. Report to Lords of Trade, 1708. *R. I. Col. Rec.* vol. iv.

Curtis, G. W. Newport Historical and Social. *Harpers' Mag.* vol. ix, 1854.

DuBois, W. E. B. The Suppression of the African Slave Trade to the U. S. 1638–1870. *Harvard Historical Monographs*, No. 1. (*Assiento;* Colonial and Federal Statutes.)

Eggleston, E. Commerce in the Colonies. *Century Mag.* vol. xxviii, 1884.

Grieve, R. The Sea Trade and its Development. Field's *R. I. at End of the Century*, 3 vols. 1902, vol. ii, chap. iv.

Hopkins, S. Report to Lords of Trade, 1760. *R. I. Col. Rec.* vol. vi.

Howland, B. R. The Streets of Newport. *Mag. of New Eng. Hist.* vol. ii.

Jenckes, J. Report to Lords of Trade, 1731. *British State Papers* (MS. copies) John Carter Brown Library.

Johnston, W. D. Slavery in R. I. 1755–76. *Pub. R. I. Hist. Soc.* vol. ii.

Kimball, G. S. Introduction to Correspondence of the Colonial Governors of R. I. (Commerce.)

Kohler, M. J. The Jews in Newport. *Pub. Am. Jewish Hist. Soc.* No. 6.

MacSparran, J. America Dissected. Updike's *Narragansett Church*, 1847. (Commerce.)

Mason, G. C. ed. Am. Hist. Rec. 1872, vol. i. (Original letters from masters of R. I. slave ships.)

Mason, G. C. ed. Annals of Trinity Church, 2 vols. 1890, 1894. (The Malbones.)

Newport Town Records, 1679–1776. MS. vol. in City Hall.

R. I. Colonial Records (10 vols.), iv and v. (Trade reports and commercial regulations.)

Richman, I. B. Rhode Island : Its Making and its Meaning, 2 vols. 1902, vol. ii, chaps. ix and xiii. (Early Newport.)

Sanford, P. Report to Lords of Trade, 1680. Arnold's *Hist. R. I.* vol. i.

Spears, J. R. The American Slave Trade, 1900.

Stiles, E. Literary Diary, 1769–95, 3 vols. 1901, vol. i, *passim.* (Slave trade, etc.)

Turner, H. E. The Two Governors Cranston, 1889 (pamphlet).

Weeden, W. B. Economic and Social History of New England, 2 vols. 1890, vol. i, chap. ix (Commerce 1690–1713) ; vol. ii, chap. xii (Slave trade, 1713–45) ; vol. ii, chap. xiv (Smuggling, 1713–45) ; vol. ii, chap. xvi (Spermaceti candles) ; vol. ii, chap. xix (Sugar Act).

CHAPTER VI. THE GOLDEN AGE OF NEWPORT — ART, LETTERS, SCIENCE. 1730–1776.

Allen, A. V. G. The Transition in New England Theology. *Atlantic Monthly*, Dec. 1891. (Samuel Hopkins.)

Arnold, S. G. History of Rhode Island, 1636–1790, 2 vols. 1859. (A strictly chronological record.)

Beardsley, E. E. Life and Correspondence of Samuel Johnson, D. D. 1874. (Berkeley.)

Callender, J. Historical Discourse, 1739. *R. I. Hist. Coll.* vol. iv.

Comer, J. Diary, 1704–33. *R. I. Hist. Coll.* vol. viii. (Berkeley.)

Foster, W. E. Some R. I. Contributions to the Intellectual Life of the Last Century, 1892. *Proc. Am. Antiq. Soc.* N. S. vol. viii.

Fraser, A. C. "Berkeley" and Berkeley's Works, 4 vols. 1871.

Goddard, D. A. The Press and Literature of the Massachusetts Provincial Period. Winsor's *Memorial Hist. of Boston*, 4 vols. 1880–82, vol. ii.

Goodwin, D. Religious Societies. Field's *R. I. at End of the Century*, 3 vols. 1902, vol. ii, chap. ii.

Jacobi, J. O. Letter on music in R. I. 1739. *Pub. R. I. Hist. Soc.* vol. vii.

Jameson, J. F. The First Public (church) Library in Rhode Island. *Pub. R. I. Hist. Soc.* vol. iv.

Mason, G. C. Reminiscences of Newport, 1884. (Printers, The Redwood Library, etc.)

Mason, G. C. Life and Works of Gilbert Stuart, 1879.

Mason, G. C. ed. Annals of Trinity Church, 2 vols. 1890, 1894, vol. i. (Biographical notices of prominent men of Newport.)

Mason, G. C. Annals of the Redwood Library, 1891. (The Philosophical Society and its members.)

Park, E. A. Memoir of Samuel Hopkins, 1854.

Parsons, C. W. Early Votaries of Natural Science in R. I. *R. I. Hist. Coll.* vol. vii.

Perry, W. S. History of the American Episcopal Church, 2 vols. 1885, vol. i. (Chapter by Moses Coit Tyler on the Berkeley era.)

Porter, N. The Two Hundreth Birthday of Berkeley, 1885.

Smith, H. P. Growth of Public Education ; The Printer and the Press ; Growth of the Public Library. Field's *R. I. at the End of the Century*, 3 vols. 1902, vol. ii. (Statistical.)

Stiles, E. Literary Diary, 1769–95, 3 vols. 1901, vol. i. (Music, Jewish Synagogue, Transit of Venus, etc.)

Stockwell, T. B. History of Public Education in R. I. 1636–1876.

Tolman, W. H. History of Higher Education in R. I. 1894. U. S. Bureau of Education, No. 18.

Waterhouse, B. Letter to Thos. Jefferson, Sept. 14, 1822. *Pub. R. I. Hist. Soc.* vol. ii. (Newport in its intellectual prime.)

Weeden, W. B. Economic and Social History of New England, 2 vols. 1890, vol. ii, chap. xiii, 1713–45. (Newport and Boston.)

CHAPTER VII. OLD NARRAGANSETT. 1720–1776.

Arnold, S. G. History of Rhode Island, 1636–1790, 2 vols. 1859. (A strictly chronological record.)

Berkeley, G. Alciphron, 1732, chap. v. (The fox hunt.)

Bowen, C. W. The Boundary Disputes of Connecticut, 1882. (Narragansett country.)

Carpenter, E. B. The Huguenot Influence in Rhode Island. *Proc. R. I. Hist. Soc.* 1885–86. (Gabriel Bernon *et al.*)

Channing, E. The Narragansett Planters. *J. H. U. Studies*, 4th ser.

Denison, F. Westerly and its Witnesses, 1878. ("New Lights.")

Douglass, W. A. Summary of the British Settlements in North America, 2 vols. 1755, vol. ii.

Earle, A. M. In Old Narragansett, 1898. (Tales and anecdotes.)

Foster, W. E. Some Rhode Island Contributions to the Intellectual Life of the Last Century, 1892. *Proc. Am. Antiq. Soc.* N. S. vol. viii.

Hazard, C. Judge Sewall's Gifts in the Narragansett Country. *Pub. R. I. Hist. Soc.* vol. vi.

Hazard, C. The Narragansett Friends Meeting, 1654–1784, 1899. (Slavery.)

Hazard, C. "College Tom," 1894. (Slavery.)

Hazard, T. R. Recollections of Olden Times. 1879. (Hannah Robinson, etc.)

Hazeltine, H. D. Appeals to the King in Council. *Brown Univ. Studies*, No. vii. (*Torrey vs. Gardner.*)

Johnston, W. D. Slavery in Rhode Island, 1755–76. *Pub. R. I. Hist. Soc.* vol. ii.

MacSparran, J. America Dissected. Updike's *Narragansett Church*, 1847.

MacSparran, J. Diary, 1743–51, 1899, Dr. Daniel Goodwin ed.

Mason, G. C. ed. Annals of Trinity Church, 2 vols. 1890, 1894. (Gabriel Bernon.)

Potter, E. R. The Early History of Narragansett. *R. I. Hist. Coll.* 1885, vol. iii.

Potter, E. R. The French Settlements in Rhode Island, 1879. Rider's *Hist. Tract No. 5*.

Rhode Island Colonial Records (10 vols.), ii–iv. (Controversies with Connecticut.)

Richman, I. B. Rhode Island: Its Making and its Meaning, 2 vols. 1902, vol. ii, chap. xv. (Pettiquamscutt, Misquamicutt, and Atherton companies.)

Stiness, E. C. The Struggle for Judicial Supremacy. Field's *R. I. at End of the Century*, 3 vols. 1902, vol. iii. (Execution of Thomas Carter on Tower Hill.)

Updike, W. History of the Episcopal Church in Narragansett, 1847. (Social life, customs, etc.)

CHAPTER VIII. GROWTH OF PROVIDENCE. 1740–1766.

Arnold, S. G. History of Rhode Island, 1636–1790, 2 vols. 1859. (A strictly chronological record.)

Bates, F. G. Rhode Island and the Formation of the Union, 1898. *Columbia Univ. Studies*, vol. 10. (Hopkins-Ward, p. 37 *et seq.*)

Brigham, C. S. History of Rhode Island. Field's *R. I. at End of the Century*, 3 vols. 1902, vol. i, chap. xiii. (Hopkins-Ward.)

Brown, M. Brown-Palfrey Correspondence. Moses Brown Papers, vol. i. (MS.) *R. I. Hist. Soc.*

Brown, M. Letter to Tristam Burges, 1836. MS. *R. I. Hist. Soc.* (Commerce.)

Census of Rhode Island, 1885. (Summary of earlier enumerations.)

Dorr, H. C. The Planting and Growth of Providence, 1882. Rider's *Hist. Tract No. 15*.

DuBois, W. E. B. The Suppression of the African Slave Trade to the U. S. 1638–1870. *Harvard Hist. Monographs*, No. 1.

Durfee, T. Two Hundred and Fiftieth Anniversary of the Planting of Providence, 1886.

Edwards, M. Materials for a History of the Baptists. *R. I. Hist. Coll.* vol. vi. (Brown University.)

Field, E. Early Habits and Customs and Old Landmarks. Field's *R. I. at End of the Century*, 3 vols. 1902, vol. iii, chap. vii.

Foster, W. E. Stephen Hopkins, a Rhode Island Statesman, 1884. Rider's *Hist. Tract No. 19*, in two parts, part i.

Gammell, W. Life of Samuel Ward, 1846. *Sparks's Am. Biog.* 2d ser. vol. ix.

Grieve, R. The Sea Trade and its Development. Field's *R. I. at End of the Century*, 3 vols. 1902, vol. ii, chap. iv. (Sea trade of Providence.)

370   BIBLIOGRAPHY

Guild, R. A. History of Brown University, 1867.

Guild, R. A. Early History of Brown University including the Life, Times, and Correspondence of President Manning, 1897.

Hazard, C. College Tom, 1894. (Slavery — Moses Brown and College Tom.)

Huling, R. G. Hopkins-Ward Letters. *Narr. Hist. Reg.* vols. iii and iv.

Johnston, W. D. Slavery in Rhode Island, 1755–76. *Pub. R. I. Hist. Soc.* vol. ii.

Jones, A. Moses Brown; a Sketch, 1892.

McClelland, T. C. Historical Address before Rhode Island Home Missionary Society, 1903. (Samuel Hopkins and Yamma and Quamine.)

Perry, W. S. History of the American Episcopal Church, 2 vols. 1885, vol. i, chapter by Moses Coit Tyler. (Education.)

R. I. Colonial Records (10 vols.), i, 243; vii, 251; x, 7 (Acts regarding slavery); vi, 385 (Act incorporative of Brown University).

Rider, S. S. The Plan of Union in 1754, with Memoir of Stephen Hopkins, 1880. *Hist. Tract No. 9.*

Stiles, E. Literary Diary, 1769–95, 3 vols. 1901, vol. i. (Brown University; Samuel Hopkins and African missions.)

Stiness, J. H. A Century of Lotteries, 1896. Rider's *Hist. Tract* (2d ser.) *No. 3.*

Weeden, W. B. Economic and Social History of New England, 2 vols. 1890, vol. ii, chap. xviii. (Sea trade of Providence, 1763–75.)

CHAPTER IX. CONSTITUTIONAL DEVELOPMENT. 1700–1800.

Acts and Laws of Rhode Island, 1730. (The Anti-Jew and Anti-Catholic Act.)

Andrews, C. M. The River Towns of Connecticut. *J. H. U. Studies*, 7th ser. (Religious foundation of Massachusetts towns.)

Arnold, S. G. History of Rhode Island, 1636–1790, 2 vols. 1859. (A strictly chronological record.)

Bates, F. G. Rhode Island and the Formation of the Union, 1898. *Columbia Univ. Studies*, vol. 10. (R. I. Judicial History, p. 136.)

Bishop, C. F. History of Elections in the American Colonies, 1893. *Columbia College Studies*, vol. 3. (Basis of suffrage.)

Channing, E. The Narragansett Planters. *J. H. U. Studies*, 4th ser. (Privileges of freemen in R. I.)

Civil Service Reform as proposed in R. I. in 1749. *Pub. R. I. Hist. Soc.* N. S. vol. vi. (Officers to retain positions during good behavior.)

Dorr, T. W. Address to the People of Rhode Island, 1843. (See pp. 43, 47, on land basis of suffrage in early R. I.)

Durfee, T. Gleanings from the Judicial History of Rhode Island, 1883. Rider's *Hist. Tract No. 18*.

Eaton, A. M. The Right to Local Self-Government. *Harvard Law Rev.* Feb. 1900.

Foster, W. E. Town Government in R. I. *J. H. U. Studies*, 4th ser.

Haynes, G. H. Representation and Suffrage in Massachusetts. *J. H. U. Studies*, 12th ser.

Hazeltine, H. D. Appeals to the King in Council. *Brown Univ. Studies*, No. vii. (Relation of legislature to courts in R. I., with sketch of the judicial history of R. I.)

Huling, R. G. The Rhode Island Emigration to Nova Scotia, 1760. *Narr. Hist. Reg.* vol. vii.

Kellogg, L. P. The American Colonial Charter. *Rep. Am. Hist. Assoc.* 1903, vol. i. (Sketch of the constitutional history of R. I.)

Kohler, M. J. The Jews in Newport. *Pub. Am. Jewish Hist. Soc.* No. 6.

Meade, J. R. Truth concerning the Disfranchisement of Catholics in Rhode Island. *Am. Rom. Cath. Quarterly*, Jan. 1894.

Osgood, H. L. The American Colonies in the Seventeenth Century, 2 vols. 1904, vol. ii, part ii. (Basis of suffrage in Massachusetts, Connecticut, Plymouth, and New Haven.)

R. I. Colonial Records (10 vols.), iii, 385 (Report by Bellomont) ; ii, 113 (Suffrage Act of 1665).

Richman, I. B. Rhode Island : Its Making and its Meaning, 2 vols. 1902, vol. ii, chap. x. (Relation of State to Town in early R. I.)

Rider, S. S. Acts and Laws of Rhode Island, 1719, with introduction, 1895.

Rider, S. S. The End of a Great Political Struggle in Rhode Island. *Book Notes*, vol. v.

Rider, S. S. Legislative History in Rhode Island. *Book Notes*, vol. iv.

Rider, S. S. The Punishment for Contempt by the Assembly. *Book Notes*, vol. iv.

Rider, S. S. An Inquiry concerning the Origin of the Clause in the Laws of Rhode Island, 1719–83, disfranchising Roman Catholics, 1889. *Hist. Tract* (2d ser.) *No. 1.*

Riley, F. M. Colonial Origin of New England Senates. *J. H. U. Studies*, 14th ser.

Stiness, E. C. The Struggle for Judicial Supremacy. Field's *R. I. at End of the Century*, 3 vols. 1902, vol. iii, chap. ii.

Stokes, H. K. Public and Private Finance. Field's *R. I. at End of the Century*, 3 vols. 1902, vol. iii, chap. iii, p. 208. (Veto power of governor.)

Washburn, E. Judicial History of Massachusetts, 1840, chap. ii. (General Court as a judicial body.)

CHAPTER X. PORTENTS OF REVOLUTION. 1763–1776.

Adams, B. The Emancipation of Massachusetts, chap. xi. (Puritan clergy and the Revolution.)

Arnold, S. G. History of Rhode Island, 1636–1790, 2 vols. 1859. (A strictly chronological record.)

Ashley, W. J. Surveys Historic and Economic, 1900. (" England and America," and " American Smuggling," 1660–1690.)

Bates, F. G. Rhode Island and the Formation of the Union, 1898. *Columbia Univ. Studies*, vol. 10. (Loyalists.)

Beer, G. L. The Commercial Policy of England toward the American Colonies, 1893. *Columbia Univ. Studies*, vol. 3. (Harmless character of Navigation Acts.)

Bigelow, M. M. Cambridge Modern History, vol. vii, 1903, (U. S.), chap. iv, " The Declaration of Independence." (Summary of Constitutional arguments.)

Brigham, C. S. History of Rhode Island. Field's *R. I. at End of the Century*, 3 vols. 1902, vol. i, chap. iv.

Chamberlain, M. John Adams, with Other Essays, 1889. (Puritanism as cause of Revolution ; Constitutional discussion.) The Revolution Impending. *Narr. and Crit. Hist. of Am.* (Winsor), vol. vi.

Channing, E. The Navigation Laws. *Proc. Am. Antiq. Soc.* Oct. 23, 1889. (Harmless character of Acts.)

Channing, E. Causes of the American Revolution. *Papers Am. Hist. Assoc.* 1887, vol. ii. (Dread of Episcopate and dislike of Sugar Act.)

Correspondence of the Colonial Governors of Rhode Island, 1723–75, 2 vols. 1902–03, G. S. Kimball ed. (Sherwood letters on detention of money due R. I. and on Sugar Act of 1733.)

Cross, A. L. The Anglican Episcopate and the American Colonies, 1902. *Harvard Hist. Monographs*, No. ix.

Doyle, J. A. Cambridge Modern History, vol. vii, 1903 (U. S.), ch. ii, " The English Colonies." (Trade policy of Great Britain.)

Doyle, J. A. Cambridge Modern History, vol. vii, 1903 (U. S.), ch. v, " The Quarrel with Great Britain." (Causes of the Revolution : Episcopate.)

Field, E. Esek Hopkins, 1898. (An Apologia.)

Foster, W. E. Stephen Hopkins, a Rhode Island Statesman. Rider's *Hist. Tract No. 19*, in two parts, 1884, part
ii, chaps. viii and ix.

Lecky, W. H. History of England in the Eighteenth Century, 8 vols. 1878–90, vol. iii, ch. xii. (Acts of Trade as
causes of Revolution; Gaspee affair.)

Osgood, H. L. England and the Colonies. *Pol. Sci. Quart.*
vol. ii. (Puritanism as cause of Revolution.)

R. I. Colonial Records (10 vols.), vi and vii. (Gaspee documents.)

Rider, S. S. Criticism of Field's Esek Hopkins. *Book Notes*,
vol. xvii.

Sheffield, W. P. John Brown of Providence. *Pub. R. I.
Hist. Soc.* vol. v. (Release of Brown by British.)

Smith, A. Wealth of Nations, 1776, Rogers's ed. 1880;
chap. vii, part ii. (Acts of Trade.)

Staples, W. R. Rhode Island in the Continental Congress,
1870, chap. i. (Naval affairs.)

Stiles, E. Literary Diary, 1769–95, 3 vols. 1901, vol. i, and
first part of vol ii. (Gaspee commission; naval situation
at Newport, 1775–76; fear of English Episcopate; Loyalists, Baptists, Quakers.)

Tyler, M. C. Literary History of the American Revolution,
2 vols. 1897, vol. i, chaps. i–vi. (Hopkins and Howard
pamphlets, etc.)

Van Tyne, C. H. Loyalists in the American Revolution,
1902.

Weeden, W. B. Economic and Social Hist. of New England, 2 vols. 1890, vol. ii, chaps. xviii and xix. (Acts of
Trade as causes of Revolution.)

Woodburn, J. A. The Causes of the American Revolution.
J. H. U. Studies, 10th ser.

CHAPTER XI. RHODE ISLAND THE THEATRE OF WAR.
1776–1780.

Almy, M. G. Journal. *Newport Hist. Mag.* vol. i. (Siege
of Newport.)

Amory, T. C. Life of Major-General John Sullivan, 1868.

Arnold, S. G. History of Rhode Island, 1636–1790, 2 vols.
1859. (A strictly chronological record.)

Balch, T. The French in America, 1777–83, 2 vols. 1891–95.
(Vol. ii contains list of regiments and officers.)

Barton, W. Seizure of Prescott. (MS. account prepared
for king of France by Barton himself. *R. I. Hist. Soc.*)

Channing, E. T. Life of William Ellery, 1854. *Sparks's Am.
Biog.* vol. vi.

Colonial Records of R. I. (10 vols.) vols. viii and ix.

Continental Congress. Journal, April, 1776. (Censure of
Esek Hopkins.)

Cowell, B. Spirit of '76 in Rhode Island, 1850. (Proceedings of New England Conventions.)

Cullum (Gen.), G. W. Fortification Defenses of Narragansett Bay, 1884. (Criticism of Sullivan.)

Diman, J. L. The Capture of General Richard Prescott,
1877. Rider's *Hist. Tract No. 1.*

Doyle, J. A. Cambridge Modern History, vol. vii, 1903
(U. S.), chap. vii, "The War of Independence."

Field, E. Esek Hopkins, 1898. (Glasgow affair; Providence
Committee and the frigates.)

Field, E. The Militia in War Time. *R. I. at End of the
Century,* 3 vols. 1902, vol. i, chap. xxiii. (Seizure of Prescott; Sullivan expedition.)

Greene, G. W. Life of Nathanael Greene, 3 vols. 1867–71.
(Vol. ii contains correspondence on Sullivan expedition.)

Greene, W. Letter to Connecticut. *Trumbull Papers, Mass.
Hist. Coll.* 7th ser. vol. ii. (Appeal for food.)

Heath, W. Correspondence. *Mass. Hist. Coll.* 7th ser. vol.
iv. (Sullivan expedition.)

Hopkins, E. Esek Hopkins Papers. MSS. R. I. Hist. Soc. Library.

Lowell, E. J. The Hessians in the Revolution, 1884, chap. xviii. (At Newport.)

Maclay, E. S. History of American Privateers, 1899, chap. vii. (Silas Talbot.)

Maclay, E. S. History of U. S. Navy, 2 vols. 1894, vol. i. (Glasgow affair.)

Mahan, Capt. A. T. Influence of Sea Power upon History, 1891. (French naval operations at R. I.)

Manners, Lord R. Letters, 1780, *Pub. R. I. Hist. Soc.* vol. vii. (British fleet operations.)

Mason, G. C. The British Fleet in Rhode Island, *R. I. Hist. Coll.* vol. vii.

McCrady, E. South Carolina in the Revolution, 2 vols, 1901– 02. (New light on military character of Gen. Nathanael Greene.)

Revolutionary Correspondence, 1775–82. *R. I. Hist. Coll.* vol. vi.

Rider, S. S. Criticism of Field's Esek Hopkins. *Book Notes*, vol. xvii. (Glasgow affair.)

Rider, S. S. The Battle of Rhode Island, 1878. Rider's *Hist. Tract No. 6.* (Sullivan's and Pigot's official reports, etc.)

Rider, S. S. The Rhode Island Black Regiment, 1880. *Hist. Tract No. 10 ; Book Notes*, vol. v.

Rosengarten, J. G. The German Soldiers in Newport, 1776– 79. *R. I. Hist. Mag.* vol. vii.

Staples, W. R. Rhode Island in the Continental Congress, 1870. (Ellery and Marchant letters.)

Stiles, E. Literary Diary, 1769–95, 3 vols. 1901, vol. ii. (Work of privateers; British at Newport; Rochambeau.)

Stone, E. M. Our French Allies, 1778–82, 1884.

Talbot, S. Capture of Pigot galley. *R. I. Hist. Soc. MSS.* vol. iii. No. 671. (MS. account by Talbot himself.)

Thurston, C. R. Newport in the Revolution. *N. Eng. Mag.* N. S. vol. ii.

Tower, C. The Marquis de La Fayette in the American Revolution, 2 vols. 1895. (Based on original French documents; best account in English of French operations from a French point of view.)

Van Tyne, C. H. Loyalists in the American Revolution. 1902.

Vernon, T. Diary. Rider's *Hist. Tract No. 13*, 1881. (A rusticated loyalist.)

Vernon, W. Papers of William Vernon and the Navy Board. *Pub. R. I. Hist. Soc.* vol. viii.

Williams, C. R. Lives of Barton and Olney, 1839.

Winsor, J. Narrative and Critical History of America, 8 vols. 1889, vol. vi, pp. 592–603. (Military operations at R. I. during Revolution.)

CHAPTER XII. RHODE ISLAND AND THE FEDERAL CONSTITUTION. 1780–1790.

Bates, F. G. Rhode Island and the Impost of 1781. *Rep. Am. Hist. Assoc.* 1874.

Bates, F. G. Rhode Island and the Formation of the Union, 1898. *Columbia Univ. Studies*, vol. 10.

Bigelow, M. M. Cambridge Modern History, vol. vii, 1903 (U. S.), chap. viii, " The Constitution."

Brigham, C. S. The Struggle for the Constitution. Field's *R. I. at End of the Century*, 3 vols. 1902, vol. i, chap. xvi.

Fiske, J. The Critical Period of American History, 1889.

Guild, R. A. Early History of Brown University, etc. 1897. (Biographical notice of David Howell.)

Harvey, G. L. How Rhode Island received the Constitution. *N. Eng. Mag.* N. S. vol. ii.

R. I. Constitutional Convention. MS. minutes. *R. I. Hist. Soc.*

Rhode Island and the Constitutional Convention of 1787. *Pub. R. I. Hist. Soc.* vol. ii. (Sentiment of the mercantile class.)

Rider, S. S. How the U. S. Senate forced R. I. to ratify the U. S. Constitution. *Book Notes,* vol. xi.

Rider, S. S. Rhode Island and a Constitutional Convention. *Book Notes,* vol. x. (Attitude by towns.)

CHAPTER XIII. DECLINE OF COMMERCE AND ESTABLISH-
MENT OF MANUFACTURES. 1790–1840.

Adams, H. History of the United States, 1801–17, 9 vols 1889–91.

Allen, G. W. Our Navy and the Barbary Corsairs, 1905.

Allen, S. H. The Federal Ascendency in 1812. *Narr. Hist. Reg.* vol. vii.

Bishop, J. L. History of American Manufactures, 1608–1860, 2 vols. 1861–64.

Bowditch, J. B. Industrial Development. Field's *R. I. at End of the Century,* 3 vols. 1902, vol. iii, chap. iv.

Brigham, C. S. The Administration of the Fenners. Field's *R. I. at End of the Century,* 3 vols. 1902, vol. i, chap. xvii.

Bristol Slave Trade in 1816. *Pub. R. I. Hist. Soc.* N.S. vol. vi.

Brown, M. Moses Brown Papers. MS. *R. I. Hist. Soc.* vols. iii, vi, vii, xviii. (Slave trade at Newport.)

Chadwick, J. W. William Ellery Channing, 1903.

Champlin Papers. MS. 2 vols. 1712–1840. *R. I. Hist. Soc.* (Commerce.)

Channing, G. G. Early Recollections of Newport, 1868. (Gibbs and Channing.)

Crèvecoeur, J. H. St. J. Lettres d'un Cultivateur Américain, 2 vols. 1787, vol. ii.

Curtis, G. W. Newport Historical and Social. *Harper's Mag.* vol. ix.

Du Bois, W. E. B. Suppression of the African Slave Trade to the U. S. 1638–1870. *Harvard Hist. Monographs,* No 1.

Eaton, A. M. The French Spoliation Claims. *Narr. Hist. Reg.* vol. iv.

Foster, T. The Foster Papers. (MS. *R. I. Hist. Soc.*) vols. i and ii. (Barbary pirates.)

Grieve, R. The Sea Trade and its Development. Field's *R. I. at End of the Century*, 3 vols. 1902, vol. ii, chap. iv.

Grieve, R., and J. B. Fernold. The Cotton Centennial, 1790–1890. (Slater, the Spragues, etc.)

Hazard, C. " College Tom," 1894, chap. x. (Slavery : Abolition movement at Providence.)

Higginson, T. W. Oldport Days, 1873.

Hunt, G. Office Seeking during Washington's Administration. *Am. Hist. Rev.* vol. i.

Jameson, J. F. The Adjustment of Rhode Island into the Union in 1790. *Pub. R. I. Hist. Soc.* vol. viii. (Office seeking under Washington.)

Jones, W. Transition of Providence from a Commercial to a Manufacturing Community, 1903. MS. monograph, Brown University.

Kimball, G. S. The East India Trade of Providence, 1787–1807. *Brown Univ. Studies*, No. 6.

La Rochefoucauld-Liancourt. Travels, 2 vols. 1795, vol. ii.

Maclay, E. S. History of American Privateers, 1899, part ii, chap. iv. (Rhode Island privateers in War of 1812.)

Maclay, E. S. History of the U. S. Navy, 2 vols. 1894, vol. i, part ii. (France and Tripoli; The President Washington.)

Mahan, A. T. The War of 1812. *Scrib. Mag.* 1905. (Perry on Lake Erie.)

Mason, G. C. Reminiscences of Newport, 1884. (Sea trade, E. G. Malbone, etc.)

Munro, W. H. History of the Town of Bristol, 1880. (The De Wolfs and the slave trade.)

President Washington — John Brown's East India Ship. *Pub. R. I. Hist. Soc.* vol. vi.

Rider, S. S. Case of the British Ship Nautilus at Newport in 1794. *Book Notes*, vol. i. (Release of impressed American seamen.)

Roosevelt, T. Naval War of 1812, 1882. (Perry on Lake Erie.)

Smith, H. P. The Sea Force in War Time. Field's *R. I. at End of the Century*, 3 vols. 1902, vol. i, chap. xxiv.

Spears, J. R. The American Slave Trade, 1900. (After the Revolution and after War of 1812.)

Stiles, E. Literary Diary, 1769–95, 3 vols. 1901, vol. ii. (Newport after evacuation by British.)

Stone, E. M. Life of John Howland, 1857.

Warville, J. P. B. New Travels, 1792. (Newport after evacuation.)

Waterhouse, B. Letter to Thomas Jefferson, Sept. 14, 1822. *Pub. R. I. Hist. Soc.* vol. ii. (Newport in its decline.)

White, G. S. Memoir of Samuel Slater, 1836.

Yankee — Private Armed Brigantine. Log-book. October, 1812–March, 1813. MS. *R. I. Hist. Soc.*

CHAPTER XIV. THE DORR REBELLION. 1834–1842.

[Bowen, F.] The Recent Contest in Rhode Island. *North Am. Rev.* April, 1844.

Brigham, C. S. The Dorr War. Field's *R. I. at End of the Century*, 3 vols. 1902, vol. i, chap. xx.

Brownson, O. A. The American Republic, 1866. (The organized and the unorganized "people" in the U. S.)

Burke, E. Interference of the Executive in the Affairs of Rhode Island, 1844. *Ho. of Rep. Doc.* No. 546.

Dorr, T. W. An Address to the People of Rhode Island, 1843. *Burke's Report.*

Dorr, T. W. Correspondence. MSS. Brown Univ. Library.

Durfee, J. Charge to the Grand Jury at Bristol. Works, 1849. ("Law of Treason.")

Durfee, T. Judicial History of Rhode Island. Davis's *New England States*, vol. iv.

Hurd, J. C. The Theory of our National Existence, 1881. (The organized and the unorganized "people" in the U. S.)

Jones, W. The Transition of Providence from a Commercial to a Manufacturing Community, 1903. MS. monograph, Brown University. (Attitude of artisan class toward the Dorr movement.)

King, D. Life and Times of Thomas Wilson Dorr, 1859.

Merriam, C. E. History of American Political Theories, 1903, chap. v.

Mowry, A. M. The Constitutional Controversy in Rhode Island in 1841. *Rep. Am. Hist. Assoc.* 1894.

Mowry, A. M. Tammany Hall and the Dorr Rebellion. *Am. Hist. Rev.* vol. iii.

Mowry, A. M. The Dorr War, 1901. (A very complete account.)

Payne, C. H. The Great Dorr War. *N. Eng. Mag.* N. S. vol. ii.

Pitman, J. S. Report of the Trial of Thomas W. Dorr for Treason, 1844 (pamphlet).

Potter, E. R. Considerations on the Rhode Island Question, 1842 (pamphlet).

Rhode Island Suffrage Association. Preamble and Constitution, March 27, 1840.

Richman, I. B. From John Austin to John C. Hurd. *Harvard Law Review*, January, 1901. (The organized and the unorganized "people.")

Rider, S. S. The Nine Lawyers' Opinion, 1880. Rider's *Hist. Tract No. 11*.

Stiness, J. H. Civil Changes in the State, 1897. (An excellent *résumé* of Dorr War issues.)

Tucker, M. Discourse, July 21, 1842 (pamphlet).

Wayland, F. Discourse, May 22, 1842 (pamphlet).

Webster, D., and J. Whipple. Arguments before U. S. Supreme Court in *Luther vs. Borden*, 1848.

CHAPTER XV. THE CIVIL WAR AND AFTER. 1842–1905.

Adams, C. F. Sexual Immorality in Puritan New England. *Proc. Mass. Hist. Soc.* 1891, vol. vi. (Antiquity of practices.)

Anthony, H. B. Defence of Rhode Island. Speech in U. S. Senate, Feb. 1881.

Anthony, H. B. Limited Suffrage in Rhode Island, 1883. *North Am. Rev.* vol. cxxxvii.

Arnold, S. G. History of Rhode Island, 1636–1790, 2 vols. 1859. (A strictly chronological record. Acts in restraint of illegal voting.)

Bowditch, J. P. Industrial Development. Field's *R. I. at End of the Century*, 3 vols. 1902, vol. iii, chap. iv.

Bradley, C. S. Methods of changing the Constitution of the States, 1885.

Brigham, C. S. History of Rhode Island. Field's *R. I. at End of the Century*, 3 vols. 1902, vol. i, chaps. xxi and xxii.

Census of Rhode Island, 1895, p. 905 *et seq.* (Foreign immigrants, especially the French-Canadians and Irish.

Census, U. S. 1900, vol i (R. I.). (Foreigners, negroes, etc.)

Davis, W. T. Constitutional History of Rhode Island. Davis's *New England States*, vol. iv.

Douglass, S. A. Speech at Rocky Point, Aug. 2, 1860. Prov. *Journal*, Aug. 3, 1860.

Durfee, T. Judicial History of Rhode Island. Davis's *New England States*, vol. iv. (*Taylor vs. Place*, etc.)

Durfee, T. Gleanings from the Judicial History of Rhode Island, 1883. Rider's *Hist. Tract No. 18.* (Early sexual laxity in R. I.)

Eaton, A. M. Constitution-Making in Rhode Island, 1899 (pamphlet).

Equal Rights Association. Constitution of Rhode Island and Equal Rights, 1881 (pamphlet).

Field, E. Wars and the Militia. Field's *R. I. at End of the Century*, 3 vols. 1902, vol. i, chap. xxiii. (Civil War.)

Foster, W. E. Providence Public Libraries. Field's *R. I. at End of the Century*, 3 vols. 1902, vol. iii, chap. vi.

Garvin, L. F. C. Special Message to the General Assembly, March, 1903. (Bribery in elections.)

Goddard, W. G. Address, May 3, 1843, to the People of Rhode Island. (With notes.)

Gorman, C. E. Historical Statement of the Elective Franchise in Rhode Island, 1879.

Greene, W. A. Providence Plantations for Two Hundred and Fifty Years, 1886.

Gregory, E. Newport in Summer. *Harper's Mag.* July, 1901.

Grieve, R. The Sea Trade and its Development. Field's *R. I. at End of the Century*, 3 vols. 1902, vol. ii, chap. iv. (Present-day commerce of Providence.)

Hale, E. E. Memorial Address on Rowland G. Hazard, Oct. 19, 1891.

Hazard, R. G. Works, 4 vols. 1889, Caroline Hazard, ed.

Jones, W. Transition of Providence from a Commercial to a Manufacturing Community, 1903. MS. monograph, Brown University. (Providence in relation to foreign commerce.)

Lincoln, A. Speech at Providence, Feb. 28, 1860. Prov. *Journal*, Feb. 29, 1860.

Lippitt, C. W. Commerce at Providence, 1883.

Lowry, E. (N. Y. *Post*). A Disclosure of Political Conditions, 1904. (Detailed survey of R. I. towns as to morals, population tendencies, etc.)

Luther, S. Address on the Right of Free Suffrage, 1833 (pamphlet).

Mowry, A. M. The Dorr War, 1901, chap. xxii. (Amendments to Constitution of 1842.)

Payne, A. The Constitution of Rhode Island and Equal Rights, 1881.

Payne, A., and W. P. Sheffield. Constitutional Reform in Rhode Island, 1886. *North Am. Rev.* vol. cxlii.

Proposed Revised Constitution of Rhode Island to be submitted to the Electors on Nov. 8, 1898. Same for resubmission on June 20, 1899.

Providence *Journal*, May 22, 1879. Newport, a City by the Sea. (A careful review of Newport history and society.)

Report of the Commission to revise the Constitution, 1898.

Report of the Constitutional Commission with Suggestions (by A. M. Eaton, C. E. Gorman, Dr. L. F. C. Garvin, *et al.*) in regard to a new Constitution, 1898.

Report of the Joint Select Committee on Changes in the Constitution, 1882.

Rhode Island Supreme Court. Opinion on Power of the General Assembly to call a Constitutional Convention, January, 1883.

Rider, S. S. Legislative History in Rhode Island. *Book Notes*, vol. iv.

Rider, S, S. The End of a Great Political Struggle in Rhode Island, 1888. *Book Notes*, vol. v. (Extension of suffrage to foreign-born citizens.)

Rider, S. S. How Rhode Island came by two Capitals, *Book Notes*, vol. viii.

Shaler, N. S. Nature and Man in America, 1891. (The French-Canadians.)

Sheffield, W. P. Random Notes on the Government of Rhode Island, 1897.

Smith, H. P. The Growth of the Library. Field's *R. I. at End of the Century*, 3 vols. 1902, vol. iii, chap. vi.

Smith, H. P. Growth of Public Education. Field's *R. I. at End of the Century*, 3 vols. 1902, vol. ii.

Smythe, E. C. French-Canadians in New England. *Proc. Am. Antiq. Soc.* N. S. vol. vii.

Steffens, L. Rhode Island: a State for Sale. *McClure's Mag.* Feb. 1905.

Stickney, C. Know-Nothingism in Rhode Island. *Pub. R. I. Hist. Soc.* vol. i.

Stiness, E. C. The Struggle for Judicial Supremacy. Field's *R. I. at End of the Century*, 3 vols. 1902, vol. iii, chap. ii. (*Taylor vs. Place; Hazard vs. Ives.*)

Stiness, J. H. Civil Changes in the State, 1897 (pamphlet).

Stiness, J. H. Two Centuries of Rhode Island Legislation against Strong Drink, 1882.

Wilson, G. G. The Political Development of the Towns. Field's *R. I. at End of the Century*, 3 vols. 1902, vol. iii, chap. i.

Woodbury, A. Major-General A. E. Burnside and the Ninth Army Corps, 1867.

Wyman, J. C. Rhode Island at the World's Fair of 1893. *N. Eng. Mag.* N. S. vol. x.

INDEX